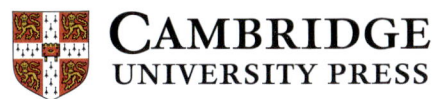

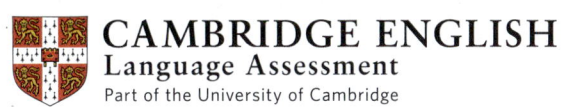

CAMBRIDGE
UNIVERSITY PRESS

CAMBRIDGE ENGLISH
Language Assessment
Part of the University of Cambridge

Cambridge English

CAMBRIDGE OFFICIAL PREPARATION MATERIAL

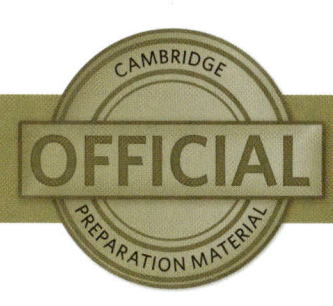

James Styring
Nicholas Tims
Series Editor: Annette Capel

Prepare!

STUDENT'S BOOK
Level 4

Cambridge University Press
www.cambridge.org/elt

Cambridge English Language Assessment
www.cambridgeenglish.org

Information on this title: www.cambridge.org/9780521180276

© Cambridge University Press and UCLES 2015

This publication is in copyright. Subject to statutory exception
and to the provisions of relevant collective licensing agreements,
no reproduction of any part may take place without the written
permission of the publishers.

First published 2015
20 19 18 17 16

Printed in Italy by Rotolito S.p.A.

A catalogue record for this publication is available from the British Library

ISBN 978-0-521-18027-6 Student's Book
ISBN 978-1-107-49785-6 Student's Book and Online Workbook
ISBN 978-0-521-18028-3 Workbook with Audio
ISBN 978-0-521-18029-0 Teacher's Book with DVD and Teacher's Resources Online
ISBN 978-0-521-18030-6 Class Audio CDs
ISBN 978-1-107-49782-5 Presentation Plus DVD-ROM

The publishers have no responsibility for the persistence or accuracy of URLs for external or third-party internet websites referred to in this publication, and do not guarantee that any content on such websites is, or will remain, accurate or appropriate. Information regarding prices, travel timetables, and other factual information given in this work is correct at the time of first printing but the publishers do not guarantee the accuracy of such information thereafter.

Contents

1	Personal profile	10
2	In fashion	14
Culture	Homes around the world	18
3	My way of life	20
4	Champions	24
PE	Sports training	28
Review 1		30
5	Take a good look	32
6	Modern life	36
Culture	Meeting and greeting	40
7	Getting on	42
8	Going away	46
Geography	Our world	50
Review 2		52
9	Shop till you drop	54
10	Taste this!	58
Culture	What I eat	62
11	A healthy future	64
12	Incredible wildlife	68
Science	Ecosystems	72
Review 3		74
13	Moods and feelings	76
14	Watch it, read it	80
Culture	World cinema	84
15	Digital life	86
16	Wish me luck!	90
Maths	Units	94
Review 4		96
17	Skills and talents	98
18	The world of work	102
Culture	Special training schools	106
19	The written word	108
20	Puzzles and tricks	112
Biology	The eye	116
Review 5		118

Pairwork	120
Word profiles	122
Vocabulary list	129
Grammar reference	138
List of irregular verbs	158

UNIT	VOCABULARY 1	READING	GRAMMAR
1 Personal profile page 10	Describing people, e.g. *bald*, *teenage*	Three friends and their profiles **EP Word profile** *right*	Present simple and continuous
2 In fashion page 14	Things to wear, e.g. *jacket*, *unfashionable*	Fashion and music **EP Word profile** *kind*	Past simple
Culture Homes around the world page 18			
3 My way of life page 20	Life events, e.g. *get a driving licence*, *get married*	Teenage life **EP Word profile** *get*	Comparatives and superlatives *not as … as*
4 Champions page 24	Sports, e.g. *athletics*, *gymnastics*, *do*, *go* and *play* + sport	Jess's blog **EP Word profile** *way*	Past continuous
PE Sports training page 28		**Review 1** Units 1–4 page 30	
5 Take a good look page 32	People and action verbs, e.g. *catch*, *clap* **EP Word profile** *take*	Caught on camera...	Past simple and continuous
6 Modern life page 36	City life, e.g. *pollution*, *public transport*	Eco heroes **EP Word profile** *light*	*some/any, much/many, a lot of, a few/a little*
Culture Meeting and greeting page 40			
7 Getting on page 42	*be*, *do*, *have* and *make* **EP Word profile** *like*	Troublespot	*have to* and *must* *should*
8 Going away page 46	Travel, e.g. *baggage hall*, *departure gate*	A cool city! **EP Word profile** *around*	Future: *be going to* and present continuous
Geography Our world page 50		**Review 2** Units 5–8 page 52	
9 Shop till you drop page 54	Money and shopping, e.g. *change*, *checkout*	Help! I just can't stop shopping! **EP Word profile** *change*	Present perfect
10 Taste this! page 58	Food and drink adjectives, e.g. *disgusting*, *juicy* **EP Word profile** *really*	Ollie, don't eat that!	Present perfect and past simple, *How long?* and *for/since*
Culture What I eat page 62			

VOCABULARY 2	WRITING	LISTENING AND SPEAKING	VIDEO
Verbs, e.g. *want*, *know*	An online profile		
Adverbs, e.g. *quickly*, *fast*		**Listening** A discussion about the past **Speaking** Talking about yourself	In fashion
too, *not enough*	An informal letter or email (1)		Life events
Words with different meanings, e.g. *coach*, *point*		**Listening** Photo of the week **Speaking** Describing a past event	
myself, *yourself*, *each other*	A story (1)		Take a look!
Compounds: noun + noun, e.g. *speed limit*, *tourist information*		**Listening** An interview **Speaking** Agreeing and disagreeing	Modern life
Phrasal verbs: friendships, e.g. *fall out*, *hang out*	An informal letter or email (2)		
Phrasal verbs: travel, e.g. *check in*, *set off*		**Listening** Travel writing competition **Speaking** Making suggestions	
been and *gone*	A story (2)		
look, *taste*, *smell*		**Listening** Food and cooking **Speaking** Ordering fast food	Taste this

UNIT	VOCABULARY 1	READING	GRAMMAR
11 A healthy future page 64	Health and illness, e.g. *ankle*, *earache*	We will live for 1,000 years **EP** Word profile *for*	*will* and *be going to*
12 Incredible wildlife page 68	Animals, e.g. *ant*, *penguin*	Animals: interesting, unusual and imagined **EP** Word profile *still*	Modals of probability, e.g. *might*, *could*
Science Ecosystems page 72		**Review 3** Units 9–12 page 74	
13 Moods and feelings page 76	Adjectives: feelings, e.g. *confused*, *stressed*	The worst day of the week **EP** Word profile *time*	*just*, *already* and *yet*
14 Watch it, read it page 80	TV, films and literature, e.g. *action film*, *historical drama*	Matt's blog **EP** Word profile *hope*	Relative clauses
Culture World cinema page 84			
15 Digital life page 86	Computing phrases, e.g. *download podcasts*, *share links*	Choosing an app **EP** Word profile *turn*	Present simple passive
16 Wish me luck! page 90	Verb + noun, e.g. *blow out candles*, *break a mirror*	Just luck? **EP** Word profile *luck*	Zero and first conditional
Maths Units page 94		**Review 4** Units 13–16 page 96	
17 Skills and talents page 98	Creative lives: nouns, e.g. *sculpture*, *studio*	Who are the *real* artists? **EP** Word profile *own*	Reported commands
18 The world of work page 102	Work, e.g. *firefighter*, *journalist*	I'm in charge **EP** Word profile *go*	Second conditional
Culture Special training schools page 106			
19 The written word page 108	Magazines, e.g. *article*, *headline*	Has it been a good year for you? **EP** Word profile *mean*	Reported speech
20 Puzzles and tricks page 112	Puzzles, e.g. *mystery*, *solve* **EP** Word profile *mind*	Tricks of the eye	Past simple passive
Biology The eye page 116		**Review 5** Units 17–20 page 118	**Pairwork** page 120

VOCABULARY 2	WRITING	LISTENING AND SPEAKING	VIDEO
Illnesses and injuries: verbs, e.g. *catch a cold*, *feel sick*	An online comment		Healthy future
Adverbs of probability, e.g. *definitely*, *probably*		**Listening** Podcast about animals at work **Speaking** Describing a picture (1)	
Adjectives: *-ed* or *-ing*, e.g. *disappointed*, *surprising*	Notes and messages		Moods and feelings
Easily confused words, e.g. *accept/except*		**Listening** Going to the cinema **Speaking** Reaching agreement	
Phrasal verbs: technology, e.g. *switch on*, *turn off*	An informal letter or email (3)		
if and *unless*		**Listening** Interview – Why do we believe in luck? **Speaking** Describing a picture (2)	Luck
Adjectives: *-al* and *-ful*, e.g. *natural*, *successful*	A biography		Talented
Suffixes: *-er*, *-or*, *-ist*, *-ian*, e.g. *director*, *journalist*		**Listening** Understanding problems **Speaking** Discussing options	Jobs
say, *speak*, *talk* and *tell*	An online review		
make and *let*		**Listening** People talking about favourite possessions **Speaking** Talking about a special object	

Word profiles page 122 **Vocabulary list** page 129 **Grammar reference** page 138 **List of irregular verbs** page 158

Welcome to *Prepare!*
Learn about the features in your new Student's Book

Your profile Start each unit by talking about you, your life and the unit topic

Word profile Focus on the different meanings of important words and phrases

Talking points Give your opinion on the topic in the text

Corpus challenge Take the grammar challenge and learn from common mistakes

Prepare to write Learn useful tips to help you plan and check your writing

Video Watch interviews with teenagers like you

Prepare to speak Learn useful words and phrases for effective communication

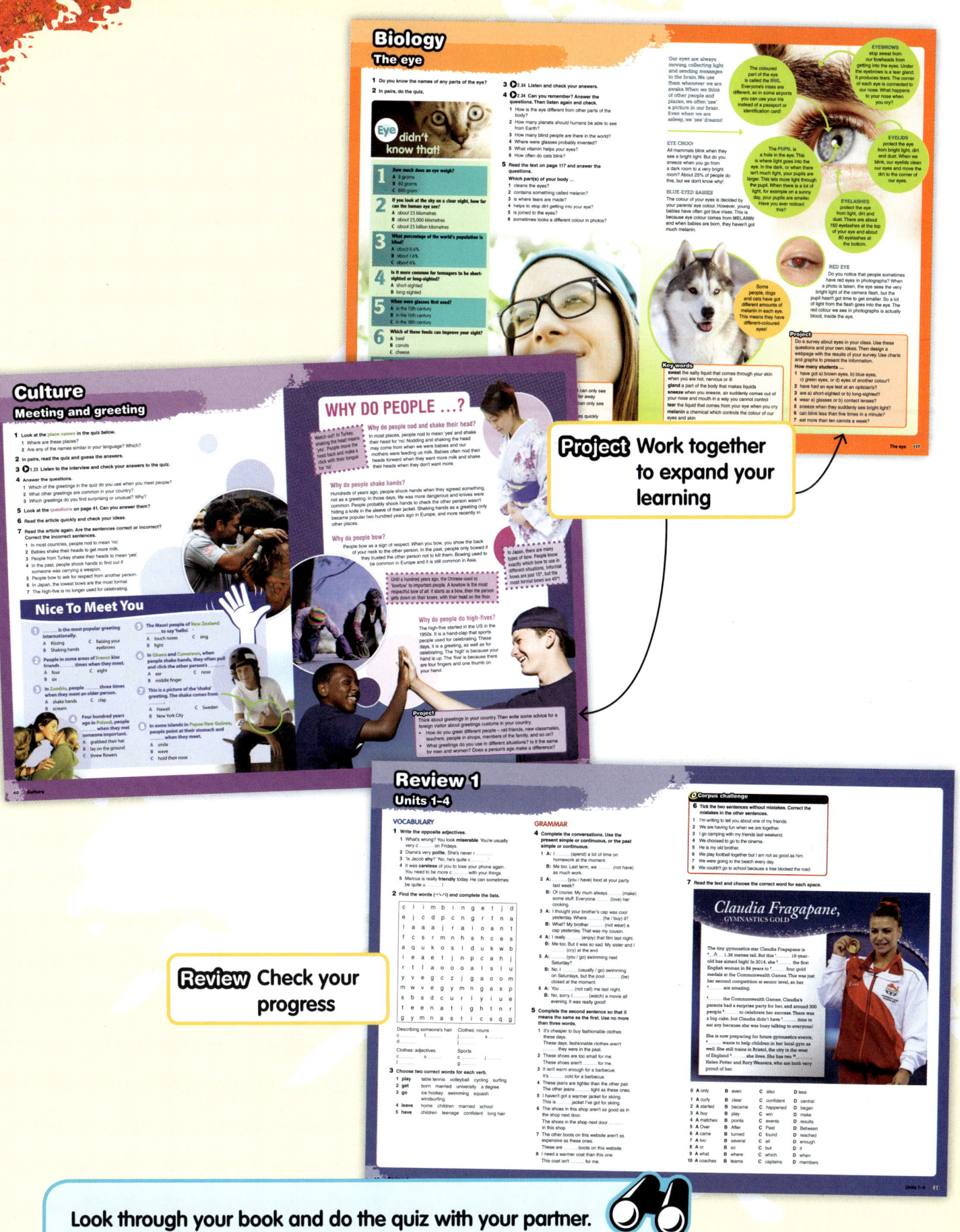

Look through your book and do the quiz with your partner.

1 What is the topic of Unit 17?
2 In which unit can you find a photo of a dolphin?
3 In which unit can you read about Barcelona?
4 In which unit can you find out about the story *Frankenstein*?
5 Can you find a famous Brazilian footballer? Who is he? What page is he on?

1 Personal profile

VOCABULARY Describing people

Your profile
What do you look like?
What type of person are you?

1 ▶1.02 Look at the photos and listen to three people talking about someone in their family. Who is each speaker describing?

2 Add the words to the table. Add other words that you know.

> ~~attractive~~   bald   curly   dark   fair
> good-looking   in his/her twenties/thirties
> straight   teenage

Age	
Looks	attractive
Hair	

3 Describe someone in the photos. Can your partner guess who it is?

A: *He's a teenage boy and he's good-looking.*
B: *Is it Matt?*

4 ▶1.03 Read the descriptions of Ali, Matt and Jess, and choose the correct words. Then listen and check.

1 Ali's really **polite** / **careless**. He always says hello at the start of lessons. He's quite clever too. He usually does well in tests.
2 My brother's called Matt. He borrows my things without asking. He thinks he's **funny** / **polite**, but he doesn't make me laugh!
3 Jess is very **friendly** / **miserable**. She lives opposite us and she always says hello. She looks after our cat when we're on holiday.
4 Matt talks a lot – like his mum! He's sometimes a bit **confident** / **careless**. I always encourage him to check his homework, but he doesn't do it!
5 Jess is a great friend. She's always smiling, and she's never **miserable** / **polite**. She really makes me laugh.
6 Ali knows what he's good at, so he's quite **careless** / **confident**. But he can also be quite a lazy person. His room's always a mess!

5 Match the adjectives below to their opposites in exercise 4.

> careful   cheerful   rude
> serious   shy   unfriendly

6 Which adjectives in exercises 4 and 5 describe you?

7 Work in pairs. Describe someone in your class. Describe what they look like, and what kind of person they are. Can your partner guess who it is?

A: *She's got straight hair and she's very confident.*
B: *Ana?*

READING

1 Read the information about part of a school website. What is it? Have you got something similar in your school?

> **NOTICES**
> **all.about.me @ Bryans High School.com**
> Would you like to meet people who share your hobbies and interests? It's easy with *all.about.me*.
> 1 Go to www.bryansschool.com/allaboutme and create an account.
> 2 Post a photo and your profile.
> 3 Click on 'Connect' to connect with new friends.

2 Ali, Matt and Jess have posted information on *all.about.me*. Match their profiles to the activities.

> designing computer games
> visiting film studios   kite surfing

3 Read the three profiles again. Who …
1 sometimes does the same thing all weekend?
2 would like to do a new activity?
3 wants someone to help with something?
4 knows how to do something but would like to do it better?
5 would like to go to another country?
6 might get a prize soon?

4 Match these texts to Matt, Ali or Jess. Then answer the questions. Choose A, B or C.

> **1 Young Game Designers' Competition!**
> Open to all teens
> Closing date September 30
> Entry fee £5

What does this text say?
A You can enter a computer game in this competition for free.
B Children of 12 and under can take part in the competition.
C The competition wants all entries by the end of September.

> **2**
> Are you free on Saturday afternoon? There's an extra film on then and I know it'll make you laugh! I've got a spare ticket, so text me today.
> Fran

What is Fran doing in this message?
A asking someone to buy a cinema ticket for her
B inviting someone to watch a comedy film with her
C telling someone about a movie she has just seen

5 Who would you most like to spend the afternoon with – Matt, Ali or Jess? Why?

Hi! I'm Jess. I live with my mum and dad. My friends say I'm a cheerful person. They're right. I enjoy having a laugh with them. In my free time, I love sport, especially tennis. I'm having lessons this term, because I want to learn how to play properly. This year I'd like to try something completely different, maybe a winter sport or even an extreme sport like kite surfing. Next month, I'm staying at an adventure centre with my youth club, so I guess we'll try something different there. I'm good friends with Matt and Ali in my class. I live right opposite Matt, so I see him a lot. **Connect**

Hi guys! I'm Ali Malik. I live with my parents and my brother and sister in a flat. Some of my classmates think I'm quite serious. I like doing things well and getting good marks. Out of school, I always have fun with my friends. My main interest is computers – I love them! I'm designing a computer game right now but I need to ask my uncle about it - he's a computer programmer. I'm taking part in the Young Game Designers competition. My mum believes I can win! **Connect**

Hello! My name's Matt. I live with my mum, dad, my little brother and my sister Alyssa. If you're feeling miserable, then I'm the right person to call! People think I'm very funny. As for my free time, I'm keen on watching films – comedies, adventure, animated films – it doesn't matter. I like them all! I sometimes spend all day Saturday and Sunday watching them. This year, I want to visit a film studio. There's one near London where they made the Harry Potter films. You can actually visit it. My dream is to fly to Hollywood and see a studio there! **Connect**

EP Word profile *right*

> I live **right** opposite Matt.
> My friends say I'm a cheerful person. They're **right**.
> I'm designing a computer game **right now**.

page 122

Talking points
" Some people think teenagers have too much free time. Do you agree?
Is it important to have the same interests as your friends? Why? / Why not? "

GRAMMAR Present simple and continuous

1 Match the examples to the rules.
1 *I'm designing* a computer game right now.
2 Next month, *I'm staying* at an adventure centre.
3 I sometimes *spend* all day Saturday and Sunday watching films.
4 *I'm having* lessons this term.
5 I *live* with my parents.

> We use the present simple for:
> a facts.
> b something that happens regularly.
>
> We use the present continuous for:
> c something that is happening right now.
> d temporary situations.
> e future arrangements.

→ Grammar reference page 138

2 Choose the correct verb forms.
1 I *get* / *'m getting* home at five o'clock every day.
2 Macy *spends* / *is spending* a lot of time online this week.
3 Look at Dan. He *doesn't concentrate* / *isn't concentrating*.
4 *Do you do* / *Are you doing* anything interesting next weekend?
5 She *plays* / *is playing* the guitar and the piano.
6 He always *goes* / *is going* swimming on Saturdays.

3 Look at the sentences in exercises 1 and 2. Complete the table with the time words/phrases.

> ~~at the moment/right now~~
> never, sometimes, always
> every day/week/year
> this month/term/week
> later, tomorrow
> on Saturdays
> next week/weekend/month

Present simple	
Present continuous	at the moment/right now

4 Make six sentences about you. Use the time words and phrases in exercise 3.

At the moment, I'm having an English lesson.
I play football on Saturdays.

5 Make questions with the present simple or present continuous. Then ask and answer them.
1 what / you / usually / do / on Sundays?
2 what subjects / you / study / this year?
3 what TV programmes / you / watch / every week?
4 what / you / do / after school / today?

Corpus challenge

Find and correct the mistake in the student's sentence.
We are going out together every week.

VOCABULARY Verbs: *want, like, love, know*

1 Read the information about the verbs. Check the meaning of verbs you don't know.

> We don't use these verbs in continuous forms:
> *believe, hate, know, like, love, mean, need, own, prefer, understand, want*
> **I don't understand** these maths questions.
> NOT ~~I'm not understanding these maths questions.~~

2 Complete the sentences with the positive or negative form of the verbs above. Sometimes more than one answer is possible.
0 My uncle ..*owns*.. three cars.
1 Ruby's very friendly. We really .... her.
2 I .... how old he is. He looks about 14.
3 What .... this word .... ?
4 I .... studying alone. I can't concentrate with other people around.
5 I'm always miserable in winter. I .... cold weather.
6 Sorry. I .... when you speak very quickly.

3 🔊 1.04 Complete the conversation with the present simple or present continuous form of the verbs. Then listen and check.

Amy: Come on, Lottie! We ⁰ *'re leaving* (leave) soon. Are you ready?
Lottie: Yeah. I ¹............ (get) my things ready now. Can you give me five minutes?
Amy: Yes, but I ²............ (not like) being late. The class ³............ (start) at seven o'clock.
Lottie: I ⁴............ (know), and we always ⁵............ (catch) the bus at six thirty. There's plenty of time.
Amy: But they ⁶............ (do) work on the roads at the moment, so the buses are all late.
Lottie: OK. I'm nearly ready. I just ⁷............ (need) to do my hair.
Amy: Your hair? Lottie, we ⁸............ (go) to the swimming pool!

WRITING   An online profile

1 Read the two online profiles. Which person is most like you? Why?

USERNAME	Snowy
AGE	13
MEMBER SINCE	January 2015
NUMBER OF POSTS	79

I'm Tom, but my online name is Snowy – my hair is very blond! I'm British, but I'm living in the USA right now. I go to Carson High School in Boston.

I'm very friendly, and I think I'm quite intelligent. Some people disagree, of course! I'm into music, especially rock. And I'm really into computers too. I'm learning to write computer programs at the moment – it's not easy!

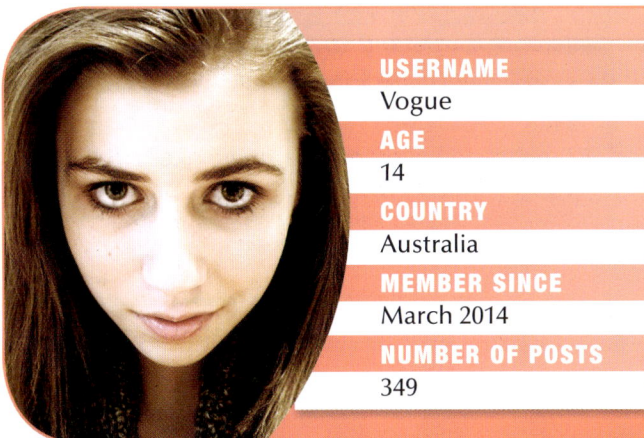

USERNAME	Vogue
AGE	14
COUNTRY	Australia
MEMBER SINCE	March 2014
NUMBER OF POSTS	349

My name's Felicity, but everyone calls me Flic. I'm from Australia. My hobbies are fashion, fashion and fashion – especially from the 1960s. Oh, and I also love music. I'm learning to play the drums at the moment. They're very loud!

I'm fairly confident, but sometimes I'm a bit careless with my school work. My friends say I'm cheerful and friendly. Oh yes, and they think I'm really good-looking (of course!).

2 Read the *Prepare* box. What phrases do Tom and Flic use to introduce themselves?

Prepare to write An online profile

In an online profile:
- introduce yourself: *I'm ... , My name's ...*
- talk about your hobbies and interests: *I'm interested in ... , I'm into ... , My hobbies are ...*
- say what you're learning at the moment: *At the moment I'm ... , Right now I'm ...*
- say what kind of person you are: *I'm very/quite ... , My friends say I'm ... , Sometimes I'm a bit ...*
- don't be too serious!

3 Look at the underlined verbs in the profiles. Answer the questions.
1. What verb form do Tom and Flic use for their likes and dislikes, and things they do regularly?
2. What verb form do they use for things they're doing at the moment?

4 Look at the highlighted adverbs in the profiles. Add them to the table.

Make adjectives stronger	Make adjectives weaker
very	

5 Complete the sentences to make them true for you.
1. I'm very …
2. I'm fairly …
3. Sometimes I'm a bit …
4. My friends say I'm really …

6 How do Tom and Flic show they aren't too serious?

7 Make notes for your online profile. Use the ideas to help you.
- My name
- Facts about me
- What I'm like
- Hobbies and interests
- Things I'm learning at the moment

8 Write your online profile.
- Use the tips in the *Prepare* box.
- Use adverbs to make adjectives stronger and weaker.
- Don't forget to check your spelling and grammar.

Personal profile

2 In fashion

VOCABULARY Things to wear

Your profile
What are you wearing today?
What fashions do you like?

1 ▶1.05 Look at the photos. Do you recognise the people? What things in the box can you see? Listen and check.

> boots   cap   jacket   jumper   necklace
> pocket   raincoat   sandals   suit
> sunglasses   sweatshirt   tie   tights
> top   tracksuit   trainers

2 ▶1.06 Listen to an interview with three teenagers, Ashley, Kelly, and Luke, about the clothes they like wearing. Answer the questions.
1 Whose clothes are quite **loose**?
2 Whose clothes are tight but **comfortable**?
3 Who doesn't like **smart** clothes?
4 Whose jeans are **narrow**?
5 Who is wearing something **brand new**?
6 Who isn't interested in **fashionable** clothes?
7 Who is very **well-dressed** today?

3 Match the adjectives below to their opposites in exercise 2.

> ~~badly dressed~~   casual   uncomfortable
> unfashionable   second-hand   tight   wide

badly-dressed – well-dressed

4 Answer the questions.
1 What do you usually wear at the weekend?
2 What types of clothes do you never wear? Why?
3 Do you prefer smart clothes or casual clothes? Why?
4 Which colours or clothes look good on you?

14 Unit 2

READING

FASHION AND MUSIC

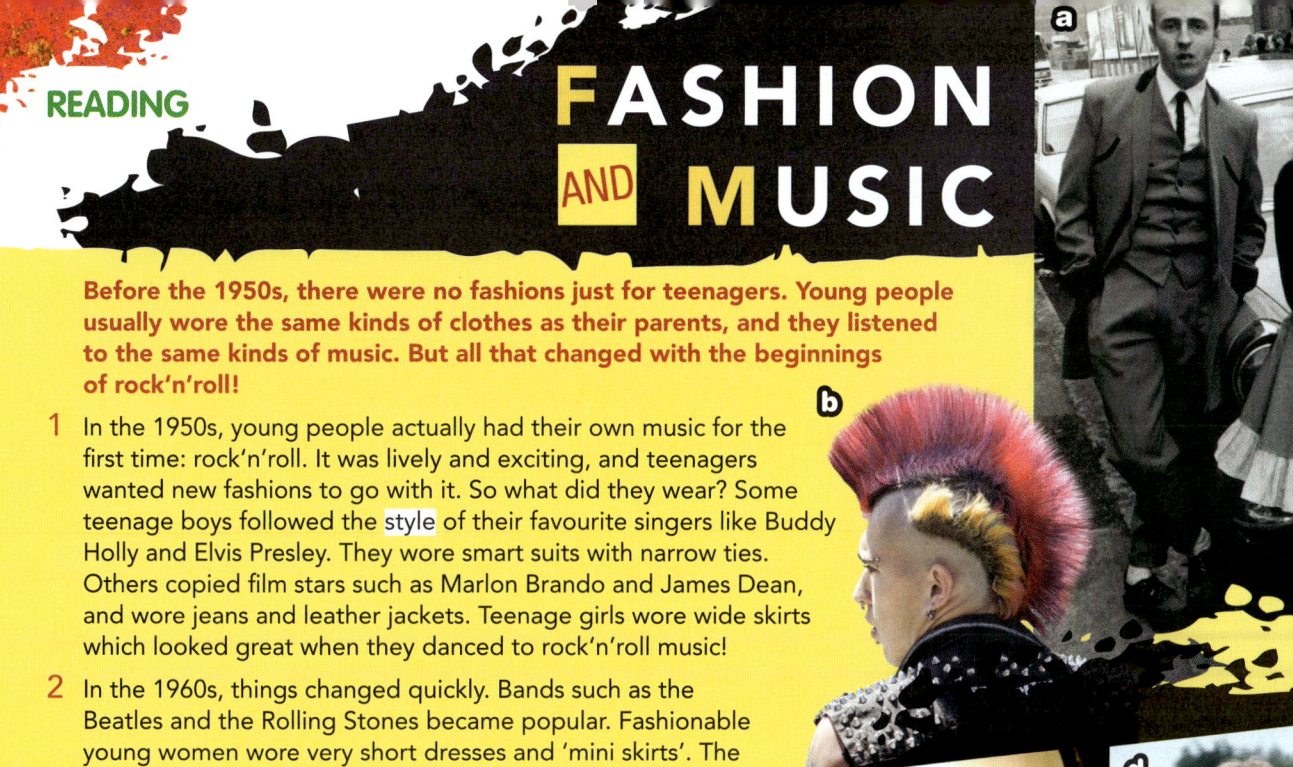

Before the 1950s, there were no fashions just for teenagers. Young people usually wore the same kinds of clothes as their parents, and they listened to the same kinds of music. But all that changed with the beginnings of rock'n'roll!

1 In the 1950s, young people actually had their own music for the first time: rock'n'roll. It was lively and exciting, and teenagers wanted new fashions to go with it. So what did they wear? Some teenage boys followed the style of their favourite singers like Buddy Holly and Elvis Presley. They wore smart suits with narrow ties. Others copied film stars such as Marlon Brando and James Dean, and wore jeans and leather jackets. Teenage girls wore wide skirts which looked great when they danced to rock'n'roll music!

2 In the 1960s, things changed quickly. Bands such as the Beatles and the Rolling Stones became popular. Fashionable young women wore very short dresses and 'mini skirts'. The older generation was shocked! The 1960s was also the time of the hippie movement. Young people were interested in ideas of peace and love, and wanted to make the world a better place. Many young men had long hair and wore sandals, some kind of loose shirt and very wide trousers.

3 The punk music of the 1970s and 80s was loud and angry, and the trends matched the music. Punks didn't want to be well-dressed or fashionable. They wanted to shock people, and they wanted to show that they didn't like the fashion industry. They bought second-hand clothes that looked old and dirty, and wore their hair in colourful and unusual ways.

4 In the 1980s and 1990s, black American music called hip hop became popular all over the world. Hip hop stars wore loose tracksuits, or jeans with trainers, and often a cap. They sang about money and fast cars. They loved to show how rich they were, so they wore lots of gold – rings, necklaces, that kind of thing. They called this 'bling'.

1 Read the article quickly. Match each paragraph to a photo.

2 Read the article again. Choose the correct answers.
1 Before the 1950s, teenagers …
 A didn't listen to music very much.
 B listened to the same music as adults.
2 In the 1950s, a lot of teenage boys …
 A joined rock'n'roll bands.
 B wore clothes similar to the pop stars.
3 In the 1960s, a lot of young men …
 A didn't like sandals.
 B grew their hair long.
4 In the 1970s, punks wanted …
 A to be very fashionable.
 B to look different.
5 In the 1980s and 1990s, hip hop singers liked …
 A wearing jewellery.
 B driving fast cars.

3 Match the highlighted words in the article to the meanings.
1 fashions
2 when there is no war
3 a way of arranging hair or designing clothes
4 a group of people of about the same age

EP Word profile *kind*

They listened to the same kinds of music.

They wore some kind of loose shirt.

They wore lots of gold – rings, necklaces, that kind of thing.

page 122

Talking points

Why do you think fashions change over time?
Why do young people like to dress differently to their parents and grandparents?

GRAMMAR   Past simple

1 Read the examples and complete the rules.
1 They **listened** to the same kinds of music.
2 They **didn't like** the fashion industry.
3 What **did** they **wear**?

> did   didn't   irregular

> We use the past simple to talk about finished past actions and states.
> a Regular verbs form the positive with -*ed*, but a lot of common verbs are ....
> b We form negative sentences with .... + the base form of the verb.
> c We form questions with .... + the base form of the verb.

→ Grammar reference   page 139

2 Choose the correct words.
1 I *see / saw* a really nice T-shirt at the market yesterday.
2 I wanted to buy some shoes, but I didn't *have / had* any money!
3 *Martha showed / Did Martha show* you her new raincoat?
4 I *went / going* shopping with my friend last Saturday.
5 I looked at a few jumpers, but I *didn't like / not like* any of them.
6 *Have / Did* you get any new clothes for your birthday?

3 Complete the sentences about you. Use the past simple positive or negative form of the verbs.
1 I .... (wear) jeans yesterday.
2 I .... (get) clothes for my last birthday.
3 My parents .... (buy) the clothes I'm wearing.
4 My family and I .... (watch) TV last night.
5 My best friend .... (text) me this morning.
6 I .... (ride) my bike last weekend.
7 We .... (play) football yesterday.
8 I .... (see) my friends before this class.

4 Complete the conversation with the past simple form of the verbs.
A: Hey, where ¹ .... (you / get) that T-shirt? It's really cool!
B: My brother ² .... (give) it to me for my birthday.
A: I really like it. Where ³ .... (he / find) it?
B: Well, he ⁴ .... (not find) it exactly. He ⁵ .... (design) it.
A: Really? How ⁶ .... (he / do) that?
B: He ⁷ .... (use) this app called UTme, on his phone. He ⁸ .... (take) a photo and then added the colours and the writing. He ⁹ .... (show) me the app. It's really cool.
A: Wow! I ¹⁰ .... (not know) you could do that. Can you show me the app?

5 Make questions about last weekend.
0 what / you / wear?   *What did you wear?*
0 you / go / shopping?   *Did you go shopping?*
1 where / you / go?
2 which friends / you / meet?
3 you / play / any sports?
4 what / watch / on TV?
5 you / go / to bed late?

6 Ask and answer the questions in exercise 5.
A: *What did you wear last weekend?*
B: *It was cold, so I wore my leather jacket.*

Corpus challenge
Find and correct the mistake in the student's sentence.
A few days ago, I meet a friend.

VOCABULARY   Adverbs

1 We can form adverbs from adjectives. Read the examples, then complete the table with adverbs from the adjectives in the box.
1 In the 1960s, things changed **quickly**.
2 He shouted at us **angrily**.
3 You need to work **hard**.

> ~~amazing~~   angry   bad   careful   fast
> good   hard   heavy   honest   polite
> rude   serious

+ -ly	y + -ily	Irregular adverbs
amazingly		

2 Complete the sentences with adverbs formed from the adjectives.
1 The sisters were chatting .... (happy).
2 She was late, so she was walking .... (quick).
3 You mustn't talk .... (loud) in the cinema.
4 My grandma is old. She walks quite .... (slow).
5 What did he say? He's talking very .... (quiet).
6 I'm studying .... (hard) for the exam.
7 I play the piano really .... (bad).
8 Alan won the tennis match .... (easy).

LISTENING

1 Look at the photos. Who are the people? What do you think they enjoy talking about together?

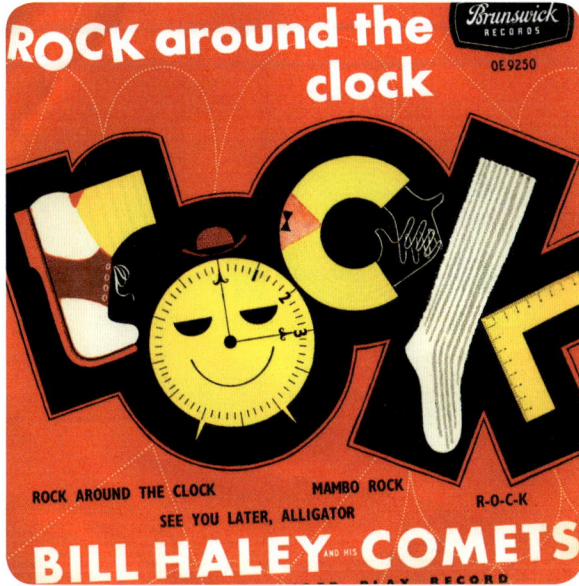

2 ▶1.07 Listen to the conversation. What does Jess's grandma talk about?
1 fashion and food
2 music and fashion
3 music and cars

3 ▶1.08 Listen to the first half the conversation again. Choose the correct words.
1 Grandma's sisters listened to the radio in the *bedroom / kitchen.*
2 Grandma *watched / didn't watch* television in the 1950s.
3 Grandma often went to the *cinema / theatre* in the evenings.
4 Grandma *didn't like / loved* rock'n'roll the first time she heard it.

4 ▶1.09 Listen to the second half of the conversation again. Complete the sentences.

| blue   dresses   fashionable   jeans   skirts |

1 Jess likes Grandma's jacket because it is the same colour as her ....
2 There weren't many .... clothes shops.
3 People made .... and .... at home.
4 Grandma made the .... jacket in 1961.

SPEAKING   Talking about yourself

1 Discuss the questions.
1 Do you enjoy shopping for clothes? Why? / Why not?
2 Who do you usually go shopping with?
3 What do you usually buy?

2 ▶1.10 Choose the correct words to make questions and think about your answers. Then listen to Harry answering the questions. Which of his answers were similar to yours?
1 *Are / Do* fashion and clothes important to you?
2 How often *you buy / do you buy* new clothes?
3 Where *do you usually / you do usually* buy your clothes?
4 How much *are / do* you spend on clothes?
5 What *do you enjoy / you enjoy* wearing?

3 ▶1.10 Listen again and complete the answers.
1 I .... having nice clothes.
2 I don't go shopping ....
3 I .... shopping in department stores because the clothes are too expensive.
4 I .... spend more when I get money for my birthday.
5 I .... jeans always look good.

4 ▶1.10 Read the *Prepare* box. Then listen again. Which phrases does Harry use?

Prepare to speak — Talking about yourself

When you answer questions:
• use the present simple and adverbs of frequency to talk about habits: *I usually ... , I always ... , I often ...*
• add reasons for your answer: *because ...*
• talk about your likes and dislikes: *I like ... , I don't like ... , I really like ...*
• give your opinion: *I think ... , I don't think ...*

5 Ask and answer the questions in exercise 2. Use phrases from the *Prepare* box.

In fashion 17

Culture
Homes around the world

1 Look at the photos on pages 18 and 19. Answer the questions. Then read the texts.
1. Where do you think each family is from? Why?
2. What can you say about the family in each photo?

2 Look at the photos for one minute. Then close your books and, in pairs, make a list of the families' possessions you can remember.

3 Read the texts again. Answer the questions.
1. Which family has got the smallest home? Which family has got the largest?
2. In which family do the children help their parents? How?
3. Which days do Mio and Maya go to school?
4. Which father enjoys watching sport?
5. Which of the families have got animals? What are they?

4 In groups, discuss these questions.
1. Why do you think Pearl Qampie lives with her aunt?
2. What do the Kalnazarovs own a lot of? Can you guess why?
3. Why do you think the Kalnazarovs live in two houses?
4. Why do you think the Ukitas' most important possessions are a ring and some ceramics?
5. How big is your home compared to these families' homes?
6. Which family is most like yours? Why?

5 ▶1.11 Listen to two teenagers talking about their homes and families. Where do they come from?

6 ▶1.11 Listen again and complete the table.

	Sanjeev	Tess
country they live in		
number of people in the family		
number of bedrooms in the home		
animals		
favourite possessions		

The Qampie family live in Soweto, near Johannesburg in South Africa.

Soweto is a famous place in South African history and Nelson Mandela had a home here for over fifty years. Over 300,000 families live in Soweto and the population is over 1 million.

The parents are Simon and Poppy. Simon's a security guard in a shop and Poppy works in an office. There are four children in the family – Pearl (14), Irene (11), George (4) and Mateo (2). Their house is small, only 37m², and Pearl actually lives with her aunt Anna. At weekends, Pearl has lunch at her parents' house with her aunt and her grandmother. Pearl's dad loves watching football – the most popular sport in South Africa.

8,500 kilometres north of Soweto is Tashkent, the capital of Uzbekistan.

In a village near Tashkent, the Kalnazarov family have got two houses: a small winter house (57m²) and a bigger summer house (93m²). It's winter, so they're sleeping in the two-bedroom winter house at the moment. There are eight people in the family so they use one bedroom for men and one for women. Bright rugs cover the floors of their houses.

Everyone works hard in the Kalnazarov family. In the mornings, Saliha, the mother, makes bread. The children help their parents when they aren't at school. Assiya (17) cuts wood for the fire. Zulfiya (14) looks after the animals. They've got three cows, for milk, and two dogs.

6,000 kilometres east of Tashkent is Tokyo, Japan.

It's 6.30 am in the Ukitas' 130m² home in Tokyo, Japan. Sayo Ukita is getting up. Her husband, Kazuo, and her two children, Mio (6) and Maya (9) are asleep. The Ukitas have a very busy life and Sayo has to be very organised.

Every morning, Sayo makes breakfast for the children. Kazuo wakes up as late as possible, has a quick breakfast of coffee and a vitamin pill, then leaves for work at 7.30. Mio and Maya start school at 8.30 am and they go every day except for Sundays. On Saturdays they go to a special school which helps them study for exams.

Their family home is full of clothes, toys and electrical equipment, but the family says that the most important thing they own is an old family ring and some family ceramics. Their wish for the future is to have a bigger house with more space for the things they own!

Project
Write a paragraph about your home and your life now. Describe:
- the town you live in and your home.
- the typical things your family does.
- your favourite possessions.

Homes around the world

3 My way of life

VOCABULARY Life events

Your profile
When did you learn to walk and talk?
How old were you when you learned to swim?

1 Match six of the phrases to the photos.

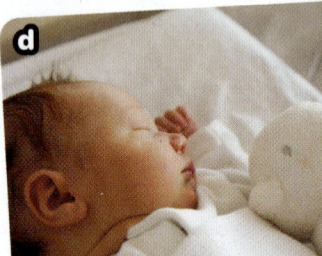

be born   get a degree   get a driving licence   get a job   get married   go to university
have children   leave home   leave school   start school

2 Read the quiz. Which event in exercise 1 is not mentioned in the questions?

Around the world: Age and events

1 In Britain, most children start school when they are ....
   a 4   b 5   c 6

2 In Belgium and Germany, students cannot leave school before they are ....
   a 14   b 16   c 18

3 In some states in the USA, the youngest age you can get a driving licence is ....
   a 14   b 16   c 17

4 In the UK, ... % of young people go to university, but only 30% get a degree.
   a 40   b 50   c 60

5 In almost all European countries, ... leave home before ....
   a men, women   b women, men

6 In the UK, children of .... are allowed to get a job.
   a any age   b 13 or over   c 16 or over

7 In .... , the average age at which women and men get married is 33.
   a Spain   b India   c Japan

8 In Sweden, approximately 55% of married couples ....
   a have children   b live with their parents   c buy their own house

3 ▶1.12 Listen and choose Ali's answers to the quiz.

4 In pairs, choose your answers to the quiz. Then check your answers on page 120. Did you get more points than Ali?

5 Look at the events in exercise 1 again. Make six sentences with *I want to …* .
I want to leave home before I'm 25.

6 Discuss the questions.
1 When can you leave school in your country?
2 At what age can you get a job?
3 How old do you have to be to get a driving licence?
4 What do you think is the best age to get married?
5 Is it important to go to university and get a degree? Why? / Why not?

READING

Teenage life – better now, or in the past?

Does this situation sound familiar?

You're complaining to your parents about something. Maybe your laptop isn't powerful enough to play the latest games. Or your friends' bikes are better than yours. Then you hear …

'When I was your age, there weren't any computers or video games. And I didn't get a bike until I was 16. And it was second-hand. And it was too big for me!'

So, is it really true that life is better for teenagers now? It's certainly true that many teenagers have got more things nowadays. A *typical* family is smaller now, so parents have got more money to spend on each child. And many things are cheaper than they were when our parents were children.

Technology is probably the greatest change. Forty years ago, no one could imagine a world with *tiny* computers, tablets and amazing smartphones. And now these things are our most *essential* possessions – we can't imagine living without them!

However, technology often means we spend more time at home. And often it's just us, with our computer or television. Teenagers aren't as healthy as they were in the past because they don't do enough exercise. And, although young people still get on well with their friends, some people think teenagers today aren't as sociable as they were in the past.

What do you think? How is teenage life better these days?

Comments

Luisa, Spain
Medicine is more advanced now. People live longer and enjoy healthier lives. This is good news for young people today!

Tom, UK
I asked my parents. My mum admits school work wasn't as hard as it is now. And my dad thinks life is too busy for teenagers nowadays. I agree. I'm always *exhausted*.

Katarina, Switzerland
Women and men are almost equal now. This is a *huge* change for female teenagers. Fifty years ago women couldn't vote in my country!

Marco, Italy
Cars are safer. This is good for teenagers as a lot of them are *awful* drivers!

Post comment

---

1 Read the article and the comments quickly. Which person thinks life is more difficult for teenagers now?

2 Read the article and comments again. Choose the correct answers.
1 Teenagers own more things now because …
   A they don't buy as many new things.
   B couples don't have as many children.
2 Technology …
   A is very important to teenagers nowadays.
   B was very expensive for people to buy in the past.
3 Teenagers need to …
   A do more sport.
   B be more polite to adults.
4 Luisa believes that …
   A teenagers don't see their parents for as long now.
   B people continue living until they are older now.
5 Tom's parents think that teenage life now is …
   A harder than it was.
   B easier than it was.
6 Katarina feels that the situation for women now is …
   A better.
   B worse.

3 Match the highlighted adjectives in the article to the meanings.
0 usual   *typical*
1 very bad
2 very small
3 very big
4 extremely important
5 very tired

EP Word profile *get*

This quiz is *getting* harder.

Let's see how many points you *got*.

Young people *get on* well with their friends.

page 122

Talking points

❝ What do teenagers need in order to be happy? What problems can modern life bring for teenagers? ❞

Video extra   My way of life

GRAMMAR Comparatives and superlatives

1 Complete the table with the correct comparative and superlative adjectives. Check your answers in the article on page 21.

Adjective	Comparative	Superlative
one-syllable adjectives		
big	bigger	the biggest
great	greater	1 ....
safe	2	the safest
two-syllable adjectives with -y		
healthy	3	the healthiest
other two-syllable and longer adjectives		
essential	more essential	4 ....
irregular adjectives		
good	5	the best
bad	worse	the worst

2 Read the examples. Then complete the rules with *comparative* and *superlative*.
  1 Your friend's bike is **better than** yours.
  2 Technology is **the greatest** change.

> We use:
> **a** *than* after .... adjectives.
> **b** *the* before .... adjectives.

→ Grammar reference page 140

3 Complete the facts with the comparative or superlative form of the adjectives. Remember to use *than* or *the*.

1 .... (old) woman in the world lived until she was 122.
2 Teenagers between 14 and 16 are generally 5kg .... (heavy) they were fifty years ago.
3 Research says that Denmark is .... (happy) country in the world.
4 University courses in the UK are usually .... (short) in other countries.
5 .... (expensive) city in the world to live in is London.
6 The north of England is generally .... (cheap) the south of England.
7 An international report says that .... (good) country in the world to live in is Australia.
8 .... (friendly) teenagers on the internet are Brazilians, with about 250 online friends.

not as … as

4 Read the example and choose the correct words to complete the rule.
Teenagers **aren't as** *healthy* **as** *they were in the past.*
(= they were healthier in the past)

> We use **not as … as** to say that people or things are *the same / not the same*.

→ Grammar reference page 140

5 Compare the people and things with *not as … as*. Use your own ideas.

> casual   fashionable   hard   messy   old   serious

0 English / maths
  English isn't as hard as maths.
1 children / adults
2 you / your best friend
3 your dad / your mum
4 your teacher's clothes / your clothes
5 you / one of your relatives

Corpus challenge

Find and correct the mistake in the student's sentence.
Suddenly the man became more happy.

VOCABULARY too, not enough

1 Read the examples and choose the correct meaning.
  1 *The coat was **too big** for me!*
    a I needed something smaller.
    b I needed something bigger.
  2 *My internet connection **isn't fast enough**.*
    a I want it to be faster.
    b It's about the right speed.
  3 *They **don't do enough** exercise.*
    a They do a lot of exercise.
    b They should do more exercise.

2 Write replies. Use *too* or *enough* and the words in brackets. Be careful with the position of *enough*.

0 A: Why aren't you coming to the concert?
  B: I'm *..too busy..* (busy) and I haven't got *..enough money..* (money).
1 A: Did you buy the trainers?
  B: No. They weren't .... (big). They felt .... (tight).
2 A: Why didn't you do the homework?
  B: I didn't have .... (time) and I was .... (tired).
3 A: Why are you getting a new laptop?
  B: My one is .... (slow) and it hasn't got .... (memory).
4 A: Why didn't your brother go to university?
  B: There weren't .... (places) and his marks weren't .... (good).

WRITING   An informal letter or email (1)

1 Jamal has moved to a new town. Read part of a letter that he receives from his friend Jack. Then read Jamal's reply. Does Jamal answer all of Jack's questions?

> Everyone here misses you, at school and in the football team!
> Tell me about your new home. Do you like the town where you're living now? What's your new school like? How are you getting on?

> Hi Jack,
>
> How's it going? We moved into our new house on Friday. The house is really nice, and I love my new room! The town is quite small, but I think there will be enough things to do. There's a cinema and a football club, so that's great.
>
> I started my new school today. It's bigger than my old school, but it isn't as modern. My first lesson was ICT, and there weren't enough laptops for everyone. Everyone's really friendly, though. I had to share a laptop with a guy called Simon. I get on really well with him. He's an Avicii fan like me and he's really funny. I guess we're going to be good mates.
>
> Speak soon,
> Jamal

2 Read the *Prepare* box. Which phrases does Jamal use to begin and end his letter?

Prepare to write An informal letter or email (1)

In informal letters and emails:
- use an informal phrase to begin your letter: *Dear … , Hi … , Hello …*
- use an informal phrase to end your letter: *Love, Write soon, Speak soon, See you soon*
- use short forms: *it's, she's, I'll*
- use informal words: *really nice, I guess*

3 Find 10 short forms in Jamal's letter.

4 Rewrite the sentences using short forms.
1. He is really nice and we are good friends.
2. How is school? I hope you are getting on well.
3. I am getting to know people and they are all really nice.
4. We have got tickets and we are going to an Avicii concert.

5 Match the highlighted informal words and phrases in Jamal's letter to the meanings.
0. How are you getting on?   *How's it going?*
1. I think
2. very
3. boy
4. very good
5. friends

6 Imagine you have moved to a new town. Read Jack's letter again and plan your reply. Use the notes to help you.
- Where is your new house? Is it nice? What's your bedroom like?
- What's the town like? Is it big or small? Are there lots of things to do?
- What's your new school like? Is it bigger or smaller than your old one? Are the lessons interesting?
- Are the people friendly? Have you got any new friends yet? What are their names? What are they like?

7 Write your letter to Jack.
- Use the tips in the *Prepare* box.
- Write about 80–100 words.
- Remember to check your spelling and grammar.

My way of life

4 Champions

VOCABULARY Sports

Your profile
Which sports do you play regularly?
Which sports do you watch?

1 ▶ 1.13 Match the photos to some of the sports in the box. Then listen and check. Check the meaning of the other sports.

a   b

c   d

e   f

g   h

athletics   boxing   climbing   cycling
gymnastics   ice hockey   ice skating   jogging
rugby   squash   surfing   swimming
table tennis   tennis   volleyball   windsurfing

2 ▶ 1.14 Listen and match the sentence halves.

1 We go   a athletics in the summer.
2 We do   b cycling all the time.
3 Do you play   c jogging quite often.
4 I go   d ice hockey?
5 My mates and I go   e tennis together.
6 We never play   f windsurfing on the lake.

3 Complete the table with the sports from exercise 1.

do	athletics
go	climbing
play	ice hockey

4 What other sports can you think of? Add them to the lists in exercise 3.

play basketball   go snowboarding

5 Discuss the questions.
1 What's your favourite sport? Why?
2 What are the most popular sports in your country?

6 Do the quiz in pairs. Then check your answers on page 120.

RACE AGAINST THE CLOCK

Answer the questions about the sports in exercise 1.

Be quick! You've got a time limit of five minutes!

1 Which nine sports can you do on your own?
2 Which four sports are for two or four players?
3 Which three sports are for teams of more than four?
4 Which five sports do you do on or in water or ice?
5 In which two sports do you use a racket?
6 In which four sports is there a net?
7 Which sport is not in the Olympic Games?
   a cycling
   b table tennis
   c ice hockey
   d rugby
8 What sports do people do in these competitions?
   a Wimbledon
   b Tour de France
   c World Heavyweight Championships

READING

1 Read Jess's profile and look at her photo. How would you describe her?

2 Look at the advertisement. What is the advertisement for? What sport can you watch at Twickenham?

Win two VIP tickets to see England v Australia at Twickenham.

Prize includes a tour of the stadium and the museum, and front row seats for the match! Email competition@greatprizes.com with your reasons why you should go.

Hi! I'm Jess. I'm 14 years old and I'm from Manchester. I love all kinds of sports. I usually play hockey in the winter and I do athletics in the summer. I also enjoy trying and watching new sports.

3 Read Jess's blog and check your ideas in exercise 2.

A LUCKY WIN AND A NEW SPORT!

I'm not normally a lucky person, but I entered a competition last month to win tickets for a rugby match at Twickenham. Two weeks ago, I was finishing my homework when my phone rang. I was one of the competition winners. No way! I couldn't believe it! A few days later, I was sitting on a coach with my dad. We were on our way to London.

When we arrived, I was amazed. I knew Twickenham was the largest rugby stadium in the world, but it is huge – there's enough room for 82,000 supporters. At the entrance we met Martin – our guide for the day. He showed us around the stadium and the museum. We learnt that the stadium is over 100 years old. Before there was a stadium there, people grew cabbages on the land, so it's also known as 'The Cabbage Patch'.

Next, Martin took us to our seats and the view was amazing. While we were waiting for the match to start, a band started playing and a group of dancers appeared. At 2.30, the referee started the match. There are several different ways of getting points in rugby, so it's always exciting to watch. After 40 minutes, it was half-time. The Australians were playing really well and they were winning 13–6. The England coach didn't look pleased. His team was losing by 7 points.

England began the second half well. Then Dad grabbed my arm and pointed at one of the England players. He was running with the ball and the Australians were trying to stop him. He scored and the crowd went crazy! At full-time, the score was England 20, Australia 13. I was really happy!

From that moment, I knew I wanted to play rugby, but there's only a boys' team at my school. With my dad's help, I found a girls' team nearby and next week I begin rugby training. My friends Ali and Matt think I'm mad, but I think they're old-fashioned. More and more women are beginning to take up sports like rugby, football and golf. Who knows? Maybe one day I'll play for England at Twickenham.

4 Read Jess's blog again. Are the sentences correct or incorrect?
1 Jess finished her homework before her phone rang.
2 People once grew vegetables on the land where the stadium now is.
3 Jess and her father could see the match very well.
4 The match started as soon as Jess and her father sat down.
5 England played better than Australia in the first half of the match.
6 Australia didn't score any points in the second half.
7 Jess can't play rugby at her school.

5 Match the highlighted words in the blog to the meanings.
1 the number of points that each person or team has in a competition
2 someone who teaches a sport or is in charge of a team's training programme
3 people who watch a player or team and want them to win
4 a big building where people watch sports events
5 the person who controls a sports game and makes sure people follow the rules

EP Word profile *way*

No way! I couldn't believe it!

We were on our way to London.

There are several different ways of getting points in rugby.

page 123

Talking points

" Should schools offer the same sports to girls and boys? Or are some sports for boys and others for girls?
Do you think there is too much sport on TV? Why? / Why not? "

GRAMMAR Past continuous

1 **Read the examples. Then choose the correct words to complete the rules.**
   1 *I **was sitting** on a coach with my dad.*
   2 *The Australians **were playing** really well and they **were winning**.*

   a We use the past continuous to talk about actions in progress at a particular time in *the present / the past*.
   b We form the past continuous with the correct *present / past* form of *be* and the *infinitive / -ing* form of the verb.

→ **Grammar reference** page 141

2 **Complete the sentences with the past continuous form of the verbs.**
   0 Mark ..*was playing*.. (play) basketball yesterday.
   1 They .... (laugh) at us.
   2 I .... (not play) ice hockey.
   3 My friends .... (not talk) about sports.
   4 What .... (he / do) on the court?
   5 .... (she / watch) the game? Yes, she ....
   6 .... (they / listen) to the match on their phones? No, they ....

3 **Look at the picture. Write positive and negative past continuous sentences.**

   0 Kim / play tennis / swim
   Kim was playing tennis. She wasn't swimming.
   1 Adam and Pete / run / skate
   2 Myla / throw a ball / hit a ball
   3 Karl and Liam / play squash / kick a ball
   4 Megan and Ana / cycle / play table tennis
   5 Lucy / catch the ball / do athletics

4 **Write questions in the past continuous.**
   0 you / do / sports at 3.30 yesterday afternoon?
   Were you doing sports at 3.30 yesterday afternoon?
   1 what / you / do / at 8.30 yesterday evening?
   2 you / read / at 10.30 / yesterday evening?
   3 what / you / wear / last / Sunday?
   4 you / sleep / at midnight last night?
   5 you / have / breakfast at 8.00 this morning?
   6 what / do / five minutes ago?

5 **Ask and answer the questions in exercise 4.**
   A: *Were you doing sports at 3.30 yesterday afternoon?*
   B: *Yes, I was. I was playing hockey.*

Corpus challenge

Find and correct the mistake in the student's sentence.
The first time I saw her was when I study in class 10.

VOCABULARY Words with different meanings

1 **Read the sentences. Choose the correct meaning of the bold words.**
   1 We got a **coach** to the volleyball match.
      a noun: a type of bus
      b noun: someone who teaches people a sport
   2 Does this tracksuit **fit** you?
      a verb: be the right size
      b adjective: healthy and strong
   3 Who won the Chelsea–Arsenal **match**?
      a verb: be the same
      b noun: a sports competition
   4 The Bulls won the basketball game by 20 **points**.
      a noun: the score at the end of a game or sports match
      b verb: show where something is using your finger
   5 The basketball team has got a new **trainer**.
      a noun: a sports shoe
      b noun: a person who helps you prepare for a sporting event

2 **Complete the sentences with the correct form of the meanings you didn't use in exercise 1.**
   0 The green colour in your shoes ..*matches*.. your top.
   1 You aren't .... enough. Do some exercise!
   2 We go jogging with the .... every day.
   3 Can you .... at the captain? I can't see her.
   4 I've got some new white ....

LISTENING

1. ▶1.15 Listen to the show and look at photos a–c. Which is the photo of the week? What happened next?

2. ▶1.15 Number the events in the order you hear them. Then listen again and check.
   a The football went into the goal.
   b The Sunderland player kicked the football.
   c A supporter threw a beach ball onto the field.
   d A Sunderland player was running towards the goal.
   e The referee decided to allow the goal.
   f The football hit the beach ball.

3. ▶1.15 Listen again. Complete the sentences.

   | Liverpool (x3)   Manchester   Sunderland (x2) |

   1 The *Sports Review* studio is in ....
   2 A .... supporter threw a beach ball onto the field.
   3 .... won the match 1–0.
   4 The .... players weren't playing well.
   5 Sara thought .... played better than ....

SPEAKING Describing a past event

1 When was the last time you watched a sports event or took part in one? What was it?

2 ▶1.16 Listen to Matt and Jess talking about sports events. Who took part in an event? Who watched an event?

3 ▶1.16 Read the *Prepare* box. Complete the sentences with the past simple or past continuous form of the verbs. Then listen again and check.
   1 Manchester City .... (win) for most of the game.
   2 Real Madrid .... (score) two goals in the last five minutes.
   3 Lots of people .... (watch) the competition.
   4 I .... (come) third in one race.

Prepare to speak — Describing a past event

When you describe a past event:
- use the past simple to talk about the main things that happened.
- use the past continuous to talk about actions in progress.
- add your opinion: *It was an amazing …, It was really exciting, It was so cool, I really enjoyed …*
- add reasons for your opinion: *because …*

4 ▶1.16 Listen again. Which phrases do Matt and Jess use to give their opinion?

5 ▶1.16 Complete the reasons that Matt and Jess give. Listen again and check.
   1 I was very happy because …
   2 I really enjoyed taking part because …

6 Think about a recent sports event. Read the questions and plan your answers.
   1 What was the event and when was it?
   2 Did you watch it or take part in it?
   3 What happened during the event?
   4 What was the final result?
   5 Did you enjoy it? Why? / Why not?

7 Ask and answer the questions in exercise 6. Use the past simple and past continuous, and use phrases from the *Prepare* box.

Champions   27

PE
Sports training

1 In pairs, look at the photos on page 29. Describe what the people are doing in each photo. What sports is each type of training useful for?

2 Read text A. Then read text B quickly. Which of points 1–4 in text A is the main idea of text B?

TRAINING FOR SPORTS

A PLANNING

It is important for athletes to plan their training. They need to think about:
1 what types of training are best for their sport.
2 how often they need to train and for how long.
3 what diet will give them the most energy and strength.
4 where they can do their training and what special equipment they need.

B TRAINING

Circuit training
Athletes run from place to place in a gym and do a different type of exercise in each place – for example, press-ups, rowing, weight lifting, running or cycling. They do each exercise for a few minutes. Circuit training helps with general fitness, speed and balance for any sport.

Continuous training
Athletes do one type of exercise for quite a long time without a rest. Continuous training gives the body stamina, and that means the body is physically and mentally strong.

Interval training
Athletes do one type of exercise very hard, for example running or swimming, and then rest. Then they do it again, then rest, and so on. Interval training is good for speed and also for muscle strength.

Weight training
Training with light weights improves stamina. Lifting heavy weights gives athletes strength.

Fartlek training
'Fartlek' means 'speed-play' in Swedish. Athletes do one type of exercise, such as running, skiing or swimming, but they change the speed a lot. Fartlek training is good for sports like football and volleyball, when players need to run very fast for short distances.

This is an example of fartlek training:
Repeat 2–6 times
1 jogging for 3km
2 running fast for 30m
3 jogging for 100m
4 running fast for 50m
5 jogging for 120m
6 running fast for 70m
7 jogging for 3km

Sport-specific training
Each sport has got different requirements. Footballers need good balance and speed, swimmers need stamina and strength, and basketball players need balance and good jumping ability. Training for basketball players, for example, includes a lot of jumping and running fast over short distances.

Parts of a training session
Warm-up
You can injure your body if you don't warm up properly before a training session. Warm up by jogging and touching your toes.

Main training exercises
Start by doing a little training and increase the amount you do every day or week.

Cool down
Always go for a slow jog after a training session. You can get a lot of aches and pains if you don't let your body cool down slowly.

Key words
press-ups lying on the ground and pushing up with your arms
weight a heavy object that athletes lift during training
fitness having a strong and healthy body
balance standing up and not falling to either side
stamina the ability to do exercise for a long period
speed how fast something moves
muscle the parts of your body that allow you to move
strength being strong

3 Read text B again and write the names of the activities in the photos.

4 Complete the text.

> circuit   fartlek   gym   interval   rowing   weight

For ¹.................. training, athletes do a variety of exercises, such as ².................. and cycling in a ³.................. . Continuous training and ⁴.................. training can give your body stamina. ⁵.................. training means training with the same activities at different speeds, and ⁶.................. training helps athletes go faster and have stronger muscles.

5 What do you think? In pairs, discuss the questions.
1 In which sports do athletes need a lot of stamina? Why?
2 What sports use weight training? Why?
3 What fartlek training would you recommend for a swimmer? Why?

6 ▶1.17 Listen to Antonia talking about her hockey training. What kinds of training does she do? Which kind does she prefer?

7 ▶1.17 In pairs, answer the questions. Use these words to help you. Then listen and check.

> jogging   passing   power   running
> shooting   standing   strength
> stretching   touching your toes   walking

1 What are hockey players doing for most of a hockey game?
2 To run fast and hit the ball hard, what do players need?
3 To change direction quickly, what do players need?
4 Why do hockey players do interval training?
5 What skills training do hockey players do?

8 ▶1.18 Listen and complete Antonia's fartlek training plan with the correct numbers.

CASE STUDY — FARTLEK TRAINING PLAN

3 kilometres jogging
¹.......... metres running
².......... metres jogging
70 metres running
150 metres jogging
³.......... metres running
⁴.......... metres jogging
70 metres running
150 metres jogging
⁵.......... metres running
⁶.......... kilometres jogging

Project
Make a training plan for a sport that you like.
- Use the internet to research the sport.
- Think about:
  1 general fitness
  2 fitness training especially for the sport
  3 skills for the sport
- Write a short training plan.

Review 1
Units 1-4

VOCABULARY

1 Write the opposite adjectives.
1. What's wrong? You look **miserable**. You're usually very c............ on Fridays.
2. Diana's very **polite**. She's never r............ .
3. 'Is Jacob **shy**?' 'No, he's quite c............ .'
4. It was **careless** of you to lose your phone again. You need to be more c............ with your things.
5. Marcus is really **friendly** today. He can sometimes be quite u............ !

2 Find the words (→ ↘ ↓) and complete the lists.

c	l	i	m	b	i	n	g	e	t	j	d
e	j	c	d	p	c	n	g	r	f	n	a
l	a	a	a	j	r	a	i	o	a	n	t
f	c	s	r	m	n	h	s	h	c	e	s
a	q	u	k	o	s	l	d	u	k	w	b
i	e	a	e	t	j	n	p	c	a	h	j
r	t	l	a	o	o	o	a	l	s	l	u
y	v	e	g	c	z	j	g	a	o	o	m
m	w	v	e	g	y	m	n	g	a	s	p
s	b	s	d	c	u	r	l	y	i	u	e
t	e	e	n	a	t	i	g	h	t	n	r
g	y	m	n	a	s	t	i	c	s	q	g

Describing someone's hair
c............   f............
d............

Clothes: nouns
j............   s............
j............

Clothes: adjectives
c............   s............
t............

Sports
c............   j............
g............

3 Choose two correct words for each verb.
1. **play** table tennis volleyball cycling surfing
2. **get** born married university a degree
3. **go** ice hockey swimming squash windsurfing
4. **leave** home children married school
5. **have** children teenage confident long hair

GRAMMAR

4 Complete the conversations. Use the present simple or continuous, or the past simple or continuous.
1. **A:** I .... (spend) a lot of time on homework at the moment.
   B: Me too. Last term, we .... (not have) as much work.
2. **A:** .... (you / have) food at your party last week?
   B: Of course. My mum always............ (make) some stuff. Everyone............ (love) her cooking.
3. **A:** I thought your brother's cap was cool yesterday. Where .... (he / buy) it?
   B: What? My brother .... (not wear) a cap yesterday. That was my cousin.
4. **A:** I really .... (enjoy) that film last night.
   B: Me too. But it was so sad. My sister and I .... (cry) at the end.
5. **A:** .... (you / go) swimming next Saturday?
   B: No. I .... (usually / go) swimming on Saturdays, but the pool .... (be) closed at the moment.
6. **A:** You .... (not call) me last night.
   B: No, sorry. I .... (watch) a movie all evening. It was really good!

5 Complete the second sentence so that it means the same as the first. Use no more than three words.
1. It's cheaper to buy fashionable clothes these days.
   These days, fashionable clothes aren't .... they were in the past.
2. These shoes are too small for me.
   These shoes aren't .... for me.
3. It isn't warm enough for a barbecue.
   It's .... cold for a barbecue.
4. These jeans are tighter than the other pair.
   The other jeans .... tight as these ones.
5. I haven't got a warmer jacket for skiing.
   This is .... jacket I've got for skiing.
6. The shoes in this shop aren't as good as in the shop next door.
   The shoes in the shop next door .... in this shop.
7. The other boots on this website aren't as expensive as these ones.
   These are .... boots on this website.
8. I need a warmer coat than this one.
   This coat isn't .... for me.

Corpus challenge

6 Tick the two sentences without mistakes. Correct the mistakes in the other sentences.

1. I'm writing to tell you about one of my friends.
2. We are having fun when we are together.
3. I go camping with my friends last weekend.
4. We choosed to go to the cinema.
5. He is my old brother.
6. We play football together but I am not as good as him.
7. We were going to the beach every day.
8. We couldn't go to school because a tree blocked the road.

7 Read the text and choose the correct word for each space.

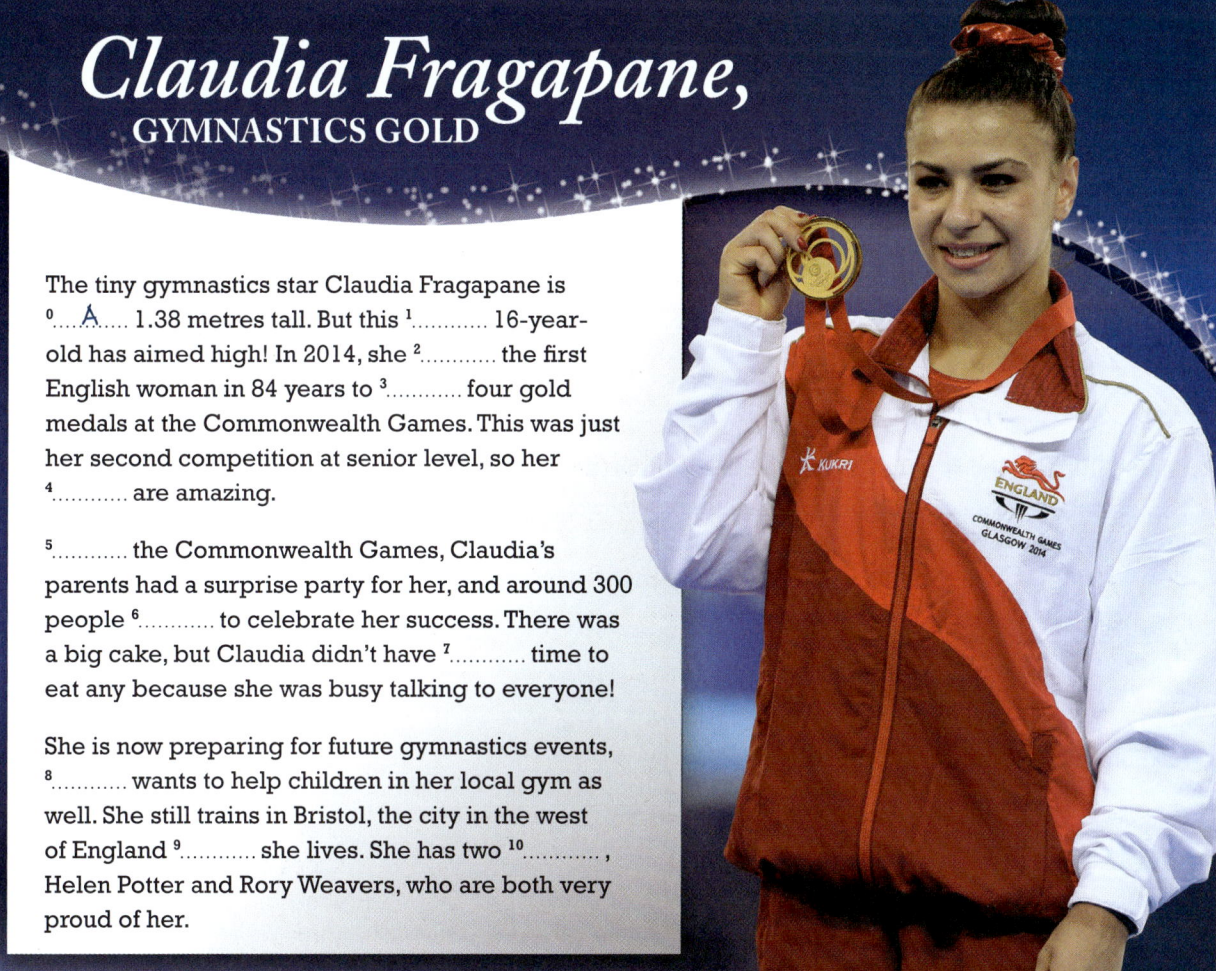

Claudia Fragapane, GYMNASTICS GOLD

The tiny gymnastics star Claudia Fragapane is ⁰...A... 1.38 metres tall. But this ¹.......... 16-year-old has aimed high! In 2014, she ².......... the first English woman in 84 years to ³.......... four gold medals at the Commonwealth Games. This was just her second competition at senior level, so her ⁴.......... are amazing.

⁵.......... the Commonwealth Games, Claudia's parents had a surprise party for her, and around 300 people ⁶.......... to celebrate her success. There was a big cake, but Claudia didn't have ⁷.......... time to eat any because she was busy talking to everyone!

She is now preparing for future gymnastics events, ⁸.......... wants to help children in her local gym as well. She still trains in Bristol, the city in the west of England ⁹.......... she lives. She has two ¹⁰.......... , Helen Potter and Rory Weavers, who are both very proud of her.

0	A only	B even	C also	D less
1	A curly	B clear	C confident	D central
2	A started	B became	C happened	D began
3	A buy	B play	C win	D make
4	A matches	B points	C events	D results
5	A Over	B After	C Past	D Between
6	A came	B turned	C found	D reached
7	A too	B several	C all	D enough
8	A or	B so	C but	D if
9	A what	B where	C which	D when
10	A coaches	B teams	C captains	D members

5 Take a good look

VOCABULARY People and action verbs

Your profile
Think about your favourite photos. Who is in them? What is happening? Why do you like the photos?

1 Match the sentences to the photos. Which sentences do not match a photo?

1 The cat and mouse are **fighting** and **hitting** their swords together.
2 The astronaut is **pointing** to the camera.
3 The player is **holding** the ball and wants to **throw** it to one of his team mates.
4 I don't know why she's **making a face**.
5 The two people are **shaking hands**.
6 The astronaut is **waving** to friends.
7 The player is trying to **catch** the ball, but he might **drop** it.
8 Someone's going up onto the stage, and people are **clapping**.

2 Look at the photos for one minute. Then cover them. In pairs, remember as much as possible about each photo.

In photo a, two men are shaking hands.

3 ▶ 1.19 Who do you think the people or characters are in each photo? Listen and check your ideas.

4 ▶ 1.19 Are the sentences correct or incorrect? Listen again and decide.

1 Canada won the final of the ice hockey at the Winter Olympics in Sochi.
2 On 4th July, 1969, Neil Armstrong was the first man to walk on the moon.
3 Katy Perry is advertising some false eyelashes.
4 Tom and Jerry have won more Oscars than any other cartoon.
5 In American football, the ball can travel at over 90 kilometres an hour.
6 Brad Pitt is happy because he's getting an award.

5 Discuss the questions.

1 What do you do when you say hello and goodbye to a friend or relative?
2 Is it rude to point at people in your country?
3 Are you good at throwing and catching?

EP Word profile *take*

Twelve teams **took part** in the men's ice hockey tournament.

It **took** them four days to get to the moon.

She's **taking a break** from singing.

page 123

READING

CAUGHT ON CAMERA...

Everyone takes photos all the time now, but this wasn't always true. In the past, taking a photo was a special event. Read about three special photos from the past.

1 On 21st July 1969, astronaut Neil Armstrong climbed down the ladder from the Eagle moon lander. Around 600 million people were watching him on television. When he got to the bottom, he carefully put his left foot on the moon. "That's one small step for a man, one giant leap for mankind," he said. This photo shows an astronaut's footprint on the moon. However, it isn't Armstrong's. Buzz Aldrin, the other astronaut on the Eagle, took the photo. It's his footprint and is the most famous photo from that incredible day. Armstrong and Aldrin spent over two and a half hours on the moon. They took photos, collected rocks and even spoke to the US President. There isn't any wind or rain on the moon, so this footprint will always be there.

2 In 1932, the photographer Charles Ebbets was working for a building company. He was taking photos of a new skyscraper in New York. He took this photo while the builders were having lunch. They were 250 metres above the ground! A New York newspaper published the photo in the same year. The photograph became very famous, but nobody knew the name of the photographer.
Ebbets died in 1978. Over 20 years later, his daughter found an old collection of her father's photos. There were some similar pictures of the skyscraper. She contacted the photo library that now owned the photo. When they saw the collection, they agreed that this famous photo was by Ebbets – 70 years after he took it!

3 This is Albert Einstein – the famous scientist – with his tongue out! It was 1951 and it was Einstein's 72nd birthday. Reporters were following him everywhere. The scientist was feeling a bit annoyed when photographer Arthur Sasse asked him to smile. So he made a face. The photo became the most popular picture of Einstein in the world. He even put the photo on cards for his friends. In 2009, a bookshop bought the original photo for $74,326.

1 Read the stories quickly and match them to the photos.

2 Read the stories again. Answer the questions.
1. How many people were watching Armstrong when he stepped onto the moon?
2. Whose footprint is in photo **b**?
3. What did the astronauts do on the moon?
4. When did people first see photo **c**?
5. How did Ebbets' daughter know that the photographer was her father?
6. How was Einstein feeling on his birthday? Why?
7. Did Einstein like the photo of him? How do you know?

3 Complete the sentences with the highlighted words in the stories.
1. Be careful on those .... ! They look dangerous.
2. Mark and I have .... hobbies, so we get on well.
3. Our .... plan was to meet here, but we've changed our mind.
4. There's a .... new shopping centre near my house with over 200 shops.
5. I get really .... when my sister takes my stuff.
6. My brother has a huge .... of old football tickets.

Talking points
What makes a good photograph?
Why do some people hate having their photo taken?

Video extra Take a good look

GRAMMAR Past simple and continuous

1 Read the examples. Which verb is in the past continuous? How do we form the past continuous?
1 *Armstrong and Aldrin **spent** over two and a half hours on the moon.*
2 *Reporters **were following** him everywhere.*

2 Choose the correct words to complete the rules.

> a We use the past *simple / continuous* to talk about a complete action at a past time.
> b We use the past *simple / continuous* to talk about actions in progress at a past time.

3 Choose the correct form of the verb.
1 Hey! Don't turn off the TV. I *watched / was watching* that programme!
2 *Did you take / Were you taking* this photo at Rachel's party?
3 My dad *left / was leaving* home on his 21st birthday.
4 I wasn't at home last night. I *travelled / was travelling* back from my aunt's house.
5 Simon couldn't answer his phone because he *had / was having* a shower.
6 I caught the ball and *didn't drop / wasn't dropping* it.

4 Read the examples. Then complete the rules with *past simple* or *past continuous*.
1 *The scientist **was feeling** a bit annoyed when photographer Arthur Sasse **asked** him to smile.*
2 *Ebbets **took** this photo while the builders **were having** lunch.*
3 *When he **got** to the bottom, he carefully **put** his left foot on the moon.*

> We often use the past continuous and the past simple together.
> a The .... talks about a past action in progress.
> b The .... talks about a complete shorter action that interrupted the action in progress.
> c If one action happens after the other, we use the .... for both actions.

→ Grammar reference **page 142**

5 Complete the story with the past simple or past continuous form of the verbs.

On a cold January morning, Flight 1549 ⁰ *was taking off* (take off) from a New York airport when it ¹............ (hit) some birds. The engines ²............ (stop) almost immediately. Captain Sullenberger quickly realised that the plane ³............ (fall) very fast. There was only one place he could land the plane: in the Hudson River in the middle of New York!

Steven Day is a photographer. That morning he ⁴............ (work) on his computer when someone passed his desk. 'What's that?' they asked, pointing to something on the river. Steven ⁵............ (find) his camera. At first, he didn't know what he ⁶............ (take) pictures of. 'It ⁷............ (move) down the river, like a boat,' he said. When he looked closely, he ⁸............ (see) it was a plane. People ⁹............ (stand) on its wings in the middle of the river!

Steven Day's photograph ¹⁰............ (appear) in newspapers and on websites all over the world.

Corpus challenge

Find and correct the mistake in the student's sentence.

She walked in the street and found £10.

VOCABULARY *myself, yourself, each other*

1 Match the examples to the pictures.

1 *They're looking at **themselves**.*
2 *They're looking at **each other**.*

2 Choose the correct words.
1 Jack bought *itself / himself* a new phone.
2 I cut *myself / itself* while I was washing up.
3 I can't believe you taught *myself / yourself* the guitar.
4 Did you and Sara hurt *herself / yourselves*?
5 They should all be ashamed of *ourselves / themselves* for behaving in that way!

3 Complete the sentences with the correct pronoun or *each other*.
1 Did you all enjoy .... at the party?
2 Tom and I often argue with ....
3 Do you and your teachers sometimes email .... ?
4 They might hurt .... if they fall off their bikes.
5 I need to buy a present for Tom. We always give .... presents on our birthdays.

WRITING A story (1)

1 Look at the photo and the title of Sam's story. What do you think happens?

> **Famous for a day!**
> Last year, we went on a school trip to Edinburgh. When we arrived, everyone was feeling <mark>exhausted</mark>.
> While we were getting off the coach, I noticed a boy. He wasn't from our school and he was walking <mark>slowly</mark> behind one of my friends. I soon realised what was happening. The boy was taking my friend's wallet from his back pocket!
> I <mark>immediately</mark> shouted 'Help! Police!' The thief started running, but <mark>luckily</mark> there were two police officers nearby. Soon the thief was in a police car and a policewoman was asking me questions.
> The next day, there was a story about it online! I felt very <mark>proud</mark>!

2 Read Sam's story and compare your ideas. What do you think of Sam's title for his story? Can you think of a different title?

3 Read the *Prepare* box. Then read Sam's story again and put events a–e in order. Decide which events belong to the beginning, middle and end of the story.

Prepare to write A story (1)
When you write a story:
- make sure there is a beginning, middle and end.
- make sure the story matches the title.
- use verbs in the past simple and past continuous.
- use adjectives and adverbs to make your story interesting.

a Sam saw the thief.
b The police caught the thief.
c Sam got off the coach.
d The story appeared on the internet.
e Sam arrived in Edinburgh.

4 Look at Sam's story again. How many verbs can you find in the past simple and past continuous? Which verb form does Sam use for the main events?

5 Look at the highlighted words in Sam's story. Which are adjectives and which are adverbs?

6 You are going to write a story with the title 'A lucky escape'. Plan the events in your story. Use the ideas to help you.
- Where does the story take place?
- Who are the characters?
- What happens at the beginning?
- What are the main events?
- What happens in the end?
- Why is it a lucky escape?

7 Compare your ideas with a partner. Can you improve your plan?

8 Write your story.
- Use the tips in the *Prepare* box.
- Write about 80–100 words.
- Remember to check your spelling and grammar.

Take a good look

6 Modern life

VOCABULARY City life

Your profile
What are the good and bad things about living in cities? Close your books and make a list.

1 ▶ 1.20 Match the words to the photos. Then listen and check.

| bin   crowd   graffiti   pollution   public transport   rubbish   street market   traffic jam |

2 What things from exercise 1 do you see in your town or city?

3 Match the sentence halves.

1 There are **street lights** in front
2 If you drive over the **bridge**,
3 There's a **bus stop** on
4 Don't cross the road here. There's a
5 When it's hot in the summer,

a you'll see a **car park** on your left. You can park there.
b West Street, next to the big **department store**.
c we sit by the **fountain** in the **park**. It's lovely and cool!
d of my **apartment block**, so it's never dark when I get home.
e **pedestrian crossing** there, at the **traffic lights**.

4 Match five **words** from exercise 3 to the meanings. Discuss the meaning of the other words.

1 a tall building where a lot of people live
2 a structure that water comes out of
3 a place where cars stop, so that people can go across the road
4 a structure that goes over a river or railway line
5 a big shop that sells lots of different kinds of things

5 Describe the place where you live. Use words from exercises 1 and 3.

36   Unit 6

READING

1 Look at the photos. What do you think these teenagers invented? Read the article quickly and check your answers.

ECO HEROES

▷ While teenager Ben Gulak was visiting Beijing, China, he was shocked at the air pollution in the city. In his home town in Canada, the traffic is quite light, but Beijing is like many big cities around the world and it has a lot of traffic. Some people drive cars, but a lot of people ride scooters. They're cheaper and they don't need much petrol. They're also lighter and easier to drive through traffic jams. There is one problem: scooters can produce ten times more air pollution than cars.

Back in Canada, Ben started thinking about the problem. He wanted to make a new type of transport – something as small as a scooter, but cleaner. He called his invention the Uno – a motorbike which looks like … half a motorbike! It doesn't use any petrol – just electricity. When people first saw the Uno, they were amazed. Ben won a prize and one day the Uno might be on our roads!

◁ Emily Cummins wasn't a typical four-year-old. She didn't just play with toys. She and her grandfather designed and created their own toys! 'Instead of watching TV, we enjoyed making things,' Emily says.

At 17, she became interested in energy problems. She was particularly interested in things we use every day, like the fridge. 'Life can be difficult without fridges,' she says. 'We need them to keep food fresh and drinks cold.' However, fridges are expensive and they need electricity. Emily decided to solve this problem.

While she was still at school, Emily invented a fridge that doesn't use any electricity. Instead, it needs just a little water and the heat of the sun. When she left school, she went to Namibia in Africa to share her invention – for free! The science of Emily's fridge isn't new, but Emily improved the idea. She designed something that costs almost nothing and only takes a few hours to make. And it works.

2 Read the article again and complete the sentences with one or two words in each space.

1 Ben was on holiday in ………… but he is actually from ………… .
2 Cars use ………… than scooters.
3 Scooters create more ………… than cars.
4 The Uno is cleaner than a normal scooter because it uses ………… .
5 When she was a child, Emily enjoyed making things more than ………… .
6 We need fridges to ………… food fresh and drinks cold.
7 Emily's fridge uses the sun and a ………… .
8 Emily's fridge ………… very little money.

3 Match the highlighted words in the article to the meanings.

1 the quality of being hot
2 make
3 in place of
4 made something better
5 surprised and interested
6 surprised and upset

EP Word profile *light*

Scooters are lighter and easier to drive.

There are street lights in front of my apartment block.

The traffic is quite light.

page 124

Talking points

What other eco inventions could improve our lives?
How could governments encourage young inventors?

Video extra Modern life 37

GRAMMAR some/any, much/many, a lot of, a few/a little

1 Read the examples. Then complete the rules with *some* or *any*.
1 **Some** people drive cars.
2 The Uno doesn't use **any** petrol.
3 Have you got **any** ideas?

> We use:
> a .... before nouns in positive sentences.
> b .... before nouns in negative sentences and in questions.

→ Grammar reference page 143

2 Complete the conversations with *some* or *any*.
1 A: We can recycle .... plastic things, but not all.
   B: They don't recycle .... plastic in our town.
2 A: There aren't .... good places for us to play.
   B: I know. We need .... more parks.
3 A: I've got .... rubbish from the picnic.
   B: Can you see .... bins?
4 A: Are there .... traffic lights in your street?
   B: No, but there are .... traffic lights outside my school.

3 Read the examples. Then complete the rules with the bold words.
1 Beijing is like **many** big <u>cities</u> around the world.
2 The city has **a lot of** <u>traffic</u>.
3 **A lot of** <u>people</u> ride scooters.
4 Scooters don't need **much** <u>petrol</u>.
5 Her fridge needs just **a little** <u>water</u>.
6 The fridge only takes **a few** <u>hours</u> to make.

> a We use *many*, ... and .... to talk about large amounts.
> b We don't use *much* or *many* in positive sentences: There is ~~much~~ a lot of time.
> c We use .... and .... to talk about small amounts.
> d We don't use *a few* or *a little* in negative sentences: He hasn't got ~~a little~~ much money.

→ Grammar reference page 143

4 Look at the <u>underlined</u> nouns in the examples in exercise 3. Are they countable or uncountable?

5 Complete the table with *a lot of*, *a few* and *many*.

Countable nouns	Uncountable nouns
1	much
2	a lot of
3	a little

Corpus challenge

Find and correct the mistake in the student's sentence.
I don't have much friends.

6 Choose the correct words.
1 A: Do you like living in the country?
   B: Yes, most of the time. There are *a few / a little* bad things. There isn't *many / much* entertainment.
2 A: It's impossible to cross this road.
   B: Yes. There aren't *many / much* pedestrian crossings.
   A: And there aren't *a lot of / much* traffic lights. The cars never stop.
3 A: Have you got *a few / a little* minutes? I'm doing a questionnaire on pollution.
   B: I'm sorry. I haven't got *a lot of / a little* time. Are there *many / much* questions?
4 A: Is there *many / much* crime near your school?
   B: There's *a little / a few* graffiti.
   A: There isn't any near our school. There are *much / a lot of* street lights.

7 Think about your perfect place to live and complete the sentences. Compare your ideas.
1 My perfect place to live has got *a lot of / a few* …
2 There are *some / a lot of* …
3 There aren't *any / a lot of* …
4 It hasn't got *much / many* …
5 There's only a *little* …

VOCABULARY Compounds: noun + noun

1 Match a word from A and B for each photo.

A
~~road~~   post   speed   tourist   car
recycling   bus   the ground

B
bin   park   box   information
stop   ~~sign~~   floor   limit

1 road sign

2 Ask and answer three questions about the words in exercise 1.

Is there a road sign near your house?

LISTENING

1. What are the advantages and disadvantages of living in the country?

2. ▶1.21 Listen to an interview with Jess and Mr Evans. In general, do they agree or disagree?

3. ▶1.21 Read the sentences carefully and check any new words. Then listen again and choose the correct words.
   1. Mr Evans lives in the *country* / *city*.
   2. Jess *lives* / *lived* in the same place as Mr Evans.
   3. Mr Evans thinks Jess is *sometimes* / *never* late.
   4. Mr Evans thinks villages need better *cinemas* / *public transport*.
   5. Jess thinks the problem with rubbish is *worse* / *better* near the school.
   6. Jess thinks people should do more *cleaning* / *recycling*.

SPEAKING   Agreeing and disagreeing

1. Look at the two photos below. What can you do in the two places? Where would you prefer to live? Why?

2. ▶1.22 Listen to Alice and Oliver talking about the places. What do they agree on?

3. ▶1.22 Read the *Prepare* box. Then listen again. Which phrases do Alice and Oliver use?

> **Prepare to speak — Agreeing and disagreeing**
>
> **Giving your opinion**
> Personally, I think …
> I don't think …
> It seems to me …
> If you ask me, …
>
> **Asking for an opinion**
> What do you think?
> Do you agree?
> Do you think …?
>
> **Agreeing**
> That's true.
> Yes, maybe you're right.
> I completely agree with …
>
> **Disagreeing**
> I'm not sure I agree.
> I don't think so.
> I don't agree.

4. Discuss which place in the photos below you would prefer to live in. Use phrases from the *Prepare* box to agree and disagree.

5. Prepare your ideas on the topics below.
   1. going to the cinema / watching movies at home
   2. going to a concert / listening to music on a music player
   3. cycling / using public transport

6. Discuss the topics in exercise 5. Use phrases from the *Prepare* box to agree and disagree.

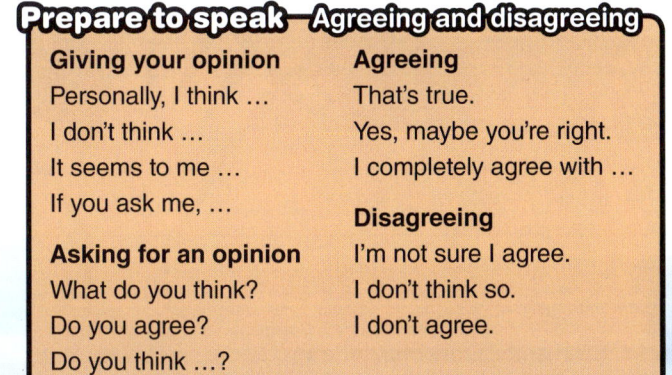

Culture
Meeting and greeting

1 Look at the **place names** in the quiz below.
  1 Where are these places?
  2 Are any of the names similar in your language? Which?

2 In pairs, read the quiz and guess the answers.

3 ▶ 1.23 Listen to the interview and check your answers to the quiz.

4 Answer the questions.
  1 Which of the greetings in the quiz do you use when you meet people?
  2 What other greetings are common in your country?
  3 Which greetings do you find surprising or unusual? Why?

5 Look at the **questions** on page 41. Can you answer them?

6 Read the article quickly and check your ideas.

7 Read the article again. Are the sentences correct or incorrect? Correct the incorrect sentences.
  1 In most countries, people nod to mean 'no'.
  2 Babies shake their heads to get more milk.
  3 People from Turkey shake their heads to mean 'yes'.
  4 In the past, people shook hands to find out if someone was carrying a weapon.
  5 People bow to ask for respect from another person.
  6 In Japan, the lowest bows are the most formal.
  7 The high-five is no longer used for celebrating.

Nice To Meet You

1 .... is the most popular greeting internationally.
  A Kissing
  B Shaking hands
  C Raising your eyebrows

2 People in some areas of **France** kiss friends .... times when they meet.
  A four
  B six
  C eight

3 In **Zambia**, people .... three times when they meet an older person.
  A shake hands
  B scream
  C clap

4 Four hundred years ago in **Poland**, people .... when they met someone important.
  A grabbed their hat
  B lay on the ground
  C threw flowers

5 The Maori people of **New Zealand** .... to say 'hello'.
  A touch noses
  B fight
  C sing

6 In **Ghana** and **Cameroon**, when people shake hands, they often pull and click the other person's ....
  A ear
  B middle finger
  C nose

7 This is a picture of the 'shaka' greeting. The shaka comes from ....
  A Hawaii
  B New York City
  C Sweden

8 In some islands in **Papua New Guinea**, people point at their stomach and .... when they meet.
  A smile
  B wave
  C hold their nose

WHY DO PEOPLE …?

Why do people nod and shake their head?

In most places, people nod to mean 'yes' and shake their head for 'no'. Nodding and shaking the head may come from when we were babies and our mothers were feeding us milk. Babies often nod their heads forward when they want more milk and shake their heads when they don't want more.

Watch out! In Turkey, shaking the head means 'yes'. People move the head back and make a click with their tongue for 'no'.

Why do people shake hands?

Hundreds of years ago, people shook hands when they agreed something, not as a greeting. In those days, life was more dangerous and knives were common. People probably shook hands to check the other person wasn't hiding a knife in the sleeve of their jacket. Shaking hands as a greeting only became popular two hundred years ago in Europe, and more recently in other places.

Why do people bow?

People bow as a sign of respect. When you bow, you show the back of your neck to the other person. In the past, people only bowed if they trusted the other person not to kill them. Bowing used to be common in Europe and it is still common in Asia.

In Japan, there are many types of bow. People know exactly which bow to use in different situations. Informal bows are just 15°, but the most formal bows are 45°!

Until a hundred years ago, the Chinese used to 'kowtow' to important people. A kowtow is the most respectful bow of all: it starts as a bow, then the person gets down on their knees, with their head on the floor.

Why do people do high-fives?

The high-five started in the US in the 1950s. It is a hand-clap that sports people used for celebrating. These days, it is a greeting, as well as for celebrating. The 'high' is because your hand is up. The 'five' is because there are four fingers and one thumb on your hand.

Project

Think about greetings in your country. Then write some advice for a foreign visitor about greetings customs in your country.
- How do you greet different people – old friends, new classmates, teachers, people in shops, members of the family, and so on?
- What greetings do you use in different situations? Is it the same for men and women? Does a person's age make a difference?

7 Getting on

VOCABULARY *be, do, have and make*

Your profile
When you have a problem, who do you ask for help? Friends or family? Why?

1 ▶ 1.24 Look at the photos and listen to two conversations. Complete the sentences with *Ali, Jess or Matt*.
1 .... has a problem with friends.
2 .... has a problem with family.

2 ▶ 1.24 Read the sentences and choose the correct words. Then listen again and check.
1 He **does** / **makes** me really **angry**.
2 You're always **making** / **having problems** with him.
3 We **had** / **made an argument** this morning.
4 **Are** / **Have** you **on your own**?
5 Why don't we **make** / **do something** later?
6 You need to **make** / **have some fun**.
7 Can you **make** / **do me a favour**?
8 What **is** / **has wrong**?
9 It's hard to **do** / **make friends**.
10 It **doesn't** / **isn't my fault**.
11 You **have** / **are** lots **in common**.

3 Complete the table with the phrases in exercise 2. Can you add any more?

be	
do	
have	
make	make someone angry

4 Complete the sentences with the correct words.
1 Oh, no! Something .... wrong with the TV. It isn't working!
2 Paul, can you .... me a favour, please?
3 Some people find it easy to .... new friends.
4 I'm really sorry the glass broke, but it .... my fault!
5 You should talk to someone if you .... problems.
6 Let's .... something together later.

5 Discuss the questions.
1 Who or what makes you angry?
2 When and why do you have arguments?
3 Do you like being on your own? Why? / Why not?
4 How do you have fun? Who with?
5 What do you have in common with your friends?

EP Word profile *like*

I **like** going running.

You have lots in common, **like** running!

I wish my brother was **like** you!

What's the club **like**?

page 124

READING

1 Look at the photo and read problems 1–3 on an internet forum quickly. Who is in the photo?

TROUBLESPOT
don't get angry – get advice

HOME | ASK US | VIDEOS | LINKS | LOGIN

1 KAITLIN, 15, DERBY

I'm quite a shy person and I haven't got a lot of friends. I was walking home from school yesterday, when I saw some boys from my class. They were laughing at me. One of them said, 'She's always on her own!' and he pointed at me. It was unbelievable! Why do I have to be with someone all the time? What's wrong with being on your own?

2 DYLAN, 14, PENZANCE

My little brother is really **annoying**. Yesterday, I found him in my room. He knows he mustn't go in there. And he was reading my diary! It made me really angry. Then we had an argument because he took my phone. He sent about 50 texts and now I haven't got any credit. Help!

3 ALEX, 15, LONDON

My best mates, Sasha and Mandy, are just like me. They're often late and they forget things, but they behave themselves (most of the time!). I was hanging out with them last Saturday and I had to get home by 10 pm, but they didn't have to get home until 11 pm. I didn't realise what the time was, and I got home a bit late. Now my parents say I can't hang out with my mates and I have to get home by 9.30 pm. It isn't **fair**! I don't want to fall out with my friends. My parents think I'm still a child. What should I do?

What you think…

a I agree. Sometimes you don't have anything in common with other people, and that's fine.

b He should **apologise**. Maybe you should **lock** your door.

c You shouldn't get angry. It's important to talk to your parents. Then you'll understand why they're worried.

d You must show them you can change, so try to be really sensible for a month – or forever!

e Maybe you should put a **password** on your phone.

f Friendship is important, but you don't have to be with someone all the time. It's good to be **independent**.

2 Read the problems again and complete the sentences with the correct names, *Kaitlin*, *Dylan* or *Alex*.

1 .... has a problem as a result of a mistake.
2 .... had a problem on her way home.
3 .... got annoyed with a family member.
4 .... doesn't mind spending time alone.
5 .... doesn't agree with someone else's decision.
6 .... can't use something essential.

3 Read the problems again and read advice a–f in the 'What you think…' section. Match two pieces of advice to each problem. What advice would you give to each person?

4 Match the highlighted words in the problems and advice to the meanings.

1 a secret word for protecting something
2 not needing to be with other people
3 say sorry
4 behaving in the same way to everyone
5 making you angry
6 shut something with a key

Talking points

Are internet forums good places to get advice? Why? / Why not?
In what ways can you help or support your friends when they have problems?

Getting on 43

GRAMMAR have to and must

1 Read the examples. Then complete the rules with the bold verbs.
1 You **must** show them you can change.
2 He **mustn't** go in there.
3 **I have to** get home by 9.30 pm.
4 You **don't have to** be with someone all the time.
5 Why **do I have to** be with someone?
6 Last Saturday, I **had to** get home by 10 pm.
7 My mates **didn't have to** get home until 11 pm.

> a We use *have to* and .... to talk about rules and things that are necessary. We don't use contractions in the positive: ~~You've to go~~.
> b We use .... when something isn't allowed by a rule.
> c We use *don't have to* when something isn't necessary and .... when something wasn't necessary in the past.
> d We use .... to talk about rules in the past. (*Must* hasn't got a past form.)
> e Remember:
> You **don't have to** go. = It isn't necessary.
> You **mustn't** go. = It isn't allowed.

→ Grammar reference page 144

2 Read the blog and choose the correct words.

> ## Life isn't fair! ☹
> My parents are really strict! I ¹*had to / have to* do my homework right after school every day. Then I can go out, but I ²*don't have to / mustn't* get home after 10 pm. That isn't fair! My best friend, Laura, ³*has / must* to do her homework, of course, but she decides when. She ⁴*mustn't / doesn't have to* do it after school. Laura ⁵*mustn't / doesn't have to* get home until 11.30 pm. Also, when my brother was my age, he ⁶*had to / must* do his homework after school, but he ⁷*mustn't / didn't have to* get home as early as 10 pm. It isn't fair.

3 Make two sentences for each idea. Compare your answers.
0 things you have to do at school
  I have to wear a uniform.
  I have to study for my exams.
1 things you don't have to do at school
2 things you mustn't do at school
3 things you must do at home
4 things you mustn't do at home
5 things you had to do when you were younger
6 things you didn't have to do when you were younger

should

4 Read the examples. Then complete the rules with the bold verbs.
1 What **should** I do?
2 He **should** apologise.
3 You **shouldn't** get angry.

> We use:
> a .... to say something is a good idea.
> b .... to say something isn't a good idea.
> c .... in questions to ask for advice.

→ Grammar reference page 144

5 Take turns to read out the problems and give advice. Use *You should* or *You shouldn't*.
1 I can never find my phone.
2 I find it hard to make friends.
3 I have a lot of arguments with my cousins.
4 My parents think everything is my fault.
5 My sister/brother uses my things without asking.
6 My friend is always borrowing money from me and never pays me back.

ⓘ Corpus challenge

Find and correct the mistake in the student's sentence.
I've to finish my homework.

VOCABULARY Phrasal verbs: friendships

1 Read the examples. Then match the bold phrasal verbs 1–4 to the meanings a–d.
1 We **hang out** in the park after school.
2 Do you **get on** well with your sister?
3 I **get together** with my mates on Saturdays.
4 I don't want to **fall out** with my friends.

a have a good relationship and not argue
b spend a lot of time somewhere
c meet someone
d have an argument with someone

2 Complete the sentences with the phrasal verbs from exercise 1.
1 I don't have anything in common with my sister. We don't .... very well.
2 Some of my friends .... at the youth centre, but I don't go there very often.
3 I usually .... with my friends after school.
4 It isn't a serious problem, and I'm sure we won't .... about it.

3 Discuss the questions.
1 Who do you get on with?
2 When do you and your mates get together?
3 Where do you usually hang out?
4 What do people often fall out about?

44 Unit 7

WRITING An informal letter or email (2)

1 Read the email from Alfons. When is he going to visit Manchester? What does he want Ali to write about?

From: Alfons Duda
To: Ali Malik

Hi Ali
I'm coming to Manchester next month on the school exchange trip. What do I need to know before I come? What's the weather like in Manchester? What should I bring with me? I'm really excited about coming to England!
Write soon,
Alfons

---

2 Read Ali's email. Does he answer all of Alfons's questions?

From: Ali Malik (home)
To: Alfons Duda
Subject: Cherwell School/GK Liceum exchange trip
1 Attachment, 241 KB

Hello Alfons
Cherwell students have to wear a uniform – look at mine! You're lucky: visitors don't have to wear a uniform. The school pays for your lunches and you don't have to pay for anything at my house, but **you should** bring some money for shopping and going out. You don't have to do any homework, but during your trip **it's a good idea to** make a note of things to include in your trip report. February is the coldest winter month here in the UK! **Remember to** pack a hat, gloves and your warmest coat. I'm really looking forward to your visit next month.
Bye for now,
Ali

---

3 Read the *Prepare* box. Look at the highlighted phrases Ali uses to give advice. Then complete the sentences.

Prepare to write An informal letter or email (2)
In informal letters and emails:
- answer all the questions you have to answer.
- use phrases to give advice if necessary:
  You should / shouldn't … , Remember to …
- try to sound friendly.
- remember to use an informal phrase to begin and end your email.

1 It's a good .... to visit in summer.
2 Remember .... say 'thank you'.
3 You .... bring a coat because it's cold.

4 Look at Ali's email again. What does Ali write to sound friendly?

5 Read Alfons's email again. Imagine he is coming to visit your school. Plan the advice you can give him about his trip.

6 Write your email.
- Use the tips in the *Prepare* box.
- Write about 80–100 words.
- Remember to check your spelling and grammar.

8 Going away

VOCABULARY Travel

Your profile
Where in the world would you most like to visit? Why?
Do you or people in your family travel abroad?
Where do you/they go?

1 ▶ 1.25 Listen to the conversation. What does Ali realise at the end of the conversation?
   1 It's his little brother's first flight.
   2 Flying isn't always fun.
   3 Flying is safe.

2 ▶ 1.25 Choose the correct answers. Then listen again and check.
   1 The Maliks have to arrive at the airport .... hours before their flight.
      a one   b two   c three
   2 At the check-in desk, they give you a ....
      a boarding pass   b passport   c ticket
   3 Customs officers look ....
      a at passports   b in luggage   c for knives

3 Look at the words in the box. Where are the things in the photos?

| backpack   baggage hall   boarding pass   check-in desk   customs   departure gate |
| passport   passport control   queue   security check   sign   ticket |

4 Work in pairs. Number the photos in order and then use them to describe what you do at the airport.

When you arrive at the airport, you go to the check-in desk and show …

READING

1 Read Ali's profile. How would you describe him?

2 Read Ali's blog entry. What's he going to see in Barcelona?

Hi, I'm Ali. I'm 14 years old and I'm from Manchester. I'm mad about new technology and I definitely couldn't live without the internet. I'm into gaming and I'm always online, either playing games or reading interesting stuff.

WE'RE OFF TO BARCELONA Posted 3.16 pm

And I can't wait! We're leaving on Saturday – a taxi is picking us up at 8 o'clock. We're going to have a great time. We're going to visit some of the museums, the Gaudí buildings and, of course, we're going to do a tour of the Nou Camp stadium. Mum says we're going to do a lot of shopping too, but that's boring. I've found this great guide to the city online, but has anyone got any cool suggestions?

3 Read the online guide to Barcelona. What things can you see and do there?

4 Read the online guide again and choose the correct answers.

1. What do we learn about Gaudí?
   - A He didn't enjoy designing buildings.
   - B He collected unusual animals.
   - C He probably didn't do well at school.
   - D He didn't like noisy places.
2. What do Dalí, Picasso and Miró have in common?
   - A They were all born in Barcelona.
   - B They all produced paintings.
   - C All their museums are in the centre of Barcelona.
   - D They all liked using bright colours.
3. What can you do at the Nou Camp?
   - A win a prize
   - B meet famous football players
   - C visit the world's biggest football stadium
   - D take photos of 100,000 people
4. What can you do at both amusement parks?
   - A eat a meal in different places
   - B enjoy amazing views of Barcelona
   - C go on a fast frightening ride
   - D climb up a mountain

5 Would you like to visit Barcelona? What would you like to see and do there?

EP Word profile *around*

There's space for **around** 100,000 people.

You can go on a tour and look **around** the museum.

Be sure to visit the amusement parks in and **around** Barcelona.

page 124

Talking points

What places do tourists usually want to visit when they come to your country?

Do you think it's better to go on holiday in your own country or go abroad?

A COOL CITY!
A GUIDE TO BARCELONA FOR YOUNG PEOPLE

PLACES TO VISIT | THINGS TO DO | WHERE TO STAY | CITY MAP

So, you're going to visit Barcelona. But what are you going to do there? Read our guide for some really cool ideas.

YOU'RE GOING TO SEE a lot of Gaudí buildings with their unusual shapes and bright colours. But who or what is Gaudí? He was an architect from Barcelona. Some people say he was a terrible student, but his buildings are amazing! One of the best places to see Gaudí's extraordinary designs is Parc Güell. Look out for the animal they call 'El Drac' (it means 'dragon' in Catalan). Parc Güell is a great place to hang out with friends and escape from the noise of the city.

DID YOU KNOW THAT three Spanish artists all have museums in or near Barcelona? Take the train to the Dalí Theatre Museum. It's pink on the outside, with giant eggs on the roof. Inside, you can see some of Dalí's paintings. Or take the funicular railway up Montjuïc, a hill in Barcelona, to look at the spectacular views of the city and visit Miró's museum. Here you'll find his fantastic colourful paintings and many of his sculptures. Or go to the Picasso Museum in the centre of the city to see a large collection of his paintings.

IF YOU'RE INTO FOOTBALL, plan a visit to the Nou Camp, home of the Barcelona football team. There's space for around 100,000 people, so it's the second largest football stadium in Europe. You can go on a tour and look around the museum. Trust us – you're going to love it! Don't forget to take a photo of yourself for the selfie competition. There's a football shirt for the best photo every month.

BE SURE TO VISIT the amusement parks in and around Barcelona. PortAventura is about an hour from the city by train, but it's worth it! If you're brave, you can ride the tallest and fastest rollercoaster in Europe, but there are also gentle rides and plenty of restaurants and cafes. Or, if you prefer to stay in Barcelona, an old-fashioned blue tram will take you up the mountain to the Tibidabo park. It's one of the oldest amusement parks in the world. Apart from looking at the city from the top of the mountain, you can enjoy 25 rides, including a big wheel and a really scary rollercoaster.

Going away 47

GRAMMAR Future: *be going to* and *present continuous*

1 Read the examples. Then complete the rules with *be going to* or *present continuous*.

1 We're **going to visit** some of the museums.
2 We're **leaving** on Saturday.
3 Trust us – you're **going to love** it!

> We use the:
> **a** .... to talk about future plans and arrangements, usually with a time reference (for example, *next week, in August*).
> **b** .... for things we intend to do some time in the future.
> **c** .... when we predict things that we know are likely.

→ Grammar reference page 145

2 ▶ 1.26 Complete the conversation with the correct form of *be going to* and the verbs. Then listen and check.

Ali: I'm really looking forward to Barcelona. We ¹............ (have) a great time.
Jess: What ²............ (you / do) in Barcelona?
Mrs Malik: We ³............ (look) at the Gaudí buildings. And it's Barcelona Fashion Week while we're there, so we ⁴............ (go) shopping!
Ali: What? I ⁵............ (not walk) around the shops! I ⁶............ (visit) the Picasso Museum and I ⁷............ (do) a tour of the Nou Camp.

3 Make sentences with the present continuous or *be going to*.

0 we / visit / Turkey one day
 We're going to visit Turkey one day.
1 I / get / the bus at 6.45 pm / tonight
2 I / cycle / to your house next time
3 they / not buy / a new TV
4 we / walk / home after school today
5 The sky is dark and cloudy. it / rain
6 we / not catch / the 5.30 train / tomorrow

4 Make notes about your plans and arrangements for next weekend. Discuss them in pairs.

> meet some friends   hang out in town
> watch a football match   go shopping
> visit my grandparents   go online   study

A: *What are you doing next weekend?*
B: *I'm going shopping on Saturday. I'm going to buy some new jeans.*

Corpus challenge

Find and correct the mistake in the student's sentence.

My best friend Amy is going to moved to a new house next year.

VOCABULARY Phrasal verbs: travel

1 Read the sentences. Choose the correct meanings of the phrasal verbs.

1 We're **going away** this weekend.
 a staying at home
 b visiting another place
2 They **set off** at 9.30 this morning.
 a left a hotel
 b started a journey
3 When are you **getting back**?
 a arriving in another place
 b returning
4 What time did the plane **take off**?
 a leave the ground
 b arrive after a fight
5 We're going to **check in** at 11 am.
 a arrive at a hotel or for a flight
 b reserve a hotel or a fight

2 Complete the questions with phrasal verbs from exercise 1.

1 What time do you .... for school every morning?
2 What time do you .... from school in the afternoon?
3 Do you usually .... or stay at home in the holidays?
4 When did you .... from your most recent holiday? Where did you go to?

3 Ask and answer the questions in exercise 2.

48 Unit 8

LISTENING

1 Look at the photo. Would you like to get around on skis? Why? / Why not?

2 Read the notes and look at the spaces. What kind of information is needed for each space?

Travel Writing Competition
Name of company running the competition: World Explorer
First prize: Trip to (1) ....
Length of trip: (2) ....

Competition details
What you must mention: (3) environment, people and ....
Maximum number of words to write: (4) ....
Closing date of competition: (5) ....
What to send with the article: (6) ....

3 ▶ 1.27 Listen and complete the notes. Compare answers with your partner.

4 ▶ 1.27 Listen again to check, and correct any mistakes.

SPEAKING   Making suggestions

1 What do you usually do at the weekend? What are you planning to do next weekend?

2 ▶ 1.28 Listen to two friends planning their weekend. What do they decide to do?

3 ▶ 1.28 Read the *Prepare* box. Then listen again. Which phrases do you hear?

4 Work in pairs. Choose three possible activities for this weekend. Use the ideas in the box or your own ideas.

go shopping	go skateboarding
go to the beach	go to the park
meet in a café	watch a sports match

Prepare to speak — Making suggestions

Suggesting ideas
Why don't we …?
What about …?
How about …?
We could …

Agreeing with ideas
That's a good idea.
That sounds great!

Disagreeing with ideas
I'm not sure.
The problem with that is …
… might be a better idea.

Making a decision
Yes, let's do that.

5 Discuss the three activities and agree what to do. Use phrases from the *Prepare* box.

Geography
Our world

1 In pairs, guess the answers to the questions. Then read part A of the text on page 51 and check.
1. What is the population of the world?
2. How many countries are there in the world?
3. How many languages are there?
4. Can you find the names of the seven continents?

   aasi — A sia
   rcaaif — A...............
   eopure — E...............
   acoenia — O...............
   nhrot imreaac — N............... A...............
   ouths iracmea — S............... A...............
   ctaacniatr — A...............

2 Work in pairs. You have two minutes. How many countries can you name in each continent?

Europe – France, the UK, …

3 Read the whole text on page 51. Match the sentence halves.

> If we imagine the world as a village of 100 people, 60 are Asian. This means that **60% (percent)** of people in the world are from Asia.

In the world, …
1. 36% of people
2. 14% of people
3. 76% of people
4. 1% of people
5. 13% of people
6. 6% of people

a. are from Oceania.
b. have got electricity.
c. are of school age but don't go to school.
d. don't eat enough food every day.
e. are of school age.
f. must find clean water every day.

4 Read the information about population density. Do you think your country has a high or low population density?

> The **population density** of a country is the number of people per square kilometre. Countries with a high population density have a lot of people per square kilometre, and countries with a low population density have only a small number of people per square kilometre.

5 ▶ 1.29 Look at the list of countries. Which do you think has the highest population density? Listen to the first part of Tina and Tom's podcast and check.
1. India
2. The Netherlands
3. Australia
4. The UK
5. Brazil

6 ▶ 1.30 Listen to the second part of Tina and Tom's podcast. Are the sentences correct or incorrect? Correct the incorrect sentences.

Case study: Australia

1. Australia is the third largest country in the world.
2. The Northern Territory and South Australia are very hot and dry.
3. In the middle of the country there are a lot of rivers.
4. 85% of Australians live in rural areas.
5. The population density of Sydney is about 400 people per square kilometre.

Imagine the world as a village

There are over seven billion people in the world. They live in 195 different countries and speak approximately 6,000 languages.

Now imagine the world as a village, with a population of just 100 people.

Where we're from
- 60 are from Asia.
- 15 are from Africa.
- 10 are from Europe.
- 9 are from South America.
- 5 are from Canada and the United States.
- 1 is from Oceania.

What we eat
There is plenty of food in the village. However, some people have got a lot more food than others. About 30 people can't always eat properly and 14 people never get enough food every day to stay healthy.

What we breathe and drink
Most of the village has got clean air and water, but 32 people in the village breathe air that is polluted and unhealthy. For 13 people, there is no safe water near their homes. These people spend a large amount of their day walking to get clean water.

What young people do
There are 36 people in the village of school age, between the ages of 5 and 24. Only 30 of them go to school. The other six must work. They need to earn money to buy food. 14 people in the village who are old enough to read cannot read or write.

What we use for power
Just over three quarters of the people in the village have got electricity at home. The rest of the village uses candles and oil lamps when it is dark. Of the electricity, 73 percent comes from fossil fuels, such as coal and gas, and only 10 percent comes from renewable energy sources, such as wind and water.

What we own
In the village, there are 45 televisions, 50 radios and 118 telephones. About 100 of these are mobile phones. Just 28 people have got a computer. There are also 10 cars and 20 bicycles.

The past and the future
In 1900, there were only 32 people in the village. Now, every year, two or three people are born, but only one or two people die. This means that by 2150 there could be at least 250 people in the village. This is an important number because experts think that this is the maximum population for a village of this size.

Or think of it like this: in 2150, there will be 14 billion people in the world – two and a half times as many people as there are today!

Key words
polluted dirty or damaged by waste
population the number of people living in an area

Project
Prepare a short presentation about a country and its population density.
- Find out the population, area and population density of the country.
- Find a map of the country. Which areas of the country have the lowest and highest population density? Why?

Our world

Review 2
Units 5–8

VOCABULARY

1 Complete the puzzle. Then write a definition for the hidden word.

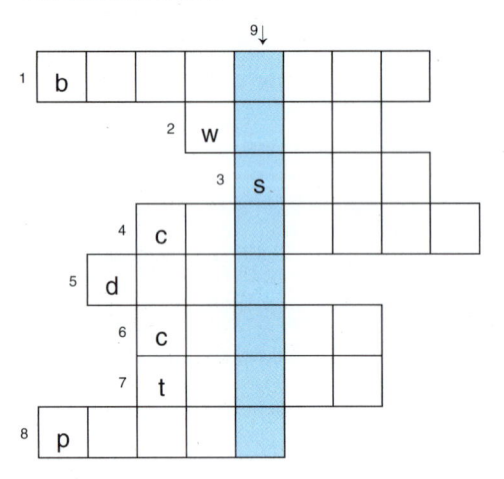

1. b _ _ _ _ _ _
2. w _ _ _
3. s _ _ _
4. c _ _ _ _ _
5. d _ _ _
6. c _ _ _ _
7. t _ _ _ _
8. p _ _ _ _

1. a bag that you carry on your back
2. move your hand from side to side, e.g. to say goodbye.
3. a written public information message
4. where airport officials might check your bag
5. fall or allow something to fall
6. a large group of people
7. make something move through the air by pushing it out of your hand
8. show where someone or something is by holding your finger towards it
9. ....

2 Match each verb with two correct answers.

		a	on my own.
		b	me really happy.
1	I am …	c	something tonight.
2	I am doing …	d	lots of things in common.
3	We have …	e	friends easily.
4	He makes …	f	fun together.
		g	you a favour.
		h	never wrong.

3 Complete the answers to the questions.

1. Where can you buy trainers?
   In a street m.......... or a d.......... store.
2. Where do you show your passport in an airport?
   At the c.......... desk, at the d.......... gate and at passport c.......... .
3. Where do people wait in queues?
   At b.......... stops and in cars at t.......... lights.
4. What do people often do after a good concert?
   They often c.......... .
5. Where should you cross the road? At a p..........crossing.

GRAMMAR

4 Complete the text. Use the past simple or past continuous.

Two boys in my school got into trouble for fighting. It was a really stupid fight! I ¹ .... (walk) into school when the fight ² .... (start). First, Simon hit Rob while Rob ³ .... (chat) to some girls. Then Rob and Simon started to argue. While they were shouting, Rob ⁴ .... (hit) Simon on the arm. Luckily, a teacher ⁵ .... (go) past and she ⁶ .... (stop) the fight.

5 Complete the sentences with the words in the box.

> few   little   many   much   some

1. I can't call her. I haven't got .... credit on my phone.
2. I've got .... new songs on my phone.
3. I want to ask you a .... questions.
4. There weren't .... people at the match last night.
5. I think there's a .... milk left.

6 Choose the correct word or phrase.

There is ¹ *a lot of / a few* pollution in the river in my town. My school is on the other side of the river, so I ² *have to / don't have to* cross the river to get to school every morning. The water always smells and it's full of rubbish. The other day, I saw ³ *some / any* old washing machines under the bridge! Everyone knows they ⁴ *have to / mustn't* put rubbish in a recycling bin or a rubbish bin, and that they ⁵ *mustn't / don't have to* throw things into the river. Unfortunately, ⁶ *a little / a few* people don't care and they throw things into the river. The problem is, nobody around here ⁷ *is cleaning / is going to clean* the river. That's why my classmates and I decided we ⁸ *mustn't / should* do something about the problem. A well-known actor ⁹ *is visiting / is going to visit* my town tomorrow, and we ¹⁰ *'re asking / 're going to ask* her to help us.

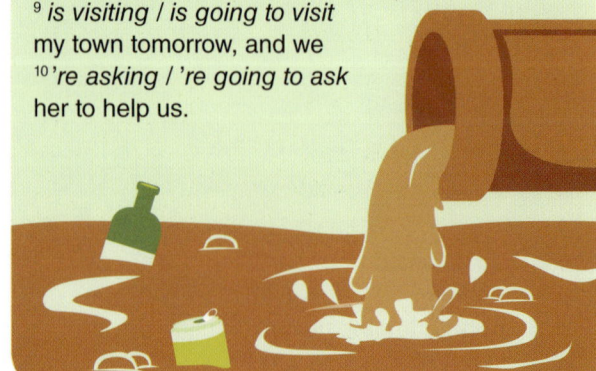

Corpus challenge

7 Tick the two sentences without mistakes. Correct the mistakes in the other sentences.

1 He played tennis when I arrived.
2 We were swimming every day.
3 The beach is just a few minutes from the hotel.
4 I have news.
5 I've to finish my homework.
6 Next Saturday, I'm going to have a picnic in the park.
7 I think I going to visit your house.
8 You will bring a ball if you want to play football.

8 Read the text and choose the correct word for each space.

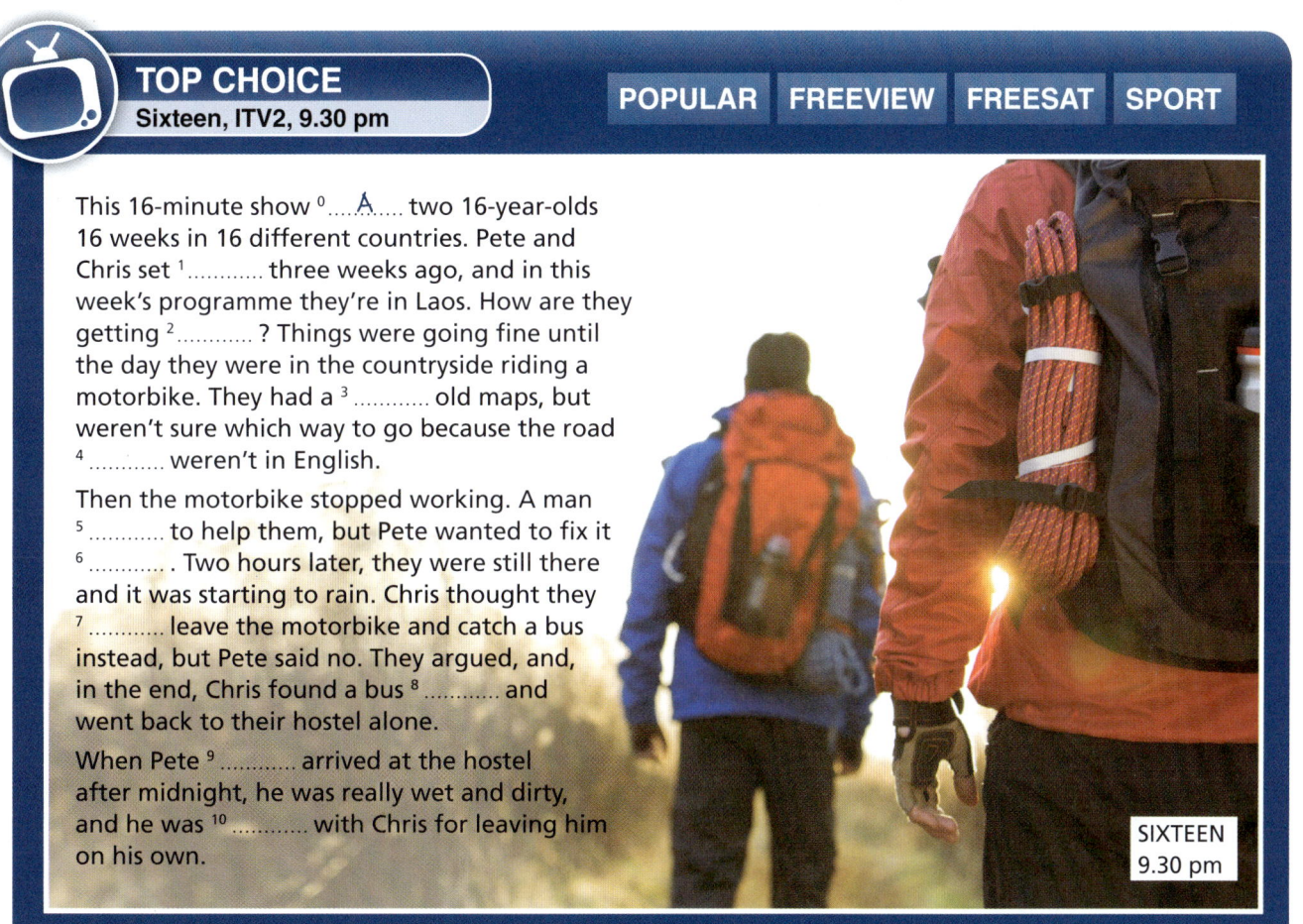

TOP CHOICE
Sixteen, ITV2, 9.30 pm

POPULAR   FREEVIEW   FREESAT   SPORT

This 16-minute show ⁰...A... two 16-year-olds 16 weeks in 16 different countries. Pete and Chris set ¹............ three weeks ago, and in this week's programme they're in Laos. How are they getting ²............ ? Things were going fine until the day they were in the countryside riding a motorbike. They had a ³............ old maps, but weren't sure which way to go because the road ⁴............ weren't in English.

Then the motorbike stopped working. A man ⁵............ to help them, but Pete wanted to fix it ⁶............ . Two hours later, they were still there and it was starting to rain. Chris thought they ⁷............ leave the motorbike and catch a bus instead, but Pete said no. They argued, and, in the end, Chris found a bus ⁸............ and went back to their hostel alone.

When Pete ⁹............ arrived at the hostel after midnight, he was really wet and dirty, and he was ¹⁰............ with Chris for leaving him on his own.

SIXTEEN
9.30 pm

0	**A** gives	**B** turns	**C** makes	**D** goes
1	**A** away	**B** in	**C** off	**D** about
2	**A** up	**B** out	**C** back	**D** on
3	**A** little	**B** few	**C** some	**D** much
4	**A** signs	**B** posts	**C** lights	**D** tickets
5	**A** checked	**B** joined	**C** tried	**D** shared
6	**A** itself	**B** myself	**C** yourself	**D** himself
7	**A** can	**B** should	**C** need	**D** will
8	**A** box	**B** park	**C** bin	**D** stop
9	**A** finally	**B** normally	**C** suddenly	**D** recently
10	**A** proud	**B** amazed	**C** upset	**D** worried

Units 5–8

9 Shop till you drop

VOCABULARY Money and shopping

Your profile
Do you get pocket money for helping at home?
How often do you go shopping? What do you like buying?

1 Read the quiz questions again. Match the **words** to photos a–h.

MONEY WIZARD OR MONEY WASTER?

1 Do you **save up** for things?
  a Yes, I'm always saving up for something.
  b Sometimes, but not often.
  c No, I never save up for anything.

2 Have you got a **bank account**?
  a Yes. I save my money in mine.
  b Yes, but I never use it.
  c No way. I'm not old enough!

3 Do you always look at the **price** of things before buying them?
  a Of course.
  b I don't always check with small things like a drink.
  c Not really. Most of the time it isn't important.

4 Do you look for **special offers**?
  a All the time.
  b Sometimes. But if I really want something, I don't care.
  c Not really. Life is too short!

5 Do you ever change your mind while you're waiting at the **checkout**?
  a Often, when I realise I don't need something.
  b Sometimes.
  c Not really.

6 Do you always check your **change**?
  a Always. Shop assistants often make mistakes.
  b Sometimes.
  c Hardly ever.

7 Do you keep **receipts** in case you need to **take something back**?
  a I keep everything.
  b Only for expensive things, like shoes.
  c Never.

8 What do you do with old clothes, CDs and other stuff?
  a I sell them to friends or online.
  b I usually **give away** everything.
  c I throw them in the bin.

2 ▶ 1.31 Listen to Ali and Jess, and read the quiz again. Write *A* next to Ali's answers for the quiz. Do you think Ali is a Money Wizard or a Money Waster?

3 Complete the sentences with **words** from the quiz.
  1 When I was at the .... in a department store yesterday, the assistant gave me too much ....
  2 I want to open a .... , so that I can put money in there and .... to buy a new tablet.
  3 Look! Those jumpers are on .... this week – there's 25% off the normal .... !
  4 I tried to .... the shoes .... to the shop, but I didn't have the .... , so they wouldn't accept them!
  5 You can .... your old clothes .... to charity shops.

4 Do the quiz and discuss your answers in pairs. Then read the key on page 121. Do you agree?

READING

HELP! I just can't stop ... SHOPPING!

Have you ever bought something and then changed your mind? For Alison Jenson, 15, this used to happen several times a week. Alison was a shopaholic. She just couldn't stop shopping and she loved special offers.

Alison's bedroom is full of stuff. 'I've been to every shop in Birmingham, I think,' says Alison. She picks up some earrings. The label is still on them. 'These were half price,' she says. 'I've never worn them.' Alison's problem wasn't just jewellery. She also bought a lot of clothes, though not many shoes, because they were usually too expensive. She has also bought hundreds of other small things – like 20 new covers for her phone. She hasn't used any of them!

According to experts, we all feel excited after we buy something new. For shopaholics, it's a little different. Soon after they buy something, they think they've made a mistake and start to feel miserable. So they buy themselves something else to feel happier.

Psychologists first described the problems of shopaholics in 1915. However, there was very little research on the subject until recently. Now, doctors think thousands of people suffer from the problem, and the situation is getting worse. There are also more teenage shopaholics now, although most young people don't have enough money to go shopping very regularly.

Alison knew she had a problem. 'I often bought something every day. Usually it was something small, but I just needed to buy it,' she says. 'I spent money that I got for my birthday, and when I was short of cash, I borrowed money from friends or my parents. When I couldn't go shopping, I felt anxious. Then one day, my mum just looked at all the stuff in my room and said, "This is crazy!" I knew she was right.' I needed some big changes in my life.

Alison now gets help with her problem and feels she has changed. She no longer thinks she's a shopaholic. 'When I want to buy something in a shop, I ask myself two questions,' she says. 'Do I need it? Can I afford it? The answer to both questions is usually "no", so I walk away. It's great!'

---

1 Read the article quickly. Which statement is not true?
1 Alison's parents know about her problem.
2 Alison's problem is a very modern one.
3 More young people are shopaholics now than fifty years ago.

2 Read the article again. Choose the correct answers.
1 What is the purpose of the article?
   A to persuade people to go shopping less
   B to encourage people to get help if they have a problem
   C to inform people about a problem
   D to warn people about the dangers of shopping
2 What kinds of things did Alison buy?
   A clothes and shoes
   B clothes, shoes and jewellery
   C only jewellery
   D clothes, jewellery and other personal things
3 What do experts say about shopaholics?
   A They feel miserable when they are shopping.
   B They soon feel unhappy after they have bought something.
   C They feel more excited than other people when they shop.
   D Shopping is the only way they can feel happy.
4 What is Alison's attitude to shopping now?
   A She doesn't often want to buy things now.
   B She doesn't enjoy shopping now.
   C She still buys things she doesn't need.
   D She is in control of her shopping now.
5 What might Alison say now?
   A I'm glad I got help.
   B I need to get help.
   C My problem wasn't too bad.
   D I need to change my life.

EP Word profile *change*

Do you always check your **change**?

Alison feels she has **changed**.

I needed some big **changes** in my life.

page 125

Talking points

What can a shopaholic do to stop shopping? Is there too much pressure on young people to buy things?

Shop till you drop

GRAMMAR Present perfect

1 Read the examples and the rules. Which verbs in the examples are irregular?
1 I've **been** to every shop in Birmingham.
2 She **hasn't used** any of them.
3 I've **never worn** them.

> a We use the present perfect to talk about past experiences in our life.
> b The positive form is: *have / has* + past participle.
> c The negative form is: *have / has* + *not / never* + past participle.
> d Regular past participles end in *-ed* and are the same as the past simple form.

→ Grammar reference page 146

2 Match the verbs to the irregular past participles. Use the list of irregular verbs on page 158 to help you.

1 eat	a caught
2 sing	b stolen
3 make	c eaten
4 write	d had
5 do	e seen
6 catch	f sung
7 spend	g written
8 win	h run
9 see	i made
10 steal	j done
11 run	k won
12 have	l spent

3 Complete the sentences with the present perfect form of the verbs.
0 My sister *'s won* (win) lots of competitions.
1 My grandparents .... (not / buy) anything online.
2 I .... (never / take) anything back to a shop.
3 I .... (save up) for lots of things.
4 My brother .... (never / borrow) any money from me.
5 We .... (visit) Ireland. My aunt lives there.
6 Tim and I .... (never / have) an argument.
7 You .... (not / meet) my brother.
8 I .... (never / steal) anything in my life!

Questions and short answers

4 Read the example. Which word means 'in your whole life'?

Have you **ever bought** something and then been unhappy with it?
Yes, I **have**. / No, I **haven't**.

5 Complete the questions with the correct past participles. Then complete the table for you with ✓ (Yes) or ✗ (No).

Have you ever …	You	Your partner
0 *sold* (sell) anything online?		
1 .... (earn) money for doing jobs at home?		
2 .... (lend) anyone any money?		
3 .... (use) a cashpoint or ATM?		
4 .... (lose) your wallet or purse?		
5 .... (receive) too much change in a shop?		

Corpus challenge

Find and correct the mistake in the student's sentence.
Have you ever have a dog?

6 Ask and answer the questions in exercise 5. Complete the table for your partner.
A: *Have you ever sold anything online?*
B: *Yes, I have. Lots of times.*

7 Tell the class what your partner has done and has never done.

VOCABULARY *been* and *gone*

1 Look at the pictures. Match the examples to the meanings.
1 My brother's **gone** to the shops.
2 My brother's **been** to the shops.
a My brother went to the shops earlier, but he isn't there now.
b My brother is travelling to the shops, or he's at the shops now.

2 Complete the sentences with *been* or *gone*.
1 Have you ever .... to London?
2 Sally isn't here. She's .... shopping.
3 Rob's .... home. He wasn't feeling well.
4 You're late home. Where have you .... ?
5 I've never .... to Spain.
6 Where's Dad .... ? I can't find him anywhere.

56 Unit 9

WRITING A story (2)

1 Look at the photo and read the first sentence of the story. What do you think happens in the story?

> It all started with a shopping trip.

2 Read Lily's story and check your ideas.

> It all started with a shopping trip. I knew as soon as I set out that something exciting was going to happen. It just felt like my lucky day! I visited a large department store first, to see if they had any special offers. While I was waiting patiently at the checkout, I noticed a leaflet about a free competition. I don't usually enter competitions, but I suddenly thought: Why not? So I filled in the form, then I forgot all about it.
> Two weeks later, a letter arrived. When I opened it, I couldn't believe my eyes. I was the competition winner, and the first prize was £2,000! I rushed into the kitchen to tell my family! They couldn't believe it. Our family never wins anything!

3 Read the Prepare box. Then read Lily's story again. Does it have a clear beginning, middle and end?

Prepare to write — A story (2)

When you write a story:
- make sure there is a beginning, middle and end.
- use interesting verbs to describe the actions of the story.
- use time adverbs and phrases to describe when things happened: *first, then, when, while, as soon as, suddenly, later*

4 Look at the highlighted verbs in Lily's story. Match them to the simple verbs below.
1 ran
2 came
3 went into
4 saw

5 Find seven time adverbs and phrases in Lily's story. Then choose the correct time adverbs in the sentences.
1 I called my friend *as soon as / while* the accident happened.
2 About an hour *then / later*, I finally arrived home.
3 He discovered the truth *while / then* he was reading some old letters.
4 She *when / suddenly* had a brilliant idea!

6 Read the task and plan your story.

- Your English teacher has asked you to write a story.
- Your story must begin with this sentence: *Tina's mum handed her a big bag from a department store.*
- Write your **story**.

7 Write your story.
- Use the tips in the *Prepare* box.
- Write about 80–100 words.
- Remember to check your spelling and grammar.

Shop till you drop 57

10 Taste this!

VOCABULARY   Food and drink adjectives

Your profile
What are your favourite types of food?
What's the most unusual thing you've tasted?

1 Look at the photos. Which of the foods have you tried? Did you like them?

2 ▶ 1.32 Listen to the first part of a conversation. What is Matt asking Ali to do?

3 ▶ 1.33 Listen to the second part of the conversation. Number the photos in the order of the taste test.

4 ▶ 1.34 Match the adjectives to the foods in Matt's project. Then listen and check.

1	juicy	a	curry
2	sour	b	pineapple
3	raw	c	lemon juice
4	spicy	d	salmon
5	bitter	e	bread
6	sweet	f	vegetables
7	frozen	g	cake
8	fresh	h	coffee

5 ▶ 1.35 Match the adjectives below that Ali used to the foods he described. Then listen again and check.

> delicious   disgusting   horrible   tasty

1 pineapple   3 sushi
2 lemon juice   4 curry

6 Discuss the questions.
1 What's the most delicious food you've ever eaten?
2 What's the most disgusting food you've ever tried?
3 What raw food do you eat?
4 What spicy food do you eat?
5 Do you often eat vegetarian meals?
6 Do you eat a lot of sweet things?

EP Word profile *really*

It's **really** juicy!

'OK then. I'll do your taste test.' '**Really?** Great!'

'Is that OK?' 'Er … **not really**.'

page 125

58   Unit 10

READING

OLLIE, DON'T EAT THAT!

When Ollie James was one, his brother had a tiny pet turtle. One day, it disappeared. Then Ollie's mum noticed a turtle's leg, hanging out of Ollie's mouth! This was the beginning of Ollie's interest in very unusual types of food. And, don't worry, the turtle was fine! Now, aged 16, Ollie's tried everything from ants to zebra. And for the last two years, he's written about them on his blog: 'Ollie, Don't Eat That!'

1 ....

Well, once my dad brought home some giant toasted ants from a business trip to Colombia. They tasted good, like salty meat. I described them on a website and I got a *lot* of replies! So I started looking for other unusual foods and I set up a blog to write about them. I've tried over a hundred different things since I started my blog.

2 ....

The strangest is the durian fruit, from South East Asia. It smells disgusting – like old fruit and rubbish! You mustn't carry them on public transport in some countries! But they taste incredible – sweet and creamy. I've also cooked with unusual ingredients. I found a recipe for an ostrich curry on the web and last week I made that. An ostrich is a bird, but its meat is dark red. I expected a strong flavour, but it isn't as meaty as lamb. I got it from an ostrich farm in England.

3 ....

That's definitely the cheeseburger in a can. A reader sent it to me from Germany. It tasted like a very bad vegetarian burger. It looked horrible and it was. I couldn't finish it.

4 ....

Oh, my favourite is miracle berries, from Africa. They taste bitter, but after a minute, you take them out. Then anything that's sour, tastes sweet. Lemon juice, for example, tastes like sweet lemonade!

5 ....

Not once. I'm always careful that the food is safe. My parents check everything. They've tried some things too. They loved my ostrich curry!

---

1 Read the interview quickly. Match questions a–e to spaces 1–5.
  a What's the most interesting thing you've ever eaten?
  b Why did you start your website?
  c Have you ever been ill because of something you've tried?
  d And what about the most disgusting?
  e What's the best food you've tried?

2 Complete the sentences with one word in each space.
  1 Ollie started his blog .... years ago.
  2 Ollie's .... gave him the toasted ants.
  3 Durian fruit doesn't smell ....
  4 Some countries don't .... people to carry durian fruit on public transport.
  5 Ollie thinks lamb is .... than ostrich.
  6 Ollie didn't eat all of the cheeseburger in a ....
  7 Miracle berries make sour things taste ....
  8 Ollie has never been .... from the unusual foods he has eaten.

3 Match the highlighted words from the article to the meanings.
  0 ingredients
    (a) food you use to cook something
    b equipment you use to cook something
  1 recipe
    a a book about food
    b instructions for cooking something
  2 flavour
    a how food or drink smells
    b how food or drink tastes
  3 lamb
    a a type of meat
    b a type of fruit
  4 vegetarian
    a not containing meat
    b raw

Talking points
" Is it good to try unusual types of food and drink? Why?
Do you think more people will eat insects in the future? Why? / Why not? "

Video extra   Taste this!   59

GRAMMAR Present perfect and past simple

1 Read the examples. Then complete the rules with *present perfect* or *past simple*.

1 Ollie's **tried** everything from ants to zebra.
2 I **made** an ostrich curry **last week**.

> a We use the .... to ask or talk about experiences in our life.
> b We use the .... to ask or say exactly when something happened.
> c We do not use past time phrases with the ....

→ Grammar reference page 147

2 Choose the correct verb forms.

1 We enjoyed the party, but there *hasn't been / wasn't* anything to eat.
2 Macy *had / 's had* an argument with her best friend yesterday.
3 We eat meat, but we *went / 've been* to vegetarian restaurants lots of times.
4 *Did you ever cook / Have you ever cooked* a meal for your friends?
5 It was Mum's birthday on Sunday and we *went / 've been* out to a restaurant.
6 I love pizza, but I *never ordered / 've never ordered* one on the phone.

3 Ask and answer questions using the present perfect and past simple.

1 go to a concert? – Who / see?
2 make anyone angry? – Who / be / it?
3 forget your homework? – What / teacher / say?
4 eat out with your friends? – Where / go?
5 win anything? – What / win?

A: *Have you ever been to a concert?*
B: *Yes, I have.*
A: *Who did you see?*
B: *I saw Katy Perry last year.*

How long? and *for/since*

4 Read the examples. Then complete the rules with the bold words in the examples.

1 '**How long** has Ollie had a blog?' 'He's had a blog **for** two years.'
2 He's tried over a hundred different things **since** he started his blog.

> We use:
> a .... to ask a question in the present perfect about a period of time.
> b .... to say when something started.
> c .... to give the period of time something has continued.

→ Grammar reference page 147

5 Write *for* or *since* for these time phrases.

> three weeks   this morning   a long time   2010
> Monday   a few years   four o'clock   midday

6 Complete the sentences about you.

0 *I've been* (be) at this school for *three years*.
1 I .... (not miss) a lesson since ....
2 We .... (be) in this classroom for ....
3 I .... (not eat) anything since ....
4 Our teacher .... (work) here for ....
5 I .... (not do) an exam since ....
6 I .... (live) in this town for ....

Corpus challenge

Find and correct the mistake in the student's sentence.
We are friends for four years.

7 Ask questions with *How long …?* Answer them with *for* or *since*.

1 you / know / your best friend?
2 you / study / English?
3 you / be / in this class?
4 you / live / in your home?

A: *How long have you known your best friend?*
B: *I've known my best friend for …*

VOCABULARY *look, taste, smell*

1 Read the examples. What type of word can we use after the verbs *look, taste* and *smell*?

1 It **looked** horrible.
2 They **taste** bitter.
3 It **smells** disgusting.

2 Describe the things using *look, taste* or *smell*. Guess what your partner is describing.

A: *It looks fresh and tasty.*
B: *The burger?*
A: *No, that probably tastes disgusting!*

Unit 10

LISTENING

1 Have you ever made a meal for anyone? Who was it for? What did you make?

2 You are going to listen to some short extracts. Read the questions and look at the pictures. What words might you hear in each extract?

1 What did the girl cook when she was younger?

A   B   C

4 What meal can you only buy today?

A   B   C

2 Where does the boy get his recipes from?

A   B   C

5 What food does Sara **not** like?

A   B   C

3 Who is a vegetarian?

A   B   C

3 ▶1.36 Listen and choose the correct picture A, B or C. Listen again and check.

SPEAKING Ordering fast food

1 Look at the menu and answer the questions.
1 What do you think 'veggie' means?
2 How much is a beef burger with cheese?
3 What is in a mixed salad?
4 What are French fries?
5 Why are there two prices for French fries and cola?

2 ▶1.37 Listen to the conversation. What does Jess order? How much is her meal?

3 ▶1.37 Read the *Prepare* box. Then listen again. Which phrases do Jess and the server use?

Prepare to speak Ordering food

Phrases the server uses	Phrases the customer uses
What can I get you?	Could I have … , please?
What would you like?	I'll have … , please.
And to drink?	I'd like … , please.
Eat in or take out?	Have you got any … ?
Here's your change.	Here you are.

BURGERS
Beef	£2.89
Chicken	£2.59
Veggie	£2.29
With cheese	+50p

SALADS AND SIDE ORDERS
Mixed salad	£3.99
Tuna salad	£4.49
French fries	£1.50/£1.80

DRINK
Orange juice	£1.90
Still/sparkling water	£1.80
Cola	£1.30/£1.70
Coffee	£2.20

4 Look at the menu again and decide what you would like to order. Then work in pairs. Practise ordering food. Use phrases from the *Prepare* box.

5 Act out your conversation for the class.

Taste this!

Culture
What I eat

1 Look at the photos on page 63.
1. Where do you think each person is from?
2. Who do you think has the healthiest diet? Why?

2 Read the profiles quickly and check your answers for exercise 1.

NAMIBIA: The long-distance lorry driver

Teri Bezuidenhout drives a lorry from South Africa to Angola – a journey of over 2,500 kilometres that takes almost three days. And then he has to come back again! It can be a tiring job and he only sees his family for about three days every month. In the mornings, he makes his only hot meal of the day at the side of the road: soup and pasta with tomato sauce. He makes a lot, so he can eat the rest later in the day. Teri doesn't usually stop driving for lunch or dinner. He has his other meals cold, while he's driving.

There are **8,400 calories** in his diet on this day.

CANADA: The green teen

Coco Simon Finken, 16, is a 'green teen'. She cycles to school every day – her family haven't got a car. She's a vegetarian and she even grows some of her own vegetables in her family's garden. The rest of her family have never eaten much meat, so they often eat the same meals as Coco. However, her mum, dad and sister all love *poutine* – a Canadian dish of fried potatoes with cheese and meat sauce. Coco never eats that.

There are **1,900 calories** in her daily diet.

> **Calories** are units of energy that tell you how much energy a food gives you. Women need about 2,000 calories every day and men need about 2,500.

CHINA: The university student

Chen Zhen is a student at university in south-west Shanghai, China. During the week, she lives at her university. She usually eats Chinese food for breakfast, lunch and dinner. However, she sometimes has lunch at a fast-food restaurant because there are always lots of special offers. Every weekend she goes home to her family's house in north-east Shanghai. Her family only eat vegetables and rice all week, so they can afford to have meat when Chen visits. Has her father ever eaten fast food? 'Never,' she says. 'He only eats Chinese food.'

There are **2,600 calories** in her daily diet.

3 Read the profiles again. Answer the questions.
1. Why doesn't Teri see his family very often?
2. Where does Teri eat most of his food during the day?
3. Why do you think Coco is called a 'green teen'?
4. Why doesn't she eat *poutine*?
5. What encourages Chen and her friends to eat at fast-food restaurants?
6. How is Chen's diet different from her father's?

4 Which of these kinds of food and drink can you see in the photos?

~~apple~~	beef	biscuits	cabbage	carrot	chicken
crisps	lettuce	mineral water	pasta	peas
popcorn	rice	soft drink	soup	strawberry

5 Put the words in exercise 4 into the correct column. Can you add three more words to each column?

Meat	Vegetables	Fruit	Drinks	Other
		apple		

62 Culture

6 ▶ 1.38 Listen to Josh, a British boy. Does his mum have a good diet? Who do you think has the healthier diet – Josh or his mum?

7 ▶ 1.38 Listen again. What things does Josh's mum eat?

> apples   biscuits   burgers   cabbage   cereal
> chicken sandwiches   chips   fish   ice cream   pasta   tea

8 In pairs, discuss the questions.
1. Think about what you eat. Which person's diet is similar to yours? Why?
2. Think about what Coco's and Chen's parents ate when they were young. What do you think was different? Why has it changed?

COCO
- **Breakfast:** bread, strawberries, soya milk (milk from soya beans, not from animals)
- **Lunch:** veggie wrap (sandwich with cheese, pepper and lettuce), apple, carrots
- **Dinner:** jyoti matar paneer (peas and Indian cheese), white rice
- **Snacks:** homemade bread with chocolate pieces, apple, milk, vegetable juice, green tea, water

TERI
- **Breakfast, lunch and dinner:** pasta, soup, tinned meat, tinned sausages, tinned meatballs
- **Snacks:** popcorn, chocolate biscuits
- **Other:** energy drink, fizzy orange drink, bottled water

CHEN
- **Breakfast:** a rice roll, vegetables, spicy cabbage, milk
- **Lunch:** chicken, chicken burger, ice cream with chocolate sauce
- **Dinner:** fried cabbage with garlic and chilli, tomato and egg soup, white rice
- **Other:** bottled water

Project
Interview someone in your family about the meals they eat.
- Write a short profile of the person you interviewed. Use the information about Coco, Chen and Teri to help you.
- Find the number of calories in their food every day.
- Find a photo of the person you interviewed. Find pictures of the food they eat on the internet or in magazines.
- Make a poster.

11 A healthy future

VOCABULARY   Health and illness

Your profile
Are you generally quite healthy?
Have you ever broken a leg or an arm?
What happened?

1 ▶ 1.39 Match the words to the parts of the body a–j. Then listen and check.

> ankle   chin   elbow   finger   forehead
> knee   shoulder   throat   thumb   toe

2 Complete the table with the words from exercise 1. Add more parts of the body you can see in the picture.

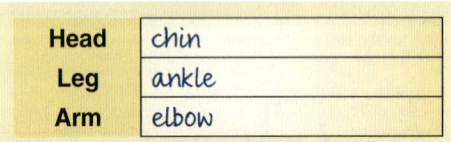

Head	chin
Leg	ankle
Arm	elbow

3 ▶ 1.40 Listen to three conversations. Match the speakers to the sentences.

> Kelly   Josh   Sam

a .... thinks he might be ill.
b .... had an accident and is injured.
c .... has sore legs and arms after doing a lot of sport.

4 ▶ 1.40 Listen again and complete the sentences with words from the box. There is one word you don't need. What does that word mean?

> aches   broken   cold   a cough   a cut   earache
> a fever   flu   sore   stomach ache   toothache

1 Sam's got .... in his arms, legs and feet.
2 Kelly's got a headache, and she has .... inside her mouth. She says it's ....
  She needs to go to the dentist because she has ....
3 The other girl hurt her nose, but it isn't ....
4 Josh feels very hot, so he thinks he's got ....
5 Dora thinks that Josh might be getting a ....
6 Josh has a sore throat and ....
  Last night he had .... , too. He hopes he hasn't got ....

5 Compare illnesses and injuries you've had.

A: *I've had a fever.*
B: *Me too. I had a high temperature last year.*

6 Work in a group. Make a chart with the information about your group's illnesses and injuries.

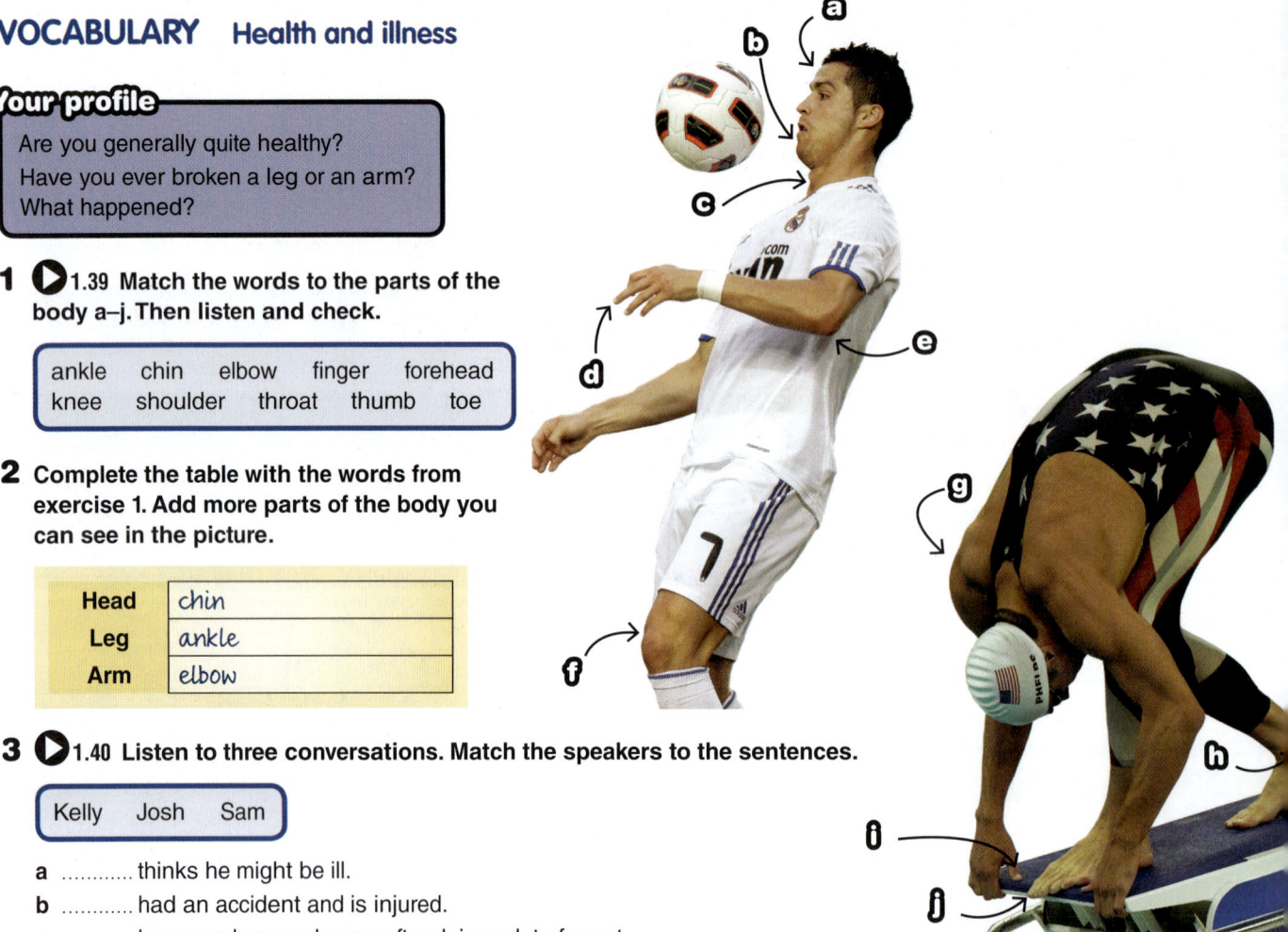

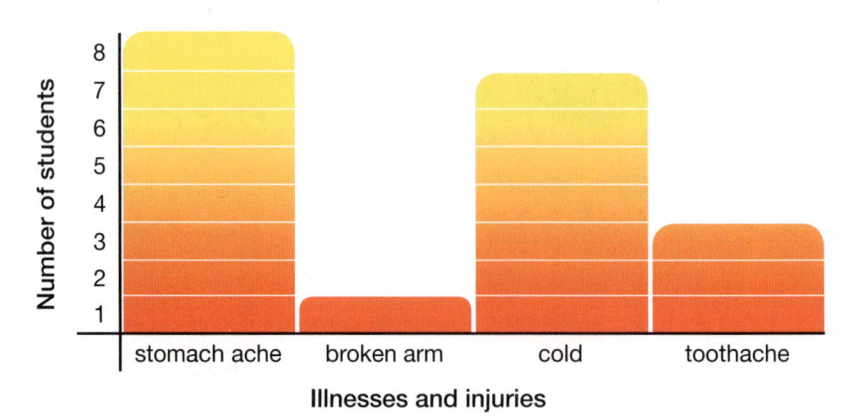

READING

News Home | World News | Headlines | Pictures

Last Updated Tues 31st

We will live for 1,000 years

How long do you expect to live for? In 1900, many people died at the age of about 50. Today, people often live for 80 years or more and doctors predict that most young people today will live to be over 100. But how much longer can people live? Some scientists believe that in the future, humans will live for 1,000 years! Dr Aubrey de Grey compares the human body with a car. Most cars last 10–15 years, but some cars are 100 years old and they're still as good as new. Why? Because their owners have repaired them and looked after them carefully. Dr de Grey believes that people can look after the human body in the same way. Scientists are now inventing drugs that can completely repair old or damaged parts of our bodies. With these drugs, people aren't going to die from common diseases. Their bodies are going to stay young and healthy.

But will it really be possible to keep people alive for 1,000 years? According to Dr de Grey, the technology to make these drugs already exists. Of course, scientists are going to do more tests on the drugs, but Dr de Grey predicts people are going to start taking them in the next few years. However, he warns that people won't live for ever. Although people won't die from old age, there will still be accidents. So the message is still to enjoy your life and make the most of it!

Comments (43)

I don't think people will live for 1,000 years. People have predicted things like this before. Dr de Grey isn't the first, and he won't be the last, person to make such promises.
Simone, Peterborough, UK

People want to live for ever, but it's impossible. You shouldn't believe everything you read!
Hannah, Sydney, Australia

I think de Grey is right. I think I'll find out more about these drugs! I think scientists will discover how to 'cure' old age one day, but not so soon. Millions of people die every year – from cancer, for instance, and we can't even cure them yet. Let's cure real diseases first!
Damian, Camden, London

---

1 Read the news report and the comments quickly. Whose comments agree with Dr de Grey's ideas?

2 Read the news report again. Decide if each sentence is correct or incorrect.
  1 In 1900, many people lived for 80 years.
  2 People usually use their cars for about 30 years.
  3 According to Dr de Grey, scientists have already created drugs to completely repair old and damaged parts of our bodies.
  4 Dr de Grey says that in the future, people won't die from common illnesses.
  5 He says that people will start taking these drugs very soon.
  6 According to Dr de Grey, one day people will live forever.

3 Read the comments again. Choose the correct answers.
  1 Simone thinks people …
    A will live about 1,000 years.
    B will live more than 100 years.
    C won't live for 1,000 years.
  2 Hannah …
    A disagrees with Dr de Grey.
    B agrees with Dr de Grey.
    C isn't sure about Dr de Grey's ideas.
  3 Damian wants scientists to cure diseases … 'cure' old age.
    A before they
    B but not
    C after they

4 Match the highlighted words in the report and comments to the meanings.
  1 making something completely new
  2 not dead
  3 people that something belongs to
  4 make someone healthy again
  5 for all time in the future
  6 makes someone realise a possible danger or problem

EP Word profile *for*

Humans will live for 1,000 years!

People won't live for ever.

Millions of people die every year – from cancer, for instance.

page 125

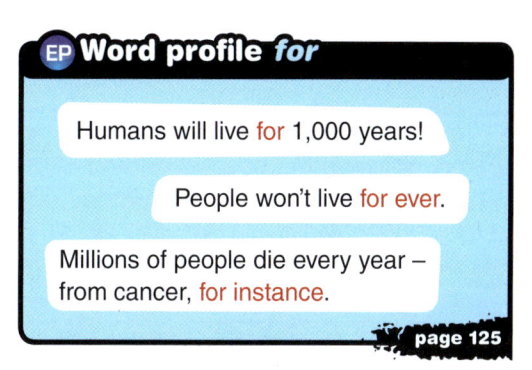

Talking points

Do you think most people would like to live to be 1,000? Why? / Why not? Are there any problems related to living to be very old? What are they?

Video extra   A healthy future

GRAMMAR will and be going to

1 Match the examples to the rules.

1 Some scientists believe that humans **will live** for 1,000 years.
2 With these drugs, people **aren't going to die** from common diseases.
3 Scientists **are going to do** more tests on the drugs.
4 I think **I'll find out** more about these drugs.

> We use *will* …
> a to predict the future generally.
> b when we decide to do something while we are speaking.
>
> We use *be going to* …
> c to talk about something we have already decided to do.
> d to predict the future based on something we can see or know now.

→ Grammar reference page 148

2 Choose the correct verb forms.

1 Do you think people *will / going to* live for much longer in the future?
2 Don't worry about buying snacks. I *make / 'll make* some popcorn later.
3 No, I don't want to come out, thanks. I *'ll have / 'm going to have* an early night.
4 Look at those black clouds! It *'s going to rain / 'll rain*!
5 I *'ll go / 'm going to go* and visit my cousins in the summer. We've already bought the tickets.
6 I hope that one day scientists *are going to find / will find* a cure for cancer.

3 Complete the sentences. Use the *will* or *be going to* future forms.

1 'Would you like some more biscuits?' 'No, I ………… (not have) any more, thank you.'
2 'Have you decided about Anita's party this evening?' 'Yes, I ………… (not come), sorry. I have to study.' 
3 'Can anyone help me?' 'Yes, I ………… (help) you!' 
4 Be careful! You ………… (crash)! 

4 Read the questions and prepare your answers. Then ask and answer the questions.

1 Is it going to rain later?
2 What are you going to do at the weekend?
3 Do you think you'll go to university? Why? / Why not?
4 What kind of job do you think you'll do?
5 Where will you live when you're older?

Corpus challenge

Find and correct the mistake in the student's sentence.

I think we go shopping at the weekend.

VOCABULARY Illnesses and injuries: verbs

1 Which verbs in the box go with the words below?

> break   catch   cut   feel   get
> have   hurt   injure   be

1 a cold   2 sick   3 your leg

2 Choose the two correct answers.

0 I was quite ill yesterday, but I'm ………… better now.
  a catching   **b feeling**   **c getting**
1 Ouch! My head ………… .
  a injures   b feels sore   c hurts
2 My sister ………… ill last night.
  a was   b caught   c felt
3 He's never ………… flu.
  a caught   b had   c felt
4 I've ………… my ankle.
  a broken   b caught   c injured
5 Be careful. Don't ………… your finger.
  a cut   b get   c hurt
6 My uncle ………… his thumb last week.
  a got   b broke   c hurt

3 ▶1.41 Complete what Matt says. Then listen and check.

> caught   feel   's got   ~~'ve got~~
> 've got   was feeling

I'm at home because I ⁰ **'ve got** flu. I ¹ ………… a bit ill at the weekend, and now I'm exhausted. My sister ² ………… flu too, so maybe I ³ ………… it from her. I ⁴ ………… a fever at the moment, and aches in my arms and legs. I've taken some medicine and my mum says I'll ⁵ ………… better soon.

Unit 11

WRITING   An online comment

1 What do you do to keep fit during the summer holidays?

2 Read Oscar's online question. What does he want advice about? What advice would you give?

> School's finished for the summer holidays, so I won't have any more basketball games. I want to keep fit over the summer. Any ideas?
> **Oscar, Leeds**
> [3 replies]

3 Read the three replies. Do they mention any of your ideas?

1 — 3.15 pm
Why don't you try swimming? It's a really good way to keep fit and it's fun too. I'm going to go swimming a lot in the school holidays. I'm sure there's a swimming pool near you. Indoor pools are OK, but outdoor pools are great when it's hot.

2 — 4.21 pm
Maybe you could try running. I started running about six months ago, and I'm definitely fitter now. The big advantage is that it doesn't cost any money. If you want to keep fit, remember to eat healthily too. That makes a big difference.

3 — 4.49 pm
You should definitely get a bike! Biking is one of the best sports for keeping fit. I'm sure you'll love it! Cycling in a big city isn't much fun, so what about getting out into the countryside? And don't forget to wear a helmet!

4 Read the Prepare box. Find the phrases in the three replies.

Prepare to write — An online comment

You can use these phrases to make suggestions in a comment, note or message:
- Making suggestions:
  Maybe you could …
  Why don't you …?
  You should definitely …
  What about …?
- Reminding someone:
  Don't forget to …
  Remember to …

5 Complete the sentences.
1 ………… about joining a gym?
2 ………… you start training for a marathon?
3 Maybe you ………… join your local sports centre.
4 You ………… definitely do exercise every day!
5 ………… to warm up before you do exercise.
6 ………… forget to ask your parents first.

6 Correct the mistakes in the sentences.
1 Maybe could you go to your local swimming pool.
2 What about sign up for a summer camp?
3 You should definitely to try to do some exercise every day.
4 Don't forget warm up before you go running.
5 Why you don't look online to find sports clubs in your area?

7 Read Oscar's question again and write your comment.
- Use the phrases in the Prepare box.
- Write about 35–45 words.
- Remember to check your spelling and grammar.

A healthy future   **67**

12 Incredible wildlife

VOCABULARY Animals

Your profile
Which of these animals have you seen? Where? Which are found in your country?

1 ▶ 2.02 Match the words to the photos of animals. Then listen and check.

> ant   bat   bear   bee   butterfly   camel
> dolphin   donkey   fly   frog   giraffe
> kangaroo   mosquito   parrot   penguin
> rat   shark   snake   tiger   whale

2 ▶ 2.03 Do the quiz. Then listen and check.

3 Read the descriptions and guess the animals.
1 It's small, with brown fur. It looks like a large mouse. People often don't like these animals.
2 It's big and dangerous. It's orange and black, and it looks like a big cat.
3 It's an insect. It moves along the ground and it lives with hundreds of others.
4 It's small and green. It can swim and jump.

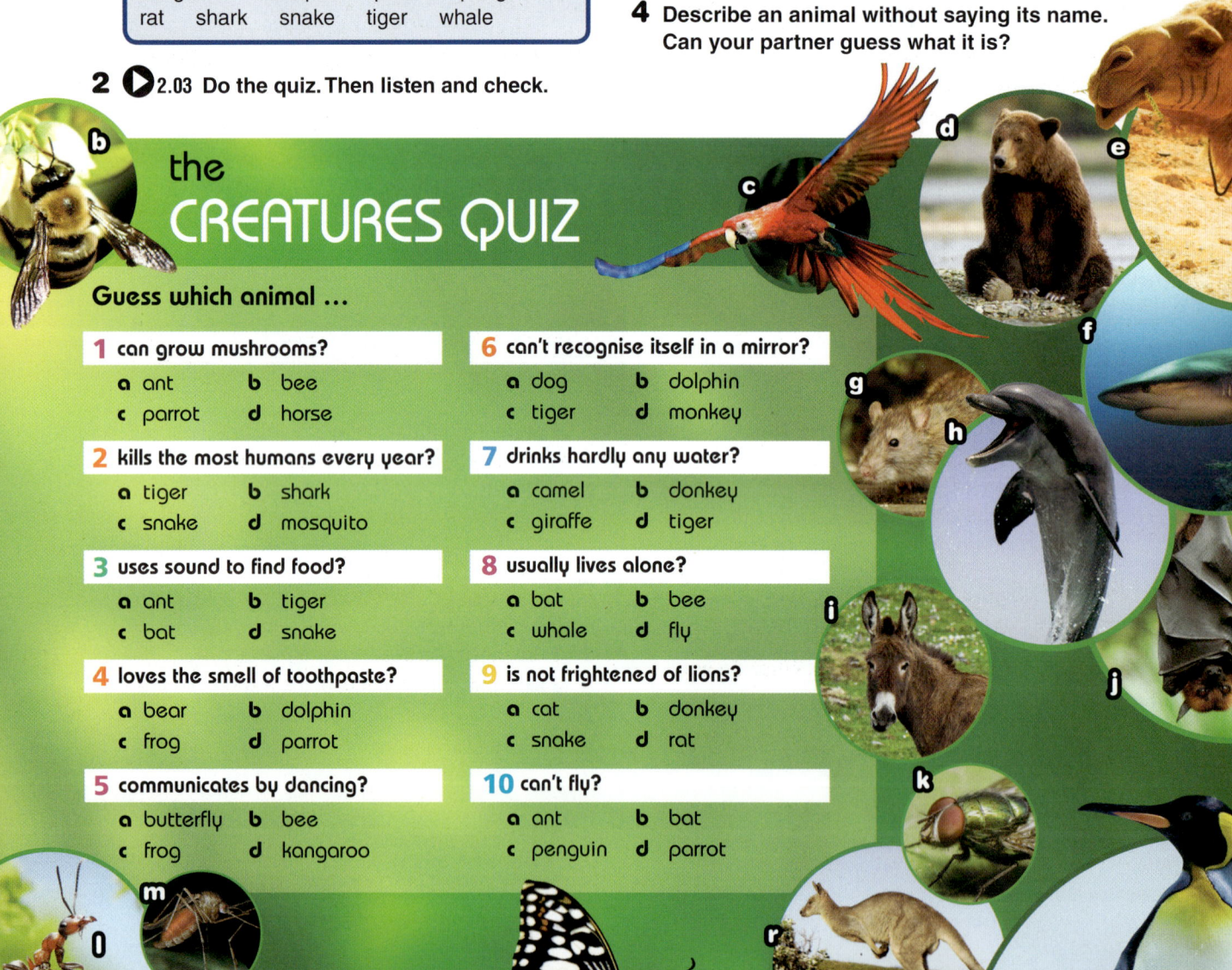

4 Describe an animal without saying its name. Can your partner guess what it is?

the CREATURES QUIZ

Guess which animal …

1 can grow mushrooms?
  a ant   b bee
  c parrot   d horse

2 kills the most humans every year?
  a tiger   b shark
  c snake   d mosquito

3 uses sound to find food?
  a ant   b tiger
  c bat   d snake

4 loves the smell of toothpaste?
  a bear   b dolphin
  c frog   d parrot

5 communicates by dancing?
  a butterfly   b bee
  c frog   d kangaroo

6 can't recognise itself in a mirror?
  a dog   b dolphin
  c tiger   d monkey

7 drinks hardly any water?
  a camel   b donkey
  c giraffe   d tiger

8 usually lives alone?
  a bat   b bee
  c whale   d fly

9 is not frightened of lions?
  a cat   b donkey
  c snake   d rat

10 can't fly?
  a ant   b bat
  c penguin   d parrot

READING

Animals: interesting, unusual and imagined

The world is full of wonderful animals, many real and a few only imagined. Read about some of these amazing animals!

A ....

Recently, some scientists were walking through a village market in Laos, in Asia, when they saw an unusual rat. They thought it might be rare, so they decided to buy it. Later, the scientists couldn't believe their eyes. They thought this species disappeared 12 million years ago!

B ....

Scientists still discover new animals every year. Most unknown wild animals live a long way from cities, so some scientists flew by helicopter into a jungle in Papua New Guinea. They wanted to find some new species and they were not disappointed. They found:
- a kangaroo that lives in trees
- a rat as big as a cat
- 20 new species of frog.

Normally, wild animals avoid being near people, and they usually run or stay very still when they see or hear humans. However, these animals weren't at all scared, probably because humans never visit that area.

C ....

The 'coelacanth', a dinosaur fish, was common 200–300 million years ago. Scientists thought the species disappeared about 65 million years ago, but a fisherman caught a healthy coelacanth in 1938, and people have seen others since then. How many more amazing animals might exist?

D ....

In the North American countryside, some people say they've seen a 'sasquatch'. It looks like a very tall human, with thick, dark hair all over its body and very large feet. Sasquatches must be shy because they always run away when they see humans. Or maybe they don't enjoy being in photos! People have seen a similar animal in the mountains of Tibet and Nepal. They call it the 'yeti'. Do sasquatches and yetis really exist? There are lots of reports, but we still can't be sure.

1 Describe the animals in the photos. What do you think they are?

2 In pairs, look at the headings below. What do you think each paragraph will be about?
1. Animals without fear
2. Does 'big foot' exist?
3. A living dinosaur
4. The species that didn't die

3 Read the paragraphs quickly and check your answers. Match the headings to the paragraphs.

4 Read the article again. Are the sentences correct or incorrect?
1. The scientists in Laos discovered a rat by chance.
2. The experts were surprised about the new species of rat.
3. The coelacanth species has lived for 200–300 years.
4. In Papua New Guinea, the wild animals weren't frightened.
5. People say that yetis have got thick hair and big feet.

5 Match the highlighted words in the article to the meanings.
1. be present or real
2. a forest in a hot country
3. not usual, or not typical
4. usual or typical

EP Word profile *still*

Scientists still discover new animals every year.

They usually run or stay very still.

We still can't be sure if sasquatches really exist.

page 126

Talking points

When people find an unusual animal like the coelacanth, what should they do with it?
Are markets the right place to sell animals?

Incredible wildlife 69

GRAMMAR Modals of probability

1 Look at the photo and read the examples. Then complete the rules with the bold verbs.

It **might** be a plant.
It **could** be a stick.
It **can't** be a bird. It hasn't got wings.
It's got feet, so it **must** be an insect.

> a We use .... / .... + infinitive to talk about things that are possible.
> b We use .... + infinitive to talk about things that we think are certain.
> c We use .... + infinitive to talk about things that are impossible.

→ **Grammar reference** page 149

2 Choose the correct words.
1 That bird flew in here. It *could* / *can't* be a penguin.
2 Our dog hasn't moved all day. It *could* / *can't* be ill.
3 Be careful. I can hear a mosquito. It *might* / *must* bite you.
4 It's on land. It *can't* / *must* be a dolphin.
5 It's big and it's got brown fur. It *can't* / *might* be a bear.
6 The cat's asleep. It *can't* / *must* be sleepy today.
7 It's got four legs, so it *could* / *can't* be a snake.
8 I can hear a voice speaking, but there's nobody here. It *must* / *can't* be that parrot!

Corpus challenge

Find and correct the mistake in the student's sentence.
This can be the best trip ever!

3 ▶ 2.04 Listen to sounds 1–8. In groups, discuss what the sounds *can't*, *might* or *must* be.

4 Look at the photos and discuss what animals they *can't*, *might* or *must be*.

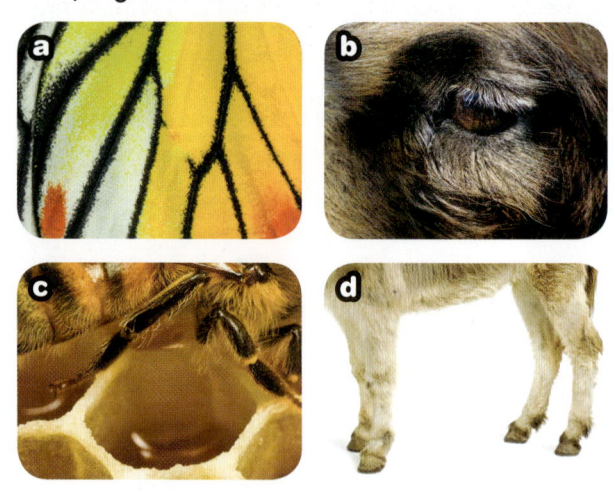

A: *It has some red on it, so it can't be a tiger.*
B: *It could be a bird …*
A: *Oh, I know. It must be a … !*

VOCABULARY Adverbs of probability

1 Read the examples. Complete the table with the bold adverbs.
1 *It has fur. It's **definitely** an animal of some kind.*
2 *It isn't in water, so it's **definitely not** a fish.*
3 *It's very small, so it's **probably** an insect.*
4 *I'm not sure what it is. **Perhaps** it's a bird of some kind.*

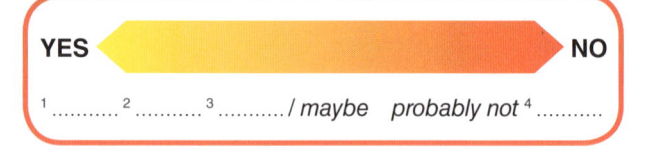

YES ─────────────────────────► NO
¹............ ²............ ³............ / maybe   probably not ⁴............

2 Look at the photos and discuss what they might be. They both have a connection to this unit. Use adverbs of probability. Check your ideas on page 121.

70 Unit 12

LISTENING

1 Read the podcast introduction and look at the photos. Discuss how the animals might help people.

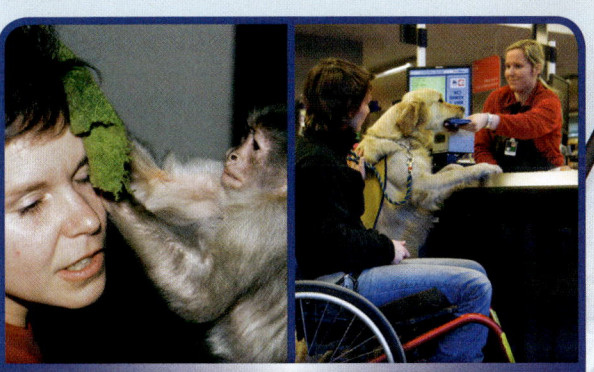

ANIMALS AT WORK

There are always stories in the news about how we need to save the planet's wildlife. But sometimes humans need help too. Hear how some clever creatures are helping us. Listen.

2 ▶ 2.05 Listen to the podcast. Which three animals do they talk about?

3 ▶ 2.05 Listen again. Complete the sentences with *dogs*, *rats* or *bees*.

1 .... avoid a problem because they aren't as heavy as humans.
2 .... can bring things to people.
3 .... can help find dangerous chemicals.
4 .... can help find bombs that are under the ground.
5 .... can help with buying things.
6 .... are cheaper to train than other animals.

4 Discuss the questions.

1 In what ways do you think Riley has improved Donna's life?
2 In what other ways can animals improve people's lives?
3 Is it fair to use animals to help us in dangerous situations? Why? / Why not?

SPEAKING Describing a picture (1)

1 Look at the photo. What do you think is happening?

2 ▶ 2.06 Listen to someone describing the photo and check your ideas.

3 ▶ 2.06 Read the *Prepare* box. Then complete the sentences about the picture. Listen again and check.

Prepare to speak Describing a picture (1)

Saying what you can see
I can see …
There's …
On the left/right, …
In the middle …

Guessing what's happening
Perhaps …
Maybe …
It's probably …
They might be …

1 The dog is .... a rescue dog.
2 On the .... one person's digging into the snow.
3 .... they're looking for someone.
4 The other person's on the ....
5 He .... be the dog's trainer.
6 I think .... the dog has found the person.

4 Work in pairs. Take turns to describe the photo in exercise 1. Use phrases from the *Prepare* box.

5 Work in pairs. Turn to page 121.

Science
Ecosystems

1 Read text A. Is a human a *carnivore*, a *herbivore*, or an *omnivore*?

A FOOD CHAINS

An **ecosystem** is any area in which certain plants and animals live, for example part of an ocean or a forest. Each type of animal feeds on the other animals or plants in that ecosystem. We can use a **food chain** to describe what the animals in an ecosystem eat. The arrows (→) in the food chain below mean 'is eaten by'.

The giraffe is a **herbivore** – it only eats plants. The lion is a **carnivore** – it only eats meat. An **omnivore** eats plants and meat.

grass → giraffe → lion

2 Look at text A and the food chain again. Then draw a food chain containing a tiger, a wild donkey and grass.

3 Read text B and look at the food web. Then complete the paragraph.

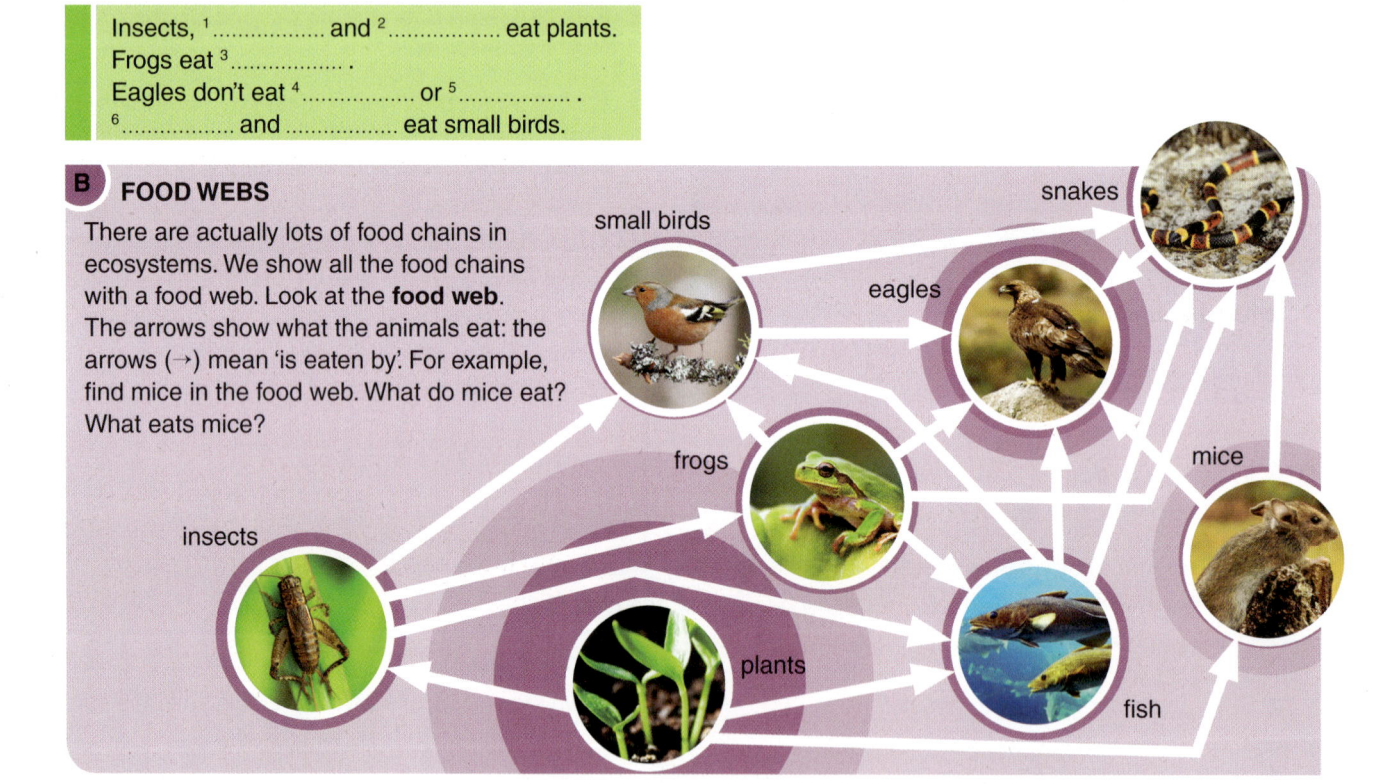

> Insects, [1]............... and [2]............... eat plants.
> Frogs eat [3]............... .
> Eagles don't eat [4]............... or [5]............... .
> [6]............... and .... eat small birds.

B FOOD WEBS

There are actually lots of food chains in ecosystems. We show all the food chains with a food web. Look at the **food web**. The arrows show what the animals eat: the arrows (→) mean 'is eaten by'. For example, find mice in the food web. What do mice eat? What eats mice?

4 Answer the questions.
1. Which animals in the food web are carnivores?
2. Which animals are herbivores?
3. Which animals are omnivores?
4. Can you name five more types of carnivore and herbivore?

5 Are these animals carnivores, herbivores or omnivores?

> bat   cat   cow   eagle   fly   mouse   mosquito   rabbit   sheep

6 Draw a food web with some of the animals in exercise 5. Add *humans, carrots* and *grass*.

7 Read text C and look at the pyramid of numbers. Are there more fish than sharks?

C PYRAMIDS OF NUMBERS

Food chains tell us what is in an ecosystem, but they don't tell us the numbers of plants and animals. We use a **pyramid of numbers** to give information about how many plants and animals live in an ecosystem. Look at the pyramid of numbers for an ocean ecosystem.

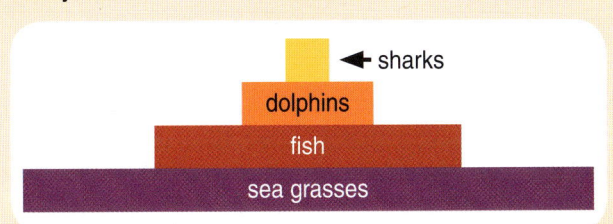

← sharks
dolphins
fish
sea grasses

The size of each block in the pyramid of numbers tells us how many animals or plants there are in each group. The animals at the top of the food chain have usually got the biggest bodies. There aren't as many of these animals, so we put them at the top of the pyramid of numbers. In the pyramid of numbers above, are there more sharks or more dolphins? Which is bigger, a shark or a dolphin?

Plants are at the bottom of the food chain, and they are normally at the bottom of the pyramid of numbers because there are a lot of them.

8 Complete the pyramid of numbers. Then discuss what the animals eat.

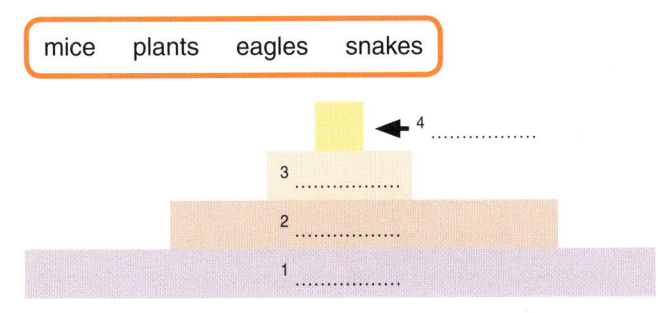

mice   plants   eagles   snakes

4 ....
3 ....
2 ....
1 ....

9 ▶ 2.07 Look at the chart. Listen to a podcast about problems in an ecosystem. Then choose the correct answers.

Pollution in a river ecosystem	
1 A some of the birds have died	B most of the fish have died
2 A frogs and small birds have less food	B the frogs move to another river ecosystem
3 A the frogs eat the birds	B some of the frogs die
4 A eagles have less food	B eagles eat the small birds
5 A the eagles fly to other areas	B most of the eagles die
6 A there are more rabbits, but not as many plants	B there are more plants, but not as many rabbits

Project

Make a poster.
- Choose an ecosystem. It can be urban or rural, and it should include at least one type of plant and four animals.
- Use the internet to research the plants and animals in the ecosystem.
- Find photos on the internet of the plants and animals.
- Label the plants and animals, and draw the arrows of a food web.
- Make a pyramid of numbers for the ecosystem.
- Explain your ecosystem poster to the rest of the class.

Review 3
Units 9–12

VOCABULARY

1 Complete the crossword.

1 a place where you put your money to keep it safe (4, 7)
2 the place where you pay in a shop (8)
3 The shop assistant gives you this piece of paper when you buy something. (7)
4 keep money until you have enough to buy something (4, 2)
5 something that is cheaper for a period of time (7, 5)
6 the money you get back at 2 (6)
7 You might do this when you buy something and then decide you don't like it. (4, 2, 4)
8 the amount of money something costs (5)

2 Match two words to each heading.

| bitter   cough   flu   forehead   fresh |
| giraffes   mosquitoes   shoulder |

1 Describing tastes .... , ...
2 The body .... , ...
3 Animals .... , ...
4 Illness .... , ...

3 Complete the sentences with the words in exercise 2.

1 Can you feel his ....? I think he's got a temperature.
2 .... use their long necks in fights.
3 I never buy fruit from that shop. It isn't ....
4 .... are the most dangerous insects in the world.
5 This chocolate isn't very nice. It's really ....
6 You haven't got a cold. You've got .... !
7 I was carrying a heavy bag all afternoon and now my .... hurts.
8 I've had a .... for over a week, and now my throat really hurts.

GRAMMAR

4 Complete the conversations. Use the past simple or present perfect.

1 A: .... you ever .... (see) a shark?
   B: No, I haven't. But last year I .... (swim) with dolphins on holiday.
2 A: How long .... Ruth .... (have) stomach ache?
   B: It started yesterday. She .... (not eat) anything since then.
3 A: We .... (go) to a Japanese restaurant last weekend.
   B: Really? I .... never .... (try) Japanese food. What's it like?
4 A: James and Tom .... (be) over 20 minutes late this morning.
   B: .... they ever .... (arrive) at school on time? They're always late!

5 Choose the correct verbs.

1 A: Don't buy those trainers now. I think they *'ll* / *'re going to* have lots of special offers after the holidays.
   B: I know, but I don't want to wait. I *'ll* / *'m going to* buy them now.
2 A: Tell your brother we *'ll* / *'re going to* have dinner in two minutes. Everything's ready.
   B: I don't think he *'ll* / *'s going to* be hungry. But I'll tell him.
3 A: Our teacher *will* / *is going to* have a baby in June. She told us today.
   B: Really? That's nice. I *'ll* / *'m going to* send her a card.
4 A: My new jacket is too small. I *'ll* / *'m going to* take it back.
   B: Are you leaving now?
   A: Yes.
   B: OK. I *'ll* / *'m going to* come with you. I need some new shoes.

6 Write a sentence that means the same as the second sentence. Use the verb in brackets.

0 He can't move his arm. *Perhaps it's broken.* (might)
   It might be broken.
1 It tastes disgusting. *I'm sure it isn't fresh.* (can't)
2 He's got a cough and a sore throat. *Perhaps he has a cold.* (could)
3 My brother often goes to that café. *I'm sure he knows your sister.* (must)
4 It looks bigger than a mouse. *Perhaps it's a rat.* (might)

Corpus challenge

7 Tick the two sentences without mistakes. Correct the mistakes in the other sentences.

1 We are friends since I was 6.
2 I know him a long time.
3 You have heard about the concert?
4 We are here since Friday.
5 We will have a lot of fun.
6 I see you at the party then.
7 Tomorrow we will go to the cinema.
8 You should bring a hat because it might be sunny.

8 Read the text and choose the correct word for each space.

EATING THE RIGHT FOOD

Eating proper meals regularly is ⁰ ..A.. important. However, when you don't ¹ .... well, you don't always want to eat. Nothing tastes good and you ² .... aren't hungry. However, your body ³ .... needs energy.

SO WHAT SHOULD YOU DO?

Try foods that are easy to eat and that will help you to ⁴ .... better. Soup and yogurt are both good. Avoid eating ⁵ .... spicy dishes, like curry, or having sour things like lemon juice, because they will ⁶ .... your stomach. You also need to eat some food with fat in it, like nuts and cheese, because a small amount of fat is good for you.

Finally, remember all the times you've ever ⁷ .... ill. Most of us ⁸ .... colds as young children. What food did your parents give you then? Some scientists advise eating the same types of food you've eaten ⁹ .... you were very young. The positive memories of these times can be very helpful in fighting ¹⁰ .... and making you better.

0	A	very	B	enough	C	too	D	even
1	A	feel	B	be	C	think	D	have
2	A	easily	B	completely	C	really	D	nearly
3	A	already	B	still	C	yet	D	once
4	A	come	B	go	C	stay	D	get
5	A	every	B	any	C	no	D	another
6	A	cut	B	hurt	C	injure	D	break
7	A	gone	B	made	C	done	D	been
8	A	caught	B	took	C	kept	D	found
9	A	before	B	for	C	since	D	from
10	A	illness	B	fitness	C	problem	D	health

13 Moods and feelings

VOCABULARY   Adjectives: feelings

Your profile
Are you usually in a good mood?
What kind of things put you in a bad mood?

1 Read the website and choose the correct adjectives.

2 Match the adjectives you <u>didn't</u> choose in exercise 1 with the definitions.
   a unhappy because you are alone
   b unhappy because something was not as good as you hoped
   c pleased about something you have done   *proud*
   d very tired
   e worried and not able to relax
   f happy to do things for other people

3 ▶ 2.08 Listen to six short conversations. Complete the sentences with the words in the box.

> confused   creative   disappointed
> embarrassed   exhausted   helpful   hopeful
> lazy   lonely   proud   relaxed   stressed

   1 Jess is feeling .... because she's got an exam tomorrow. Matt thinks she'll work better if she's ....
   2 Ali is feeling .... because he's just finished football training. His mum thinks he's being ....
   3 Rob is .... School was closed the last time it snowed, but Matt thinks it will be open today. Rob is .... that they can't go outside to play now.
   4 Matt is feeling .... because he has no one to talk to. Ali is trying to be ....
   5 Jess is .... of her poster. Ali thinks she's very ....
   6 Matt feels .... because he made some stupid mistakes in his exam. He's still .... that he has passed.

4 Complete the sentences. Then compare them with your partner.
   1 I get embarrassed when …
   2 On Friday afternoons, I usually feel …
   3 At the weekend, I sometimes feel …
   4 I get stressed when …
   5 I feel a bit disappointed when …

   I get embarrassed when I have to talk in front of the class.

LOGOUT

Ellen Gardner
Birthday: September 5
132 friends See all

Recent activity

Evie Turner doesn't want to do anything except watch TV!
Feeling: ¹*lazy / proud*
7 minutes ago

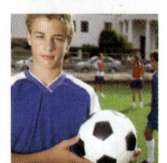

Alfie Dale has already made (yes, made!) two birthday presents this evening.
Feeling: ²*creative / helpful*
22 minutes ago

Lily Gates is enjoying her Sunday night on the sofa with a DVD and some snacks.
Feeling: ³*stressed / relaxed*
1 hour ago

Ollie Parks has just watched 'Sherlock', but didn't understand the ending.
Feeling: ⁴*confused / lonely*
1 hour ago

> **Ellen Gardner** says: I haven't seen it yet! Don't tell me what happens!

Jack Forrest thought that Sydney was the capital of Australia! Oops!
Feeling: ⁵*embarrassed / exhausted*
2 hours ago

> **Ollie Parks** says: I made the same mistake with Rio and Brazil recently.

Grace Buxton has just scored 92% in a practice maths test. The real thing is in the morning!
Feeling: ⁶*hopeful / disappointed*
2 hours ago

READING

The WORST day of the week

Ask someone who goes to school from Monday to Friday for the worst day of their week. Most people will say Monday. The fun of the weekend has just finished and the week has just begun. Everyone is back at school, or work, and the next weekend is five days away.

However, two maths professors in the USA believe this isn't true, and they can explain why. Peter Dodds and Christopher Danforth studied ten million sentences on social networking websites like Facebook and Twitter. The sentences all included the phrase 'I feel' or 'I'm feeling'. Then, they invented a system of scores for words, between 1 and 9. Positive words like 'hopeful' and 'cheerful' had high scores. Words like 'stressed' and 'exhausted' had low scores.

They used the scores of each sentence to decide how happy people were on each day.

Their surprising results could change your life – or at least your week! According to the professors, Sunday is the happiest day of the week. On Sunday, people think and write about the fun things they did on Saturday. Monday is actually the second happiest day of the week. People haven't forgotten about their weekends yet. However, Wednesday is most people's worst day of the week. They have already been at school or work for two days. Their memory of the previous weekend has gone and there are two more days before the next one.

Dodds' and Danforth's research found another interesting fact: people between 45 and 60 are the happiest people online, but the most unhappy group is … teenagers!

Comments

Ryan, Cambridge	Sunday evening is definitely the worst evening of my week. I always put off starting my homework until then and I have to work until midnight!
Zaura, Riyadh	It's different here. Our schools are closed on Friday and Saturday. So Thursday is definitely one of my favourite days of the week!
Anna, Kraków	They're completely right! I always feel terrible on Wednesday mornings.

1 Read the article quickly. Do you agree with the professors?

2 Read the article again. Choose the correct words.
1. Peter Dodds and Christopher Danforth are *teachers / students*.
2. Dodds and Danforth gave low scores to *positive / negative* words.
3. Dodds and Danforth found that *Saturday / Monday* is the next happiest day after Sunday.
4. According to Dodds and Danforth, people aged *12–19 / 45–60* are the unhappiest group online.
5. Ryan does his homework on *Sunday evenings / Monday mornings*.
6. Zaura doesn't *like / go to* school on Fridays.

Talking points
Should the weekend be three days rather than two? Why? / Why not?
Would it be a good idea to have a day off during the week? Why? / Why not?

3 Match the highlighted words in the article to the meanings.
1. happy
2. as said by someone
3. decide to do something at a later time
4. designed or made something new
5. in every way
6. your ability to remember things

EP Word profile *time*

I haven't got **time** to talk now.

It's **time** for school.

Last **time** it snowed, our school was closed.

If you hurry, you'll get there **in time**.

page 126

Video extra — Moods and feelings

GRAMMAR just, already and yet

1 Read the examples. Then complete the rules with *just*, *already* and *yet*.

1. On Mondays, the week has **just** begun.
2. They haven't forgotten about their weekends **yet**.
3. They have **already** been at school or work for two days.
4. Have you finished your homework **yet**?

> We often use *just*, *already* and *yet* with the present perfect to talk about recent actions.
> a .... means that something happened before now or sooner than expected.
> b .... means a short time ago.
> c .... means that the speaker expected something to happen before now.

2 Choose the correct words.

1. A: Do you understand question six, Jess?
   B: Yes. Matt has *already / yet* explained it to me.
2. A: Have you tidied your room *just / yet*?
   B: No, sorry, I'll do it now.
3. A: You look relaxed.
   B: Yes. I've *yet / just* been for a swim.
4. A: You look stressed.
   B: I am! I haven't done any revision *yet / already*!

3 Look at the examples in exercise 1 again and complete the rules.

> We use ¹............ and ²............ in positive sentences. They come after *have*, but before the main verb.
> We use ³............ in negative sentences and questions. It comes after *have* and the main verb.

→ Grammar reference page 150

4 Make sentences using the present perfect and *just*, *already* and *yet*.

1. I / finish / my homework (just)
2. I'm feeling quite confident. I / do / lots of revision (already)
3. Jack's so lazy! It's eleven o'clock now and he / not / get up (yet)
4. Sara's feeling a bit lonely. Her best friend / move / to a new town (just)
5. Freddie! Why can't you be more helpful? you / do / the washing up? (yet)
6. I can't play any more tennis. I'm exhausted! I / play / three times today (already)

Corpus challenge

Find and correct the mistake in the student's sentence.
I just have found a new computer game.

5 Kate is getting ready for a party. Look at the picture. Say what Kate *has already done* and what she *hasn't done yet*. Use the words in the box.

| ~~have a shower~~ | wrap the present | write the card |
| iron her T-shirt | tidy her room | wash her hair |

She's already had a shower.

VOCABULARY Adjectives: -ed or -ing

1 Look at the picture. Match the examples to the meanings.

This story is really confusing.

Yes, I'm completely confused!

1. I'm confus**ed** / disappoint**ed** / surpris**ed**.
2. It's confus**ing** / disappoint**ing** / surpris**ing**.
a. This is how something makes me feel.
b. This is how I feel.

2 Complete the adjectives with *-ed* or *-ing*.

1. I'm tidying my room and I'm bor......... .
2. Did you hear what happened? It's really shock......... .
3. I want to go to bed. I've had a really tir......... day.
4. I think my brother's failed his driving test. He looks really disappoint......... .
5. I've just bought that game and now it's 50% off. That's really annoy......... .
6. When my parents dance, it's really embarrass......... .

78 Unit 13

WRITING   Notes and messages

1 Read the notes and messages quickly. Which note is …

1. saying thank you for something?
2. inviting someone to something today?
3. wishing someone good luck?
4. reporting something lost?

2 Read the *Prepare* box and find examples of the phrases in the notes and messages.

Prepare to write Notes and messages

You can use these phrases when you write a note or short message:
- Apologising: *Sorry I couldn't …, Sorry about …*
- Thanking someone: *Thanks a lot for …, Thank you for …*
- Asking someone to do something: *Please could you …? Can you …?*
- Inviting someone: *Would you like to …? Do you want to …?*
- Wishing someone luck: *Good luck! Hope …*

3 Complete the sentences with phrases from the *Prepare* box.

1. ………… helping me clear up after the party. It was very kind of you.
2. Hi, Jen. ………… come round to my house tomorrow? I've got a great new game!
3. ………… come to your party last weekend. I was visiting my grandparents.
4. ………… call me later? I need some help with my maths homework.
5. ………… with your job interview! ………… it goes well!

4 Which phrases from the *Prepare* box can you use in these situations?

a. You've just lost something.
b. Your friend has given you a great present for your birthday.
c. You want to invite a friend to go shopping with you at the weekend.
d. Your sister has got a driving test later today.
e. You forgot your friend's birthday last week.

5 Write notes and messages for the situations in exercise 4.
- Use phrases from the *Prepare* box.
- Remember to check your spelling and grammar.

---

a My mum's just invited you to dinner. Would you like to come round after school? Tell me at lunchtime, if possible.

b HELP!
I left a red phone in room D3 on Monday lunchtime.
Please could you call or text Evie if you have seen it?

c **Dad** Hi! Has your exam started yet?
Ruby Not yet. 2 pm. Remember?
Dad OK. Good luck! Hope it all goes well today. Try not to get stressed. We know you'll pass. We're thinking of you and love you very much!

d MYBOOK
Hi Libby
Thanks a lot for a great party last night! Sorry I couldn't stay and tidy up.

Moods and feelings

14 Watch it, read it

VOCABULARY TV, films and literature

Your profile
What films have you seen recently?
What are your favourite TV shows?
What novels have you read recently?

1 Match the types of TV show, film and novel to the photos. Which type of film or TV show can you not see?

action film   animated film   chat show   comedy   documentary   historical drama   horror film/story
love film/story   murder mystery   science fiction film/story   soap opera   ~~thriller~~

a) thriller

2 ▶ 2.09 Listen and check your answers to exercise 1. What type of TV programme is *Hollyoaks*?

3 Complete the definitions with words from exercise 1.
1 A .... is a film or TV programme that gives information about a subject.
2 A book or film with a very exciting story is called a ....
3 A .... is a TV drama series about people's daily lives.
4 A book or film about the future is called a ....
5 A .... is a movie that takes place in the past.
6 A TV programme in which people talk and discuss things is called a ....

4 Think of two examples of each type of TV show, film and novel from exercise 1.
A: *Despicable Me 2 is an animated film.*
B: *Yes. And Kung Fu Panda is an animated film too.*

5 Complete the sentences with the kinds of books and films that you like and dislike. Compare your opinions.
1 I'm a big fan of …
2 I can't stand …
3 I love …
4 I'm not a big fan of …
5 I'm really into …
6 I'm not into …

READING

1. Read Matt's profile. How would you describe him?
2. Matt wants to set up an after-school film club in his school. What questions do you think he has?
3. Read Matt's post and check your ideas in exercise 2.

Hello, I'm Matt. I'm 13 years old and I'm from Manchester. I spend a lot of my free time watching films and reading about cinema. I suppose my dream is to work in the film industry, possibly in Hollywood.

moviefanbase.com

Matt, Manchester asks…

Hi! I've read on the internet that a lot of schools have film clubs. What exactly do you do in a film club? Are they easy to set up? Do you need a special room where you can watch films, or can you use a classroom? I'd like to start one at my school, and I'm hopeful plenty of people will be interested. Has anyone got any ideas or tips that they can give me?

Hello Matt! I belong to a film club at my school. Before you start your club, I'd advise you to find a teacher or a parent who can help you. There's a lot to do, and it's good to have an adult that you can ask sometimes. You also need to think about the practical details like when and where you'll show your films. I hope this helps. **Liz, Manchester**

Hey! Great advice, Liz! You don't need a special room. I suggest you find a big classroom with furniture which you can move easily. As for help, I think it needs to be a teacher who's interested in films and is willing to stay after school. A film club has to be after school really, because there isn't time to watch a whole film at lunchtime. **Steve, Nottingham**

Hi, Matt! A film club should be more than just watching films, or your members will lose interest. At our film club, we hold our own Oscars ceremony and give prizes to the best film, actor, director, etc. We also go to the cinema twice a year, and last year someone came and gave us a talk about making films. **Jenny, London**

Hi, guys! Interesting posts! I have a couple of suggestions which hopefully you can use. There are lots of organisations which can offer help with setting up your club. Have a look online and I'm sure you'll find websites where there's some useful advice. Apart from that, have you thought about selling snacks and refreshments? It'll create a nice relaxed atmosphere and you'll make money for the school. **Phil, Bristol**

4. Read the comments. Do they answer all of Matt's questions?

5. Read the comments again. Who advised Matt …
   1. to look for help on the internet?
   2. to think about offering a variety of different activities?
   3. to offer food and drink?
   4. to get support from an adult with a connection to the school?
   5. not to hold the club at midday?
   6. to consider the time and place of the club carefully?
   7. that he might want to move chairs and tables for the club?
   8. that people may leave the club if they get bored?

6. Read the comments again. Complete the sentences with highlighted words from the text.
   1. Our cinema sells soft drinks and other ....
   2. At the end of the year, our school gives out prizes at a ....
   3. Our teacher wants to .... a book club where we can talk about books.
   4. The .... told the actors to do the scene again.
   5. Do you .... any clubs at your school?

Talking points
" Is it better to watch films at home or in the cinema? Why?
Are school clubs a good idea? Why? / Why not? "

EP Word profile *hope*

I **hope** this helps.

I'm **hopeful** plenty of people will be interested.

I have a couple of suggestions which **hopefully** will help.

page 126

Watch it, read it 81

GRAMMAR Relative clauses

1 Read the examples. Then complete the rules with the words in the box.
1. *Find a big classroom with furniture **which** you can move easily.*
2. *Has anyone got any ideas or tips **that** they can give me?*
3. *Find a teacher or parent **who** can help you.*
4. *It's good to have an adult **that** you can ask.*
5. *Do you need a special room **where** you can watch films?*

> that   ~~that~~   where   which   who

> We use relative clauses to explain who, what or where we are talking about.
> We use:
> a ..that.. and .... to talk about things.
> b .... and .... to talk about people.
> c .... to talk about places.

→ Grammar reference page 151

2 Read the text and choose the correct words.

Frankenstein is one of the most famous science fiction horror stories ever. There are a lot of films of the story, but the original *Frankenstein* wasn't a film. It was actually a novel ¹*that / who* was published in 1818. Nobody knew the name of the person ²*who / which* wrote it for many years. In those days, people were shocked by a story ³*that / where* described such a terrible monster. Years later, readers discovered that the author was Mary Shelley, a woman ⁴*who / which* was married to the famous English poet, Percy Shelley.

Many people think Frankenstein is a monster, but this is wrong too. In fact, the story's main character is a crazy scientist ⁵*which / who* is called Dr Frankenstein. He's got a laboratory ⁶*where / that* he is trying to create a beautiful, new kind of creature. Eventually, he makes a monster ⁷*that / where* is huge – and ugly. Frankenstein's monster has got yellow and green skin, and a face ⁸*where / which* is very frightening.

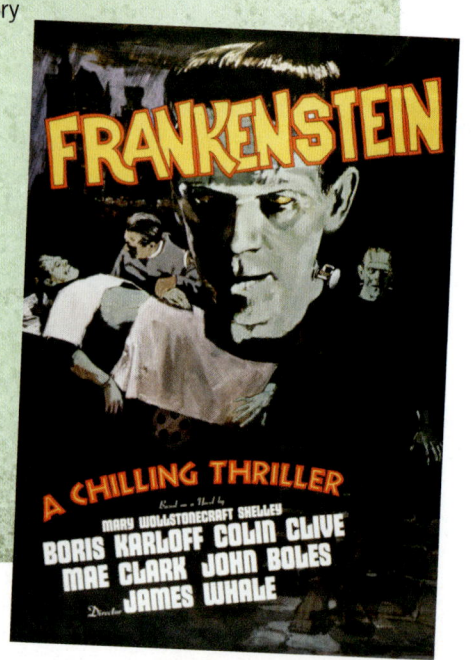

3 Connect the sentences with relative pronouns.
0. Johanna Spyri was a Swiss author. She wrote the famous book *Heidi* in 1880.
   Johanna Spyri was a Swiss author who wrote the famous book Heidi in 1880.
1. Jane Lynch is a funny actor. She is in *Glee*.
2. This is a great book. Philip Pullman wrote it.
3. There's a new bookshop. You can buy English books there.
4. Angelina Jolie is a Hollywood star. She has appeared in lots of great films.
5. Anthony Horowitz is an English novelist. He wrote the *Alex Rider* series.
6. This is a brilliant film. I watched it last week.

> **Corpus challenge**
> Find and correct the mistake in the student's sentence.
> *There are a lot of visitors visit the waterfall.*

4 Student A, turn to page 120. Student B, turn to page 121.

VOCABULARY Easily confused words

1 Check the meaning of the words. Then choose the correct words.
1. *They're / Their* brother is a famous actor.
2. I *passed / past* the remote control to my sister.
3. What did the teacher *advice / advise* you?
4. Did the teacher *accept / except* your excuse?
5. I like wearing *loose / lose* clothing.
6. The *whether / weather* is terrible today.

2 Check the meaning of the words in brackets. Then complete the sentences.
1. My cousin said we could .... this game. (lend / borrow)
2. I'm sorry, I didn't .... that you hate historical dramas! (notice / realise)
3. I never buy new books. I always go to the .... (library / bookshop)
4. I was telling the truth, but my dad didn't believe my .... (history / story)
5. Did you .... to bring my jacket? (remember / remind)
6. My brother's .... He never does anything wrong. (sensible / sensitive)

Unit 14

LISTENING

1 Look at the photo. Answer the questions.

1 What kind of film are the people watching? How do you know?
2 How often do you go to the cinema? Who do you usually go with?
3 What good films have you seen at the cinema recently?

2 ▶2.10 Match the film titles with the types of film. Listen again and check.

1 *Long Live the King*   a comedy
2 *Moscow*   b historical drama
3 *After Dark*   c action film
4 *Silly Money*   d horror film

3 ▶2.10 Listen again. Are the sentences correct or incorrect? Correct the incorrect sentences.

1 Jess likes historical dramas.
2 Ali went to the cinema last week.
3 Jess has seen *Moscow*.
4 Ali and Jess like comedies.
5 Ali and Jess agree to go to the cinema at 10.15.

SPEAKING   Reaching agreement

1 You are planning a movie night with some friends. Look at the list of films. Which one would you like to watch? Why?

This week's best new films on DVD!

- **Planet Alpha**   A film for all science fiction fans. Captain Mark Adams and his crew travel to a new planet. What will they find there?
- **Superdog**   The best animated film this year! Funny and clever, with great animations!
- **Watching You**   Don't watch this thriller alone! Very exciting, and very scary!
- **Jerry's Vacation** Jerry is planning a normal holiday with a friend. But things don't go to plan, with very funny results. A laugh a minute!

2 ▶2.11 Listen to two friends discussing which film to watch. Which one do they choose?

3 ▶2.11 Read the *Prepare* box. Then listen again. Which phrases do you hear?

Prepare to speak — Reaching agreement

Giving reasons	Reaching agreement
because …	Let's decide.
It's too …	Yes, that's a good choice.
It looks/sounds …	I think we're both happy with that.

4 In pairs, make a list of four films you would like to watch. Discuss the films, and reach agreement on which one to watch. Use phrases from the *Prepare* box.

Culture
World cinema

1 In pairs, do the quiz.

FILM QUIZ

1 The Lumière brothers made the first ever film. What was the year?
 a 1895 b 1905 c 1959

2 The world's first full-length movie was *The Story of the Kelly Gang*. Where was it made?
 a Australia b the UK c the USA

3 Where was the world's first cinema?
 a Tokyo, Japan b Los Angeles, USA c Pisa, Italy

4 The earliest films were silent. When was the first film with speaking and music?
 a 1927 b 1957 c 1987

5 The longest film ever made is *Cinématon*. How long is it?
 a 56 hours b 106 hours c 156 hours

6 Which famous character has appeared in the most films?
 a James Bond b Mickey Mouse c Sherlock Holmes

7 What is the name of the famous film-making area in India?
 a Nollywood b Bollywood c Hollywood

8 Number the countries in order of how many films they make every year. Write *1* for the smallest number and *5* for the largest number of films.
 ☐ China ☐ India ☐ Nigeria ☐ Spain ☐ the USA

9 Where do people go to the cinema the most frequently?
 a Iceland b the USA c Poland

10 Number the countries in order of the number of cinema screens they've got. Write *1* for the smallest number and *4* for the largest number of screens.
 ☐ Brazil ☐ India ☐ China ☐ the USA

Charlie Chaplin starred in nearly 90 silent comedy films.

2 ▶ 2.12 Listen and check your answers.

3 ▶ 2.13 Read the sentences and guess the missing numbers and dates. Then listen and check.

| 31 | 215 | 550 | 850 | 1902 |
| 1950s | 2,300 | 40,000 | | |

1 The world's first cinema opened in ....
2 There weren't many colour films before ....
3 It took .... years to make *Cinématon*.
4 The character Sherlock Holmes has appeared in more than .... movies.
5 Over .... films are made every year in Nigeria. Only .... films are made in the USA.
6 There are at least .... cinema screens in the USA and .... in Brazil.

4 ▶ 2.14 Order the events. Write *1* for the earliest event and *5* for the most recent. Listen and check.
 a films were colour and with sound
 b films were black and white, and silent 1
 c cinemas became popular
 d films were made with computers
 e films were black and white but with sound

5 Look at the country information on page 85. Have you seen films from any of these countries?

6 Read the country information and answer the questions.
 1 Which is one of the best films of the last 100 years?
 2 What kind of films do they make in the UK?
 3 Which festival do film-makers go to every year?
 4 Where is Andrzej Jakimowski from?
 5 Which two movies are comedies?
 6 Which country specialises in cartoons?

FRANCE	Films per year: 250

The film industry was born in France about 120 years ago. Hundreds of new films are shown at the annual film festival in Cannes.

You must see: *Jean de Florette* and *Manon des Sources* (both 1986), classics of the French cinema. The well-known French actor Gérard Depardieu stars as a young man in *Jean de Florette*.

ITALY	Films per year: 150

Italian films have been popular internationally since the 1960s, thanks to famous directors such as Federico Fellini.

You must see: *The Best of Youth* (*La Meglio Gioventù*, 2003), about the adventures of two brothers from Rome.

JAPAN	Films per year: 400–450

The monster Godzilla has appeared in dozens of Japanese films and many have been dubbed into English.
Film fans say *Seven Samurai* (1954) by Akira Kurosawa is one of the most important films of the twentieth century.

You must see: the 'anime' film *Paprika* (2007), a colourful film about dreams. Over 60% of Japanese films are 'anime' cartoons.

MEXICO	Films per year: 70

You must see: *Cantinflas* (2014), a lovely movie set in the 1940s–50s. It tells the story of the famous Mexican comedy actor, Mario Moreno.

POLAND	Films per year: 40

You must see: *Tricks* (*Sztuczki,* 2009). This beautiful film really captures the atmosphere of a young boy's life in the Polish countryside one summer. *Squint Your Eyes* (*Zmruz Oczy,* 2003) by the same director, Andrzej Jakimowski, is also well worth watching.

SPAIN	Films per year: 150–200

You must see: *Spanish Affair* (*Ocho Apellidos Vascos,* 2014), a popular comedy with great acting. It was filmed in the Basque country, in the north-east of Spain.

THE UK	Films per year: 100

The British make lots of romantic comedies and historical dramas.

You must see: The *Sherlock Holmes* murder mystery/action films directed by Guy Ritchie and set in nineteenth century London.

THE USA	Films per year: 550

Most actors would love to win an award at the annual Oscars ceremony in Los Angeles.

You must see: *Avatar* (2009) directed by James Cameron. This beautiful science fiction adventure was the first 3-D film made completely with CGI (computer-generated images).

TURKEY	Films per year: 35

You must see: *The Magician* (*Hokkabaz,* 2006), a funny father-and-son comedy directed by Cem Yilmaz.

7 Discuss the questions.
1. What are the biggest differences between the films of 75 years ago and modern films?
2. Do you watch films in the original language, or do you prefer films 'dubbed' (translated) into your language? Why?
3. Have you ever watched films with Sherlock Holmes or James Bond? Who are your favourite film characters? Why?

Project

In pairs, go online to research one of your favourite films. Plan a presentation about it. Then give your presentation to the class.
- What kind of film is it (horror film, thriller, etc.)?
- Who directed the film? Where and when did they make it?
- What happens in the story?
- Which actors are in it and what roles do they play?
- Has it won any awards, for example an Oscar?
- Why do you like it?
- If possible, find photos and music from the film.

15 Digital life

VOCABULARY Computing phrases

Your profile
What do you use your phone or tablet for? Make a list.

1 ▶ 2.15 Match the beginnings and ends of the quiz questions. Then listen and check.

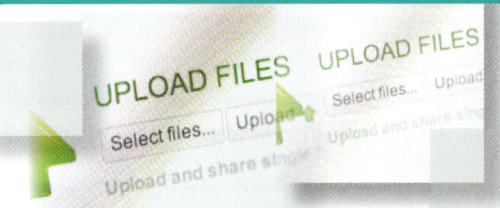

1 Have you ever **deleted** an
2 Have you ever got
3 Do you think of a
4 Do you often **share**
5 Have you ever **done**
6 Do you **upload**
7 How many new **apps** have you
8 Do you ever **download**

a photos or videos to the internet to share with friends?
b different **password** for each website you use?
c important **file** by mistake?
d **podcasts**?
e **a search for** your own name online?
f a **virus** on your computer?
g **installed** on your phone this week?
h **links** to interesting websites with friends?

2 ▶ 2.16 Listen to Matt's answers to the quiz. Ali asks follow-up questions to get more details. Complete the questions.

1 What did ...you...do.. ?
2 How did you .... ?
3 How do you .... ?
4 What kinds of things .... ?
5 What did .... ?
6 Which apps do you use .... ?
7 How many do you .... ?
8 Which ones do you .... the most?

3 ▶ 2.16 Complete the sentences about Matt with words from exercise 1. Then listen again and check.

1 Matt ...deleted... a school project, but his dad helped him to get it back.
2 He got a .... when he installed a game.
3 He uses a different .... for each website.
4 He often .... to funny videos or photos.
5 He has .... his name and found it in some football reports.
6 He .... a lot of .... and mainly uses Instagram.
7 He has .... about 10 .... this week and has over 200 altogether.
8 He doesn't often .... and listen to ....

4 In pairs, answer the quiz questions in exercise 1. If you can, use the follow-up questions in exercise 2 to find out more information.

5 Tell the class something interesting you found out about your partner.

Sara got a virus on her dad's computer and they had to buy a new one!

86 Unit 15

READING

1 Emre wants an app to help him with learning English. Read about Emre and notice the key underlined information a–c.

1 Emre often <u>ᵃ finds language apps easy and wants some difficult practice</u>. He <u>ᵇ would like to improve his reading and listening skills</u> and he <u>ᶜ intends to use it on his short journey to and from school</u>.

2 Read the descriptions of the first three apps (A–C). Find apps that:
   a mention difficult activities.
   b improve reading and listening skills.
   c have activities suitable for use on short journeys.

Which app is best for Emre?

3 Read about three more teenagers who want apps to help them with learning English. Underline three key things that each person wants.

2 Anna enjoys all subjects at school but finds she needs more help in English. She is bored of doing traditional vocabulary and grammar exercises and is looking for something else, that is quick to complete.

3 Luis likes watching movies and TV comedy shows in English, but would like to understand them better. He expects apps to look good and is prepared to spend a lot on the right one.

4 Evie likes fun language apps that allow you to compete. In particular, she's interested in developing her vocabulary skills. She doesn't mind paying for something if it's worth the price.

4 Read the descriptions of the apps (A–F). Decide which app would be the most suitable for each teenager in exercise 3.

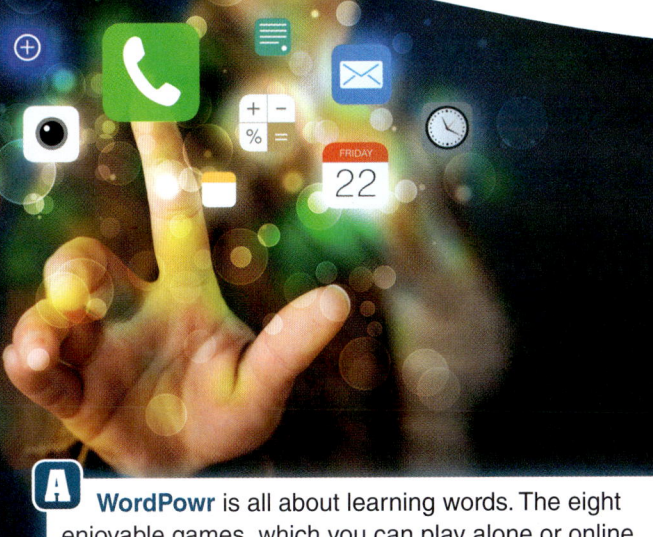

A **WordPowr** is all about learning words. The eight enjoyable games, which you can play alone or online against other users, provide good value for money. And games last just a few minutes, so it's perfect for a bus ride. Turn down the annoying music though!

B **EnglishScene** is expensive, but the app is often given five stars in reviews. The design is attractive, with professional quality videos and excellent activities to go with them. It takes time to use this app properly and it is most suitable for higher-level learners.

C **Newscast** is a free app that helps you understand stories from online newspapers and podcasts. You can set time limits for the activities and the questions are often quite challenging. The app includes a simple dictionary to help with word problems.

D Practise the 3000 most frequent words with **PassWords3000**. This app is for low-level students and includes a very common range of activity types. It's free, so you sometimes have to watch a video advertisement to continue using it. New questions are added every month.

E The design of **VidEnglish** is bright and attractive. However, the app is mostly a series of links to short, but sometimes quite advanced, video clips from documentaries. The clips aren't downloaded with the app, so you need a fast internet connection to watch them.

F **Themez** is a fresh and unusual app that teaches English through topics like science and history. It includes several games that you can play by yourself or with other Themez users. There is a lot of support for learners who find it harder to make progress.

Talking points

❝ How can apps help you to learn languages?
How can computers be useful in the classroom? ❞

EP Word profile *turn*

Take **turns** to do the quiz.

Turn down the annoying music!

page 127

Digital life **87**

GRAMMAR Present simple passive

1 Read the examples. Then complete the rules with the words in the box.

1 The app **is** often **given** five stars (**by** reviewers) in reviews.
2 New questions **are added** every month.
3 The clips **aren't downloaded** with the app.

> past participle   by   be

> a We use the passive when the person or thing that causes the action is unknown or unimportant.
> b We form the present simple passive with the correct form of .. and the .... of the verb.
> c When we include *who* or *what* did the action, we use ....

→ Grammar reference page 152

2 Complete the text with the present simple passive forms in the box.

> is thought   are shared   is used
> are given   is owned   is often added

Instagram is an online photo and video sharing app and ¹ .... by Facebook. It cost the social networking site $1 billion in 2012, but now the app ² .... to be worth over $20 billion.
The app is extremely popular and ³ .... by over 150 million people regularly. Over 60 million photos ⁴ .... every day and a word or phrase ⁵ .... to the photo, called a 'tag'. People often vote for other photos they like by clicking 'Like'. Over 10,000 'Likes' ⁶ .... to photos every day on Instagram!

3 Complete the text about how computer viruses work. Use the present simple passive form of the verbs.

Computer viruses ¹ .... (not create) by computers. They ² .... (write) by computer programmers. The virus ³ .... (download) by people, often in emails. Sometimes it ⁴ .... (hid) in software. Viruses ⁵ .... (delete) by special software on some computers. But if a virus ⁶ .... (not find), sometimes copies of it ⁷ .... (send) to other people by email.

4 Answer the questions with your own ideas. Turn to page 120 to check.
1 Which countries are most computers made in?
2 Which type of program is downloaded from the internet the most often?
3 Which password is used by people most often online?
4 Which female singer is searched for online the most often?
5 Which male actor is searched for online the most often?

Corpus challenge

Find and correct the mistake in the student's sentence.
The game called Empire Earth.

VOCABULARY Phrasal verbs: technology

1 Complete the phrasal verbs.

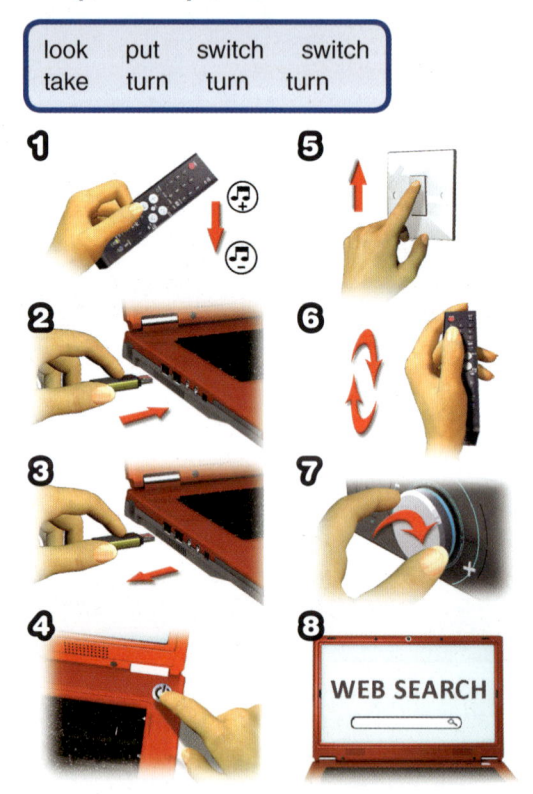

> look   put   switch   switch
> take   turn   turn   turn

1 .... down   5 turn off / .... off
2 .... in   6 switch over / .... over
3 .... out   7 .... up
4 turn on / .... on   8 .... up

2 Complete the sentences with the phrasal verbs in exercise 1.
1 Can you .... the train times on your phone?
2 .... that music! It's too loud!
3 Please .... your mobiles before the film begins.
4 This is an awful programme. Let's .... and watch something else.
5 .... the old memory card from your camera and .... a new one.

Unit 15

WRITING An informal letter or email (3)

1 Read part of an email that Paul receives from his friend Ivan. What information does Ivan want from Paul?

> I'm going on holiday next week and we'll be in the car for about six hours. I need some new games for my phone, so I don't get bored. What's your favourite at the moment? Can you recommend any others?

2 Read Paul's reply. Does he answer all Ivan's questions?

> From: Paul
> To: Ivan
>
> Hi Ivan,
> I've got loads of cool games on my phone. In my opinion, the simplest games are the best. My favourite is Doodlejump. The idea is to make a little animal jump as high as you can. It has to land on the green steps, or it falls down and the game's over. Very annoying, but I can't stop playing it! You should definitely try it! Another one I would recommend is Whale Trail. I would say it's quite a relaxing game. You keep the whale flying through the air, and all you have to do is avoid the angry clouds!
> For me, these two games are great for long journeys. Have a great time on holiday!
> See you soon,
> Paul

3 What games does Paul suggest? What phrases does he use to recommend them?

4 Read the *Prepare* box. Find three phrases that Paul uses to give his opinion.

Prepare to write – An informal letter or email (3)

In an informal letter or email:
- use phrases to give your opinion:
  I really think …,
  I don't think …,
  For me, …,
  In my opinion, …,
  If you ask me, …,
  I would say …
- use phrases to make suggestions: *You should …,*
  I would recommend …
- remember to answer all the questions.
- remember to use an informal phrase to begin and end the email.

5 Complete the sentences with your opinions about game apps. Compare your opinions with a partner. Do you agree with your partner's opinions?
  1 In my opinion, …
  2 I really think …
  3 For me, …

6 What informal phrases does Paul use to begin and end his email?

7 Read Ivan's email again. Plan your reply and make some notes. Here are some ideas to help you.
- How many games do you have on your phone?
- How often do you play?
- What's your favourite game? Why do you like it?
- What do you have to do in the game?
- What games would you recommend for a long journey? Why?

8 Write your email to Ivan.
- Use the tips in the *Prepare box*.
- Write about 100 words.
- Don't forget to check your spelling and grammar.

Digital life

16 Wish me luck!

VOCABULARY Verb + noun

Your profile
What do you understand by 'luck'?
What things do you think are lucky or unlucky?
Do you know anyone who is lucky?

1 ▶ 2.17 Use words from each box to make phrases that match the photos. Then listen and check.

| blow out   give   pour   spill   break | a bunch of flowers   candles   coffee   fingers   a grey hair |
| cross   touch   step   pull out | a mirror   on gaps in the pavement   salt   wood |

2 Complete the sentences with verbs and nouns from exercise 1.

Good or bad luck?

a It's *good / bad* luck to ..pull out a grey hair... If you do, ten more grey ones will grow in its place.
b It's *lucky / unlucky* to .... on .... in the pavement.
c If you .... all the .... on a cake, you can wish for something and it *will / won't* come true.
d In some countries, they say touching a piece of .... brings *good / bad* luck.
e After you .... on the table, you *should / mustn't* throw some over your left shoulder.
f It's *good / bad* luck to .... your fingers in many countries.
g If you .... a .... , you'll have seven years of *good / bad* luck.
h It's *lucky / unlucky* to put the sugar in the cup before you .... your .... If you do this, you'll become rich!
i In China, chrysanthemum flowers bring *good / bad* luck. However, in some parts of Europe, it's *lucky / unlucky* to .... someone a .... of chrysanthemums.

3 ▶ 2.18 Read the sentences in exercise 2 again and choose the correct words. Then listen and check.

4 Discuss the questions.
   1 Which of the ideas in exercise 2 do people have in your country?
   2 Do you believe any of the ideas? Why? / Why not?

READING

Just luck?

Not everyone agrees on what is lucky or unlucky. 'If a black cat walks in front of you, it'll bring good luck.' That's true in the UK, but Americans think the opposite. For Russians, a grey cat is lucky and for the Chinese, it's a red bat. They can't all be right! Why do some people believe certain things are lucky or unlucky? We don't know for sure, but we can probably explain *some* ideas about luck.

In the past, people thought that being healthy or happy was all because of luck. British people followed the old idea that 'An apple a day keeps the doctor away.' Now we know apples aren't lucky, they're just healthy. So you're more likely to be healthy if you eat lots of apples.

People also used ideas about luck to avoid danger. The traditional idea that 'If you walk under a ladder, you'll have bad luck' is easy to explain for this reason. It isn't a good idea just in case something falls on your head!

People who did dangerous jobs also believed in the 'good luck' that kept them safe. Sailors always said, 'If you see a dolphin, your ship won't sink.' They believed these friendly animals brought good luck. Now we know that dolphins like staying near the coast. If you're lost and you see dolphins, luckily you're probably close to the coast – and you're also probably safe.

So, a lot of ideas about luck are not as silly as they seem, and sometimes science can explain why a traditional idea works. For example, it seems that the old phrase, 'You'll have bad luck if you get out of bed on the wrong side' may have some truth in it. Scientists now know that when we always do things in the same way, our mind works better. Maybe as science understands more about us and our world, we'll find that most traditional ideas about luck are also based on facts.

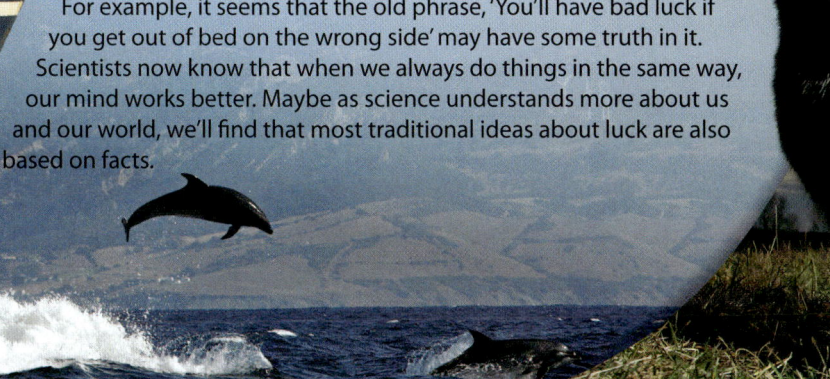

1 Read the article quickly. Choose the best answer.

The text is about …
a how to be lucky.
b people who avoid bad luck.
c how science can sometimes explain luck.

2 Choose the correct answers, according to the text.

1 .... are considered unlucky in the USA.
   A Black cats   C Grey cats
   B Red bats   D Red cats
2 In the past, British people thought that apples were …
   A unlucky.   C better than doctors.
   B lucky.   D bad for you.
3 It is unlucky to walk under a ladder because …
   A you could fall over.   C things might fall on you.
   B the ladder could fall. D you might hurt someone.
4 Dolphins …
   A often swim close to boats.   C aren't safe.
   B are friendly.   D are silly.
5 Scientists agree it is a good idea to .... things each day.
   A avoid difficult   C work hard at
   B try new   D do the same

EP Word profile *luck*

Not everyone agrees on what is **lucky** or **unlucky**.

They believed dolphins brought good **luck**.

Luckily, you're probably close to the coast.

page 127

Talking points

Why do you think some people believe in good and bad luck?

Do you think that science will be able to explain everything in the future? Why? / Why not?

Video extra   Wish me luck!

GRAMMAR Zero and first conditional

1 Read the examples. Then choose the correct words to complete the rules.

1 *If you **see** dolphins, you **are** probably close to the coast.*
2 *You **are** more likely to be healthy if you **eat** lots of apples.*

> **Zero conditional**
> a We use the zero conditional to talk about actions or situations that are always *true / false*.
> b We use the *present simple / past simple* in both clauses.
> c The *If* clause can come first or second in the sentence. The meaning is the same.

→ Grammar reference page 153

2 Complete the zero conditional sentences.

1 If something bad .... (happen), some people .... (think) it's because of bad luck.
2 My grandma .... (feel) happy if she .... (see) a black cat.
3 If you .... (believe) in science, you .... (not trust) ideas about good and bad luck.
4 We .... (understand) traditional ideas better if we .... (know) they have a scientific explanation.
5 .... (it / be) unlucky if you .... (step) on gaps in the pavement?

3 Complete the sentences with your own ideas. Then compare your sentences in pairs.

0 I feel tired all day *if I get up too early.*
1 If I get home late, my parents …
2 I don't watch TV …
3 If I don't have any homework, …
4 When I haven't got music to listen to, …
5 If we don't pass a test at school, …

4 Read the examples. Then choose the correct words to complete the rules.

1 *If a black cat **walks** in front of you, it'**ll bring** good luck.*
2 *You'**ll have** bad luck if you **get** out of bed on the wrong side.*

> **First conditional**
> a We use the first conditional to talk about possible or probable future events.
> b We use *if + present simple / past simple* and *will + infinitive / -ing form*.
> c The *if* clause can come first or second in the sentence. The meaning is the same.

→ Grammar reference page 153

5 Choose the correct words.

1 If you help us, we *are / 'll* pay you.
2 What *will / do* you do if you get lost?
3 If Chelsea *don't / won't* win, I won't mind.
4 Where will you go if it *will rain / rains* later?
5 My mum won't mind if we *'re / will be* late.
6 If you join my team, you *don't / won't* regret it.

6 Complete the first conditional sentences.

0 If you ..see.. (see) one magpie, you ..'ll have.. (have) bad luck all day.
1 It .... (bring) good luck if you .... (see) more than one magpie.
2 If you .... (open) an umbrella inside the house, it .... (bring) bad luck.
3 If you .... (find) a spider in your house, someone .... (visit) you soon.
4 If you .... (say) goodbye to a friend on a bridge, you .... (never see) each other again.
5 You .... (not get) unwelcome visitors if you .... (put) a brush behind the front door.
6 If fishermen .... (not put back) the first fish they catch each morning, they .... (not catch) many fish that day.

> **Corpus challenge**
>
> Find and correct the mistake in the student's sentence.
> *If you bring the crisps, I bring the juice and fruit.*

VOCABULARY *if* and *unless*

1 Read the examples. Notice that *unless* means the same as *if not*.

1 *You won't fail the test **if** you study harder.*
2 *You'll fail the test **if** you **don't** study harder.*
3 *You'll fail the text **unless** you study harder.*

2 Complete the sentences with *if* or *unless*.

1 The computer won't work .... you enter the password.
   .... you enter the password, the computer will work.
2 It's raining. We won't play football .... the weather gets better.
   We'll play football .... the weather gets better.
3 I hate soap operas. I'll watch TV with you .... you turn to another channel.
   .... you turn to another channel, I won't watch TV with you.
4 It's unlucky to spill salt, but .... you throw some over your left shoulder, you won't have bad luck.
   You'll have bad luck .... you throw some of the salt over your left shoulder.

Unit 16

LISTENING

1 ▶ 2.19 Listen to the interview and look at the photos. Which two photos aren't mentioned?

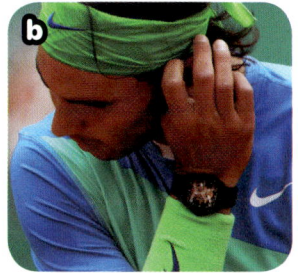

a
b
c
d

2 ▶ 2.19 Read the sentences and choose the correct answers. Then listen again and check.

1 What do people think is lucky?
   A crossing fingers
   B white cats
   C football shirts
2 When do we start to believe that objects have got special qualities?
   A as adults
   B as teenagers
   C as young children
3 Why don't people want to touch the murderer's pen?
   A it might be dirty
   B they don't need it
   C it has negative qualities
4 When does Cristiano Ronaldo change his hairstyle?
   A before a match
   B during a match
   C after a match
5 What does Rafael Nadal wear during a match?
   A a special T-shirt
   B special socks
   C a special watch
6 Who has got the funniest habit, according to Dr Davies?
   A Serena Williams
   B Rafael Nadal
   C Laurent Blanc

SPEAKING Describing a picture (2)

1 Look at the photo. Where do you think it is? What do you think is happening?

2 ▶ 2.20 Listen to someone describing the photo. Compare your ideas.

3 ▶ 2.20 Read the *Prepare* box. Then listen again. Which phrases do you hear?

Prepare to speak — Describing a picture (2)

When you aren't sure	When you don't know the word
It looks like …	I don't know what it's called.
It could be …	
It might be …	
They seem very …	
I'm not really sure.	
I can't make it out very well.	

4 Look at another photo. Take turns to describe it. Use phrases from the *Prepare* box.

5 The photographs in this section show two celebrations. Work in pairs. Choose a celebration in your country. Discuss the questions.

1 When and where does it take place?
2 Who comes to the celebration?
3 What do people do to celebrate?

Wish me luck!

Maths
Units

1 Read the news article. What do you think of the scientists' plan? Is there a better way to find the tallest building?

SCIENTISTS TO FIND WORLD'S TALLEST BUILDING

Scientists are planning to find the world's tallest building. They are going to move the world's five tallest-looking buildings to one place. Engineers will take down each building carefully, take them to Texas in the USA, and then rebuild them. Then they can compare them, next to each other, and see which is the highest.

2 Read and complete text A on page 95.

3 What units do we usually use to talk about 1–3?

> kilograms   hours   litres   tons   grams
> centilitres   minutes   millilitres   seconds

1 volume
2 weight
3 time

4 Which unit(s) do you usually use to describe these things?
1 a person's height
2 a bottle of water
3 the distance between two cities
4 the weight of fruit
5 the time of a long-distance flight

5 ▶ 2.21 Listen to the conversations. What are the people describing with the units of length? Number the pictures in the correct order 1–4.

6 ▶ 2.21 Listen again and complete the sentences.
1 Ben's height is .... feet .... inches.
2 The size of the TV that the customer wants is .... inches.
3 The player scored a goal from .... yards.
4 Sally's house is .... miles from Ellen's house.

7 Use the information in text A and a calculator to find the answers in exercise 6 in …
1 metres.
2 centimetres.
3 metres.
4 kilometres.

8 Read text B on page 95. Which unit …
1 could we use to describe a Ferrari?
2 do you think a famous website is named after?
3 is used to say how pure something is?
4 could we use to describe a USB drive?
5 is named after a person?
6 do people worry about when they are trying to lose weight?
7 do you think is very unusual?

9 Find real examples of these measurements.
- some jewellery (carats)
- the amount of storage on your phone or tablet (gigabytes)
- TV size (centimetres, inches)
- your favourite meal (calories)
- your height (feet/inches, metres/centimetres)
- the distance from your school to your house (kilometres, miles)
- the power of a car (horsepower)

My mum's got a 24-carat gold ring.

A

Ten thousand years ago, people had simple lives. They didn't need to measure things. They just guessed the length of things or how long it took to walk to places. However, over time, we developed **units**. These units helped us measure distances, time and many more things.

Almost all countries now use kilometres (km), metres (m), centimetres (cm) and millimetres (mm) to measure length and distances.

1km = ... m = ... cm = ... mm

In the UK, Australia and the USA, people also use other units to measure length and distances.

1 **inch** = 2.54cm   1 **yard** = 0.91m
1 **foot** = 30.5cm   1 **mile** = 1.61km

We say numbers like 2.54 as two point five four.

How old are you?

B

All information in a computer is binary (1s and 0s).
Each 1 or 0 is called a **bit**.
8 bits is called a **byte**.
1 **megabyte** (1MB) = about a million *bytes*
1 **gigabyte** (1GB) = about a thousand *megabytes*.

What parts of a computer are described in *megabytes* or *gigabytes*?

IT'S GOT 128 GIGABYTES!
REALLY?

A **googol** is not really a unit but it's used to describe very big numbers. A googol = 1 with a hundred zeros after it.

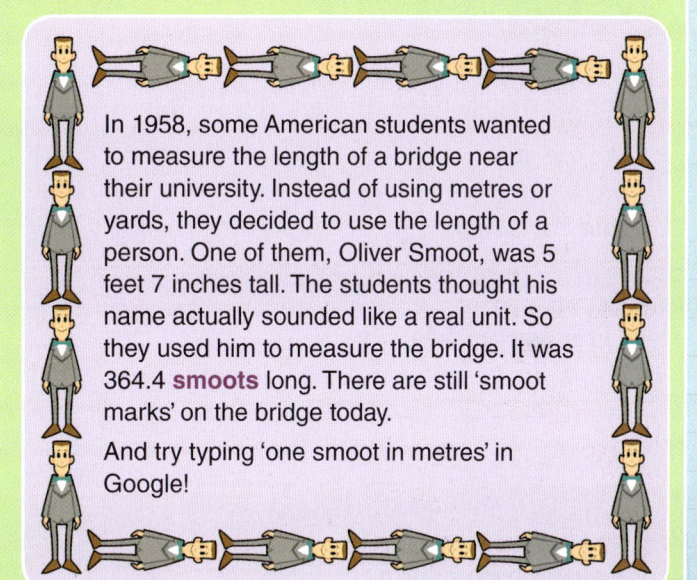

The **calorie** is used to describe how much energy there is in food or drink. If a food has got a lot of calories, it also makes you fat.

In 1958, some American students wanted to measure the length of a bridge near their university. Instead of using metres or yards, they decided to use the length of a person. One of them, Oliver Smoot, was 5 feet 7 inches tall. The students thought his name actually sounded like a real unit. So they used him to measure the bridge. It was 364.4 **smoots** long. There are still 'smoot marks' on the bridge today.

And try typing 'one smoot in metres' in Google!

When gold is described as 24-**carat**, it is (almost) 100% gold. And 18-carat gold has 75% gold and 25% other metals. How many carats are there in gold that has 50% gold and 50% other metals?

Key words
measure discover the exact size or amount of something

Project
Imagine you are selling something, at school or online. Write an advertisement describing the object. Use these ideas or your own.

a bicycle   your TV/computer   a car
some jewellery   some cakes

When people used horses to pull transport, we measured the pulling power of something in the number of horses or **horsepower**. And even today we use the same word to describe the power of a car. If you want a fast car, look for a high horsepower (and low weight)!

COWPOWER!

- Write a description of the object, using appropriate units.
- Give each object a price.
- Find pictures from the internet or magazines for your advertisement.

Review 4
Units 13-16

VOCABULARY

1 Find the words (→ ↘ ↗ ↓) and complete the lists.

d	o	c	u	m	e	n	t	a	r	y	s
m	i	d	e	r	l	f	i	l	e	p	e
b	i	s	e	j	a	b	l	e	s	r	m
o	v	r	a	i	z	e	r	l	l	o	b
c	d	e	d	p	y	l	a	d	i	u	a
o	e	n	n	y	p	n	r	n	n	d	r
m	l	o	h	u	r	o	s	t	k	t	r
e	e	s	t	e	w	o	i	s	t	d	a
d	t	r	t	s	t	e	h	n	r	o	s
y	e	a	s	v	i	r	u	s	t	e	s
e	c	a	m	t	o	r	n	c	h	e	e
e	p	c	h	a	t	s	h	o	w	r	d
g	t	h	r	i	l	l	e	r	o	m	e

Adjectives: feelings
p............ d............
l............ e............

Computing phrases
p............ l............
v............ d............

TV, films and literature
d............ c............
c............ t............

2 Complete the sentences with the words in the box.

> confused   deleted   exhausted
> did a search   soap opera   stressed

1 I .... for a cheap ticket online, but there weren't any.
2 This .... is on TV five times a week.
3 I've just run 15km. I'm .... !
4 She's upset because she .... her homework by mistake.
5 I'm .... I don't understand this homework.
6 I'm feeling very .... this evening. I need to sit down and relax.

3 Match the verbs and nouns to make phrases about luck.

1 touch   a salt
2 break   b wood
3 cross   c on gaps in the pavement
4 spill   d all the candles
5 blow out   e your fingers
6 step   f a mirror

GRAMMAR

4 Complete the sentences. Use the correct form of the verbs.

1 .... you .... this book yet? (read)
2 When I switch off the lights, it .... always very dark in here. (be)
3 This table .... of wood. (not make)
4 He never .... much homework when he's in his room. (do)
5 Look! The teacher .... just .... (arrive)
6 Breakfast .... every day between 7 and 10 am (serve)
7 Don't worry. I'll remind her if she .... (forget)
8 I'm not hungry. I .... already .... lunch. (have)
9 If you click 'yes', the film usually .... quite quickly. (download)
10 Unless he arrives soon, we .... leave without him. (have to)

5 Complete the second sentence so that it means the same as the first sentence. Use no more than three words.

1 They produce most Indian films in Bollywood.
  Most Indian films .... in Bollywood.
2 If you don't come to the cinema, you'll be really bored tonight.
  .... be bored tonight if you come to the cinema.
3 They don't sell comics in this bookshop.
  Comics .... in this bookshop.
4 I finished watching the documentary a few minutes ago.
  I've .... watching the documentary.
5 She's the new actor. She plays Juliet.
  She's the new .... Juliet.
6 Do you sell DVDs here?
  Are .... here?
7 This is a really funny comedy. You should watch it.
  This is a really funny .... should watch.
8 Unless someone can remember the password, we can't use the computer.
  We .... the computer if someone can remember the password.

96 Review 4

Corpus challenge

6 Tick the two sentences without mistakes. Correct the mistakes in the other sentences.

1. I've just spend some money on lunch.
2. My friend hasn't arrived already.
3. I like the pizza restaurant is near my house.
4. I want to tell you about a computer game that I bought three weeks ago.
5. I haven't seen yet my new shoes!
6. I have just received this letter from you.
7. If you come with us, it be fun.
8. If you have a problem, I would help you.

7 Read the text and choose the correct word for each space.

PRIZES FOR YOUNG ENGINEERS

Any student ^{0} ...A... the ages of 12 and 19 can enter the *Young Engineers for Britain* competition. This annual event challenges students to be ^{1} .... in developing their own idea. Their ^{2} .... is to design a useful item that could be produced and ^{3} ....

Ruth Amos won the prize a few years ago for her invention, the 'StairSteady', ^{4} .... helps old people to go up and down stairs. It is ^{5} .... from a strong metal and is very safe, as well as being ^{6} .... to use. Ruth has now left school and has ^{7} .... sold thousands of StairSteadys all over the country.

More ^{8} .... , Matthew Hunter developed a product to charge a mobile phone that will fit ^{9} .... a bicycle. He won the *Young Engineers' Duke of York Award* and ^{10} .... prize money of £1,000 for his invention.

	A	B	C	D
0	between	from	through	with
1	lonely	confused	embarrassed	creative
2	file	map	project	work
3	paid	sold	cost	earned
4	where	which	what	who
5	put	done	switched	made
6	correct	right	simple	pure
7	already	yet	ever	still
8	nearly	usually	recently	suddenly
9	on	at	by	in
10	passed	received	picked	realised

17 Skills and talents

VOCABULARY Creative lives: nouns

Your profile
Have you ever tried: creating art / playing music / performing on a stage / writing stories or poetry?
When, and what was it like?

1 Look at the photos and discuss what you can see in each one.

2 ▶2.22 Listen to three conversations and check your answers.

3 Add the words to the table. Some words match more than one list. Can you think of any other words for the lists?

~~audience~~ biography director gallery
novel painter painting poet
poetry sculpture studio writer

Actor	audience,
Artist	
Author	

4 Complete the newspaper articles with the correct form of some of the words in exercise 3. Then add the words to the table in exercise 3.

Young Talent
There's an **exhibition** of new ⁰ ...artists... called Young Talent at the university ¹ .... this month. It's mainly ² .... and **drawings**, but there are a few massive outdoor ³ .... situated in the park next door.

Secrets Told
A revealing ⁴ .... of the best-selling ⁵ .... Jonathan Lee is out now. It tells the story of the writer's life, from his childhood experiments with writing ⁶ ...., to how he came up with the ideas for his **series** of murder mystery ⁷ ...., X-Filed. He spoke to a lively ⁸ .... at The King's Arms in Manchester last night.

Hollywood Hopes
There's trouble in Hollywood this week for the *Project Z* movie. The **script** has been rewritten, and the ⁹ .... of the original script is complaining that a lot of her good ideas have now gone. But the ¹⁰ .... have already been in the ¹¹ .... for several days ready to start **filming**. Time is money in showbusiness, so the ¹² ...., Frankie Jones, needs to show that he's in charge and end this argument quickly.

5 Discuss the quiz questions.

What's the difference between …
1. a *studio* and a *gallery*?
2. a *director* and a *writer*?
3. an *artist* and a *painter*?
4. a *novel* and a *biography*?
5. an *author* and a *poet*?
6. a *sculpture* and a *painting*?

Unit 17

READING

WHO ARE THE REAL ARTISTS?

THE SONGWRITERS

When you hear a new song, you probably don't think about who wrote it. And although certain performers like Lady Gaga always write their own songs, hundreds of others perform songs written for them by songwriters. Jessie J is a famous singer who has toured the world several times and sold millions of her own albums. She's also a successful songwriter who has written hits for some of the biggest stars in the pop world. Next time you hear a song you love, why not look it up online and see who actually wrote it?

THE GHOSTWRITERS

Wayne Rooney is a busy professional footballer, yet somehow a publisher convinced him to write an autobiography, *My Story So Far*. How did Rooney manage that? The truth is, he didn't write it on his own. A journalist called Hunter Davies helped Rooney to write it. Davies is a ghostwriter – he writes celebrities' books for them. Celebrities often use ghostwriters, either because they don't have time, or because they aren't natural writers. Ghostwriters' names don't usually appear on book covers, so it looks as if the celebrity is the author, and often they ask writers not to discuss anything with journalists.

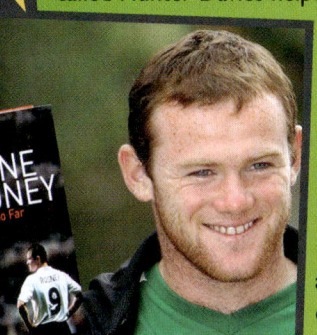

THE STUNT DOUBLES

Daniel Craig has an action-hero reputation thanks to his performances as James Bond. But does the actor appear in all the dangerous scenes himself? Not always. Instead, a stunt double does lots of them. Ben Cooke was competing in a martial arts tournament when a film-maker saw him and advised him to become a stunt double. Ben Cooke looks a bit like Daniel Craig, so he became Craig's double. He's won a lot of prizes, including one for an incredible jump in *Casino Royale*. After the stunt, Daniel Craig gave Ben a watch as a thank-you present.

THE SECRET PAINTERS

Damien Hirst produces hundreds of paintings every year. How does one man produce so many? Like da Vinci and Michelangelo before him, he employs assistants in a studio. He usually tells them to do the easy jobs, but they often do whole paintings too. Rachel Howard was 22 when she started working for Hirst. According to Hirst, he only ever made five "spot" paintings himself and the best spot painting is one painted by Rachel! Nowadays, Rachel Howard doesn't work for Hirst. She is a well-known artist whose work fills galleries all around the world.

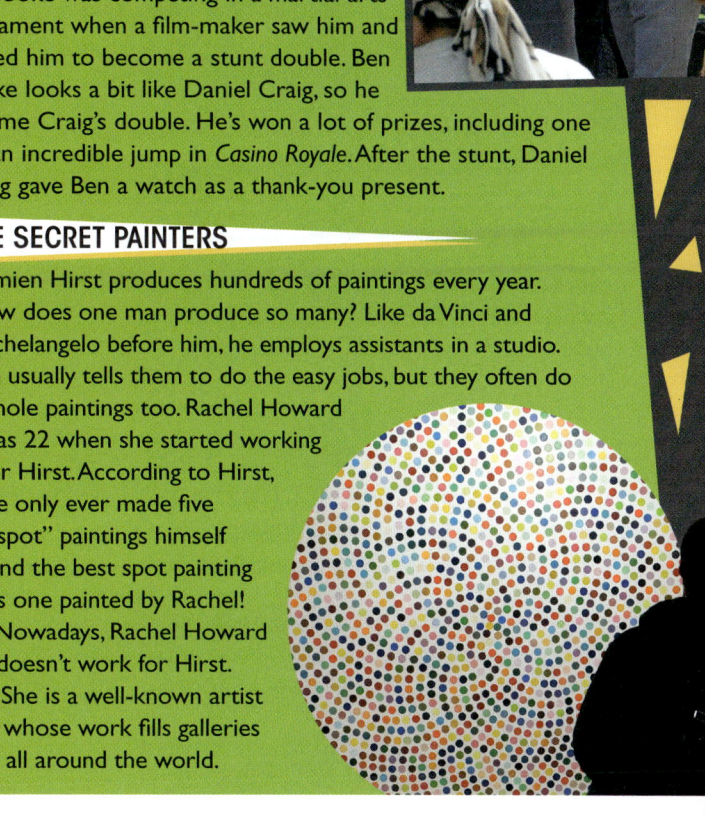

---

1 Look at the photos. Who or what can you see?

2 Read the article quickly. What do these people have in common?

> Jessie J   Hunter Davies   Ben Cooke   Rachel Howard

3 Read the article again and choose the correct answers.
1 Jessie J has written songs for ....
   A movie stars   B sports stars   C pop stars
2 Wayne Rooney's ghostwriter is also a ....
   A footballer   B celebrity   C journalist
3 .... received a gift for a stunt in *Casino Royale*.
   A Daniel Craig   B James Bond   C Ben Cooke
4 .... was a famous painter's assistant.
   A Rachel Howard   B Michelangelo   C Damien Hirst

4 Match the highlighted words in the article to the meanings.
1 travelled around, playing in concerts or appearing at events
2 people who entertain others by acting, singing, dancing or playing music
3 a person who writes stories for a newspaper, or who broadcasts them on radio or TV
4 act in a film or a play
5 a short part of a film, play or book in which the events happen in one place
6 entertain people by acting, dancing, singing or playing music

Talking points

Do you think it's fair that famous people get others to do things for them? Why? / Why not?

Should the 'secret' artists be more famous than they are?

EP Word profile *own*

Certain performers always write their own songs.

She has sold millions of her own albums.

He didn't write it on his own.

page 127

Video extra — Skills and talents

GRAMMAR Reported commands

1 Read the examples and choose the correct commands, a or b.

1 A publisher **convinced him to write** an autobiography.
2 They **ask writers not to discuss** anything with journalists.
3 A film-maker **advised him to be** a stunt double.
4 He usually **tells them to do** the easy jobs.

1 a 'Please write these books about your life.'
    b 'Don't write any books, thanks.'
2 a 'You mustn't discuss anything with the press!'
    b 'You must discuss this with the press!'
3 a 'You shouldn't be a stunt double!'
    b 'You should be a stunt double!'
4 a 'Don't do the easy jobs.'
    b 'Do the easy jobs, please.'

2 Complete the rules with *to* or *not*.

> We report:
> a positive commands using a reporting verb + object pronoun + ... infinitive.
>   The teacher **ordered us to be** quiet.
> b negative commands using a reporting verb + object pronoun + ... + *to* infinitive.
>   The teacher **reminded us not to talk**.

→ Grammar reference page 154

3 Complete the reported commands. Use the reporting verbs in brackets.

0 Mum: 'Help in the kitchen, please.'
   Mum *asked* them *to help* in the kitchen.' (ask)
1 Karen: 'You mustn't touch my things!'
   Karen .... me .... her things. (warn)
2 Police officer: 'Stop!'
   A police officer .... us .... (order)
3 Anna: 'You must be more careful.'
   Anna .... him .... more careful. (tell)
4 Sara: 'You shouldn't worry so much.'
   Sara .... her .... so much. (advise)
5 Diane: 'Come on! Let's go!'
   Diane .... us .... (persuade)
6 Lulu: 'Don't hand the work in late.'
   Lulu .... us .... the work .... late. (remind)

4 Report the commands. Use reporting verbs from exercise 3.

0 A thief to his friend: 'Don't move!'
   The thief warned his friend not to move.
1 A teacher to her students: 'Don't forget your homework on Monday.'
2 A man to his son: 'Pass the salt, please.'
3 A girl to her brother: 'Get out of my room!'
4 A woman to her daughter: 'Do your homework soon.'
5 A taxi driver to his passenger: 'Don't get out yet.'
6 A boy to his friend: 'Why don't we go to the cinema? Come on! There's a new movie you'll love!'

Corpus challenge

Find and correct the mistake in the student's sentence.
He said to me to look at the picture.

VOCABULARY Adjectives: -al and -ful

1 Read the examples and answer questions a–b.

1 He's a busy profession**al** footballer.
2 She's also a success**ful** songwriter.
3 They aren't natur**al** writers.

a Which part of speech (verbs or nouns) do we use to make adjectives with *-al* and *-ful*?
b What spelling changes do you notice in one of the adjectives?

2 Complete the sentences with adjectives formed from the nouns.

1 The exhibition at the new gallery is very .... (colour)
2 I love the countryside here. It's really .... (peace)
3 That's a really .... idea. (origin)
4 Ouch! Don't touch my leg. It's still quite .... (pain)
5 My brother laughs a lot. He's very .... (cheer)
6 The articles aren't at all .... (politics)

3 Complete the questions using adjectives formed from the nouns in the box. Then ask and answer the questions.

> culture   environment   help
> music   stress   tradition

1 Can you cook any .... dishes from this region?
2 Can you play any instruments, or aren't you terribly .... ?
3 Are you worried about .... issues like global warming?
4 Do you like .... TV shows about art and literature?
5 What's the most .... advice you've ever received?
6 Have you been in any .... situations recently? What was happening?

WRITING A biography

1 Look at the photo. What do you know about Taylor Swift? Read the biography and check your ideas.

Taylor Swift

Taylor Swift was born in 1989 in Reading, Pennsylvania. **As** a child, she lived on her family's Christmas tree farm. She became very interested in country music **at the age of** nine and she often travelled 200km to New York for singing lessons. Then, **as soon as** she learnt to play the guitar, people started noticing her talent. She was only 12! In 2004, her family moved to Nashville, the centre of country music in the US, because they wanted to help her career. **By the time** Taylor was 16, her first album was already successful. Her songs were popular with fans of both pop and country music, and her second album *Fearless* (2008) was both a country and a pop hit. **Nowadays**, Taylor enjoys the life of an international celebrity, but she is also keen to use her success to help other people. In 2010, she paid for an education centre in Nashville.

2 Read the *Prepare* box, then read the biography again. What interesting facts do you learn about Taylor Swift?

Prepare to write — A biography

When you write a biography, include:
- interesting or unusual facts about the person.
- important dates from the person's life.
- information about what the person did at different ages:
    As a child, …
    At the age of …,
    As soon as he / she …,
    By the time he / she was …,
    Nowadays, …

3 How many important dates are mentioned in the biography? What happened in each year?

4 Complete the sentences about someone's age with one word in each space.
1 He left home .... the age of 14.
2 She got married .... soon .... she was 21.
3 He started playing football .... a young child.
4 .... , she's a well-known guitarist.
5 .... the .... he started at college, he was already in two bands.

5 You are going to write a biography. Choose a famous person or someone you know. Plan your biography and make some notes. Here are some ideas to help you.
- When was he/she born?
- What are the important dates in his/her life?
- What are his/her main achievements?
- What interesting facts do you know about him/her?

6 Write your biography.
- Use the tips in the *Prepare* box.
- Write about 100 words.
- Don't forget to check your spelling and grammar.

Skills and talents

18 The world of work

VOCABULARY Work

Your profile
What jobs do people you know do?
What job might you want to do? Why?

1 ▶ 2.23 Listen to eight people describing their jobs. Match them to the photos.

2 ▶ 2.24 Label the photos with eight of the jobs in the box. Then listen and check.

| author | babysitter | builder | coach | designer | detective | DJ | film director |
| firefighter | journalist | lawyer | mechanic | model | musician | scientist | vet |

3 Answer the questions, using the jobs you didn't use in exercise 2.

Who …
0 gives advice to criminals? *a lawyer*
1 plays music on the radio?
2 appears in photographs to advertise things like clothes?
3 tries to discover information about a crime?
4 plays a musical instrument?
5 writes books?
6 draws and plans how something is made?
7 studies and works in science?

4 Discuss the questions.

Which job(s) …
1 do you usually need to pass exams for?
2 are people usually paid the most for?
3 can school students in your country do?
4 do people usually do alone?
5 do people usually do as part of a team?

I think that you need to pass exams to be a vet.

READING

1 Read the introduction and look at the photos. What jobs do you think the three young people did? Read the article quickly and check.

I'M IN CHARGE

Would you like to be a football coach, a model or a musician? If you could do any job for a day, what would it be? Every year, Takeover Day offers thousands of young people this chance. Read more to find out what jobs they chose, and what they learned.

Takeover Day is an annual event and about 40,000 young people 'take over' from adults. They're in charge for the day! Of course, it's difficult to give someone the job of a celebrity or a model. However, Takeover Day has offered young people jobs as journalists, radio DJs, film directors, teachers and even politicians.

The event has two aims. Firstly, it gives young people experience in a wide range of jobs. Secondly, adults can learn from young people's opinions and fresh ideas.

Simon Evans and some friends had a day at Coventry Football Club. He became coach of the football team for a day. 'Having a go at training professional players was an unforgettable experience,' said Simon. 'If I had the chance, I would do this job every day.'

Paul Saunders spent the day with an important politician. He even went to a meeting with the Prime Minister! Paul thought that if everyone had the chance to follow a politician for a day, they'd be amazed. 'It isn't a nine-to-five job,' he said. 'It's 24/7 and there's no time for lunch!'

Sally Cameron, 15, became the headteacher of her school. 'I'd go mad if I were a headteacher!' she said. 'There were so many meetings and some of them went on for ages!' Sally thinks she learned a lot. 'My favourite part of the day was meeting the school chef and approving the school menus for the week. It was a great opportunity to tell her what we *really* like eating!'

2 Read the article again. Answer the questions.
1. How many young people usually take part in Takeover Day?
2. What jobs are mentioned in the text?
3. Who does the day help? How?
4. What was Simon's opinion of his day?
5. What surprised Paul about a politician's work?
6. What did Sally dislike about her day?

3 Match the highlighted words in the article to the meanings.
1. a lot of different types
2. new and different
3. a long time
4. a normal job
5. exciting and impossible to forget
6. happening every year

EP Word profile *go*

Having a go at training professional players was an unforgettable experience.

Some of the meetings went on for ages.

I'd go mad if I were a headteacher.

page 127

Talking points
Is Takeover Day a good idea? Why?
What do you think young people can gain from doing a part-time job?

Video extra   The world of work

GRAMMAR Second conditional

1 Read the examples. Then choose the correct words to complete the rules.

1 If I **had** the chance, I **would** do this job every day.
2 I'**d** go mad if I **were** a headteacher!

> We use the second conditional to talk about an unlikely or impossible situation in the present or future, and its results.
> **a** We form the second conditional with: If + *present simple / past simple*, + *will / would* + infinitive
> **b** The short form of *will / would* is '*d*.
> **c** We can use *were* instead of *was* in the *if* clause of the second conditional.
> **d** The *if* clause can come first or second in the sentence.

→ Grammar reference page 155

2 Match the sentence halves and choose the correct verbs.

1 You probably *didn't / wouldn't* earn much money
2 I *made / 'd make* thrillers
3 *Did / Would* you be worried
4 If I *were / would be* the headteacher of my school,
5 If I *wanted / would want* to be a vet,
6 If Dad *worked / would work* nine-to-five in an office,

a if your dad *was / would be* a firefighter?
b he *got / 'd get* very bored.
c if you *became / would become* a musician.
d what subjects *did / would* I have to study?
e if I *became / 'd become* a film director.
f lessons *started / would start* at 10 am.

3 Complete the second conditional sentences.

1 You .... (sleep) better if you .... (do) more exercise.
2 If you .... (fail) the end-of-year exam, what .... your parents .... (say)?
3 If my brother .... (not take) my things, we .... (not have) so many arguments.
4 You .... (finish) your homework before dinner if you .... (not waste) so much time on the internet.
5 If I .... (can) live anywhere in the world, I .... (choose) somewhere hot.
6 .... you .... (be) upset if your best friend .... (not give) you a birthday present?

4 Complete the sentences with your own ideas. Compare your answers.

0 If I were an author, …   *I'd write horror stories.*
1 If I could do any job for a day, …
2 If I had €100,000 to spend on equipment for my school, …
3 I wouldn't ever be bored again if …
4 If I were in charge of my school, …
5 My parents wouldn't be pleased if …
6 If I could be the coach of any team, …

5 Tell the class about your partner's answers in exercise 4.

If Luca could do any job for a day, he'd be a photographer.

Corpus challenge

Find and correct the mistake in the student's sentence.
If you met her, you will really like her.

VOCABULARY Suffixes: -er, -or, -ist, -ian

1 Read the examples. Then make nouns for people from the words in the box.

1 He spent the day with an important politic**ian**.
2 It isn't easy being a teach**er**.
3 Would you like to be a journal**ist**?
4 I'd love to be a film direct**or** for a day!

| ~~act~~ art clean music reception run visit |

actor

2 Complete the definitions.

0 A blogger …   *writes a blog.*
1 A competitor …
2 A scientist …
3 A football supporter …
4 A vegetarian …
5 A guitarist …
6 A novelist …
7 A television actor …
8 A goalkeeper …

3 Mime a job. Can your classmates guess what it is?

LISTENING

1 ▶ 2.25 Listen to the conversations. Answer the questions.

1 What are Jess and Matt's problems?
2 Who are they asking for advice?
3 Do you agree with the advice?

2 ▶ 2.25 Listen again. Are the sentences correct or incorrect?

Conversation 1
1 Ali already does a weekend job.
2 Jess's parents have said she can't get a weekend job.
3 Ali thinks Jess might be able to earn some money at home.
4 Jess wants to avoid asking her parents.

Conversation 2
5 Matt knows what he wants to do in the future.
6 Mrs Elson already knew that Matt was a film fan.
7 Matt thinks he might change his mind about doing a film degree.
8 Mrs Elson thinks that ten subjects might be too many for Matt.

SPEAKING Discussing options

1 Look at the pictures. The student is thinking about getting a weekend job. Which one would you prefer to do? Why?

2 ▶ 2.26 Listen to two friends discussing the jobs. Which one do they agree would be best?

3 ▶ 2.26 Read the *Prepare* box. Then listen again. Which phrases do you hear?

4 Work with a partner. Talk together for three minutes about the different jobs the student could do and decide which would be best.

Prepare to speak — Discussing options

Making suggestions
What about …?
I think … might be a good idea
What do you think about …?

Agreeing
Yes, you're right.
That's true.
Maybe you're right.
I see what you mean.

Disagreeing
I'm not so sure.
The problem with that is …
… might be better.
No, I don't agree.

Reaching agreement
Yes, that's a good choice.

The world of work

Culture
Special training schools

1 Work in pairs. Look at the four talented young people. What do you think each of them has achieved? Use the words in the box.

climb Mount Everest   take part in a Formula 1 race
star in a film   record a number 1 hit record

2 ▶ 2.27 Listen and check your answers. What else do you learn about each person?

3 Look at the three photos in the article on page 107. Match the special training schools below to the countries. Then read the texts quickly and check your answers.

1 circus school   a Cuba
2 martial arts school   b Russia
3 ballet school   c China

4 Read the texts again. Which school(s) …
1 has students who get up before 6 am?
2 is free for people from that country?
3 isn't located in a city?
4 has the highest number of students?
5 was the first of this type of school to open in the world?
6 accept foreign students?

5 Discuss the questions.
1 Would you like to go to any of these training schools? Why? / Why not?
2 What other kinds of special training schools are there?
3 What do you think are the advantages and disadvantages of going to a special training school when you are young?

circus school

1

In Russia, the circus is an important cultural activity just like the opera or ballet, so it's no surprise that in the 1920s, the first circus school in the world opened in Moscow. Russian students don't have to pay to go there, but foreign students pay fees. Circus school is not an easy option. For 6 hours a day, 5 days a week, 200 students are taught how to jump, dance and fly by around 70 different teachers – a lot of them retired performers themselves. Foreigners also have Russian lessons.

2

People believe that martial arts developed in ancient China as self-defence, a hunting technique and also as a way to train for war. Nowadays, there are hundreds of martial arts schools across China. The largest is Tagou School, which is on Mount Song, in the middle of beautiful countryside. This school teaches both Kung Fu and Chinese kick-boxing to around 35,000 male and female students, aged between 5 and 35. The day begins early at 6.30 am.
School-aged students do some school subjects but spend most of their time training. All students pay fees for the school but it takes pupils from all over the world.

3

Ballet is an important part of Cuban culture. Its national ballet company is one of the best in the world. At the moment, around 3,000 students are studying at the Cuban National Ballet School in the capital, Havana, which means it's the biggest school of its kind in the world. The training doesn't cost anything but the students need to have talent and be strong. Many of the students get up at 5 am and do 90 minutes of ballet training before they even start their lessons. The teachers make their students work hard but the results are spectacular. The best ballet companies around the world all have at least one Cuban dancer.

ballet school

martial arts school

6 ▶ 2.28 Listen to an interview with Carolina Woods. What is her special talent? Where did she go to finish her training?

7 ▶ 2.28 Listen again. What advantages and disadvantages does Carolina mention of training in Russia?

Project

Find out some information about a training school in your country and prepare a presentation for your class. Include information about:
- where it is
- what you can study there
- what a typical day is like
- what the advantages and disadvantages are

Special training schools

19 The written word

VOCABULARY Magazines

Your profile
What types of magazines do you enjoy reading? (football? gaming? celebrity news?)
Do you prefer printed magazines or digital ones? Why?

1 Look at photos a–c. What types of magazine are they?

2 ▶2.29 What types of magazines do the people read? Listen and check.

1 Ali   a celebrity magazines
2 Jess   b music magazines
3 Jess's mother c computer games magazines
4 Matt   d fashion magazines
                 e car magazines

3 ▶2.29 Look at the magazine words below. Who mentions each one? Listen again and write *A* (Ali), *J* (Jess) or *M* (Matt).

1 advert   4 front cover   7 line
2 article   5 headline   8 paragraph
3 comments section   6 interview   9 title

4 ▶2.30 Complete the sentences with the correct form of words from exercise 3. Listen and check.

1 Some of the reviews are several pages long, and some are just a ....
2 I always read the .... People always post really interesting stuff in them.
3 There's an amazing American gaming magazine but I can't remember the ....
4 I sometimes look at celebrity magazines in the shop if I like the ....
5 The .... can be a bit long so I don't read every ....
6 I'm really into music magazines that have .... with bands and singers.

5 Discuss the questions.

1 How or why do you choose which magazines to read?
2 What are the most important things in a good magazine?
I always look for great photos and articles about my favourite bands.

READING

HAS IT BEEN A GOOD YEAR FOR YOU?

Well guys, the school year is nearly over. Has it been a good one for you? What's the most interesting thing you've done? Post your experiences here and we'll then invite some of you to write a longer article for the school website.

Volunteering on a city farm

JESS

I had an amazing time when I won the trip to Twickenham, but working on a city farm was a more interesting experience. Our teacher told us that a city farm in our **neighbourhood** was looking for young people to help with the animals. City farms are a great way for people to get experience of life in the country – but in a city. You can learn about animals and plants and you can even take part in working on the farm. Anyway, I spoke to the farm manager and a few days later I was looking after the horses on the farm! I was really proud of myself when I helped a young girl to ride a horse for the first time. It really meant a lot to her – and to me!

Making my first film

MATT

I made my first film this year, which was definitely the best moment for me. It all started when I read an interview with a young film-maker who said he made films using his phone. I told my friends I was interested in trying this and they all said it would be really cool. First, I had to think of an idea. Everyone said that the film needed to be short and simple. In the end, I decided to make an animated film called 'Into Space'. It's now on the school website if you **fancy** watching it. For my first film, I think it's **pretty** good.

Climbing the highest mountain

ALI

You're all expecting me to tell you about creating a new app or building a better computer. But actually my experience is about reaching the top of a mountain. In May, my uncle told me that he was going to climb Scafell Pike – the highest mountain in England. He also said I could go with him if I wanted to! It takes about four hours to climb Scafell Pike, which meant we had to set off at about 7 am, to avoid climbing in the heat of the midday sun. It was a lot more **challenging** than I expected it to be, but fortunately the weather was beautiful. The views from the top were **spectacular** and I took a lot of photos!

---

1 Read the beginning of Matt, Jess and Ali's class blog. What do they have to write about? What do you think each one will write?

2 Read Matt, Jess and Ali's posts and check your ideas in exercise 1.

3 Read the class blog again and answer the questions.
   1. What is a city farm?
   2. What did Jess do on the city farm?
   3. What did Matt use to make his film?
   4. What sort of film did Matt make?
   5. What did Ali decide to do? Who with?
   6. Why did Ali have to start his adventure early?

4 Complete the sentences with highlighted words from the blog.
   1. Did you see Neymar's goal in the Brazil match? It was .... !
   2. Do you want to go to the cinema? I .... seeing a film tonight.
   3. We live in a big city, but our .... is really friendly.
   4. I found maths quite .... this term, but I did well in my exams.
   5. There are about 1,000 students at my school, so it's .... big.

5 What is the most interesting thing that has happened to you this year?

EP Word profile *mean*

It really **meant** a lot to her.

It takes about four hours to climb Scafell Pike, which **meant** we had to set off at about 7 am.

page 128

Talking points

" Do young people have enough free time to do all the things they enjoy?

Is it necessary to spend money if you want to have fun? "

The written word 109

GRAMMAR Reported speech

1 Match the speech bubbles to the examples.

> a I make films using my phone.

> b A city farm is looking for young people to help with the animals.

> c You can go with me.

> d It will be really cool!

1 My uncle said I **could** go with him.
2 They all said it **would** be really cool.
3 He said he **made** films using his phone.
4 Our teacher told us that a city farm **was looking** for young people to help with the animals.

2 Match the examples 1–4 in exercise 1 to the rules.

> We use reported speech to repeat what someone said earlier.
> We change the tense in reported speech.
>
> | **Direct speech** | **Reported speech** |
> |---|---|
> | a Present simple | Past simple |
> | b Present continuous | Past continuous |
> | c can | could |
> | d will | would |
>
> We also often change pronouns:
> 'I make films.' → He said **he** made films.

→ Grammar reference page 156

3 Complete the second sentence so it means the same as the first. Use no more than three words.

0 Clare: 'I love writing about fashion.'
   Clare said that ..she loved writing.. about fashion.
1 Ewan: 'I don't want to write about sport!'
   Ewan said he .... to write about sport.
2 Anita: 'My article will be really funny.'
   Anita said her article .... really funny.
3 Paul: 'I'm writing about the cafeteria.'
   Paul said that he .... about the cafeteria.
4 James: 'The story can't be true.'
   James said the story .... true.
5 Sophie: 'The photos look amazing.'
   Sophie said the photos .... amazing.
6 Dan: 'You'll enjoy the movie.'
   Dan said I .... the movie.
7 Sarah: 'There won't be any more shows in that series.'
   Sarah said there .... any more shows in that series.
8 Chris: 'I'm not listening to a word you say!'
   Chris said that he .... to a word she said.

4 Report what the people said.

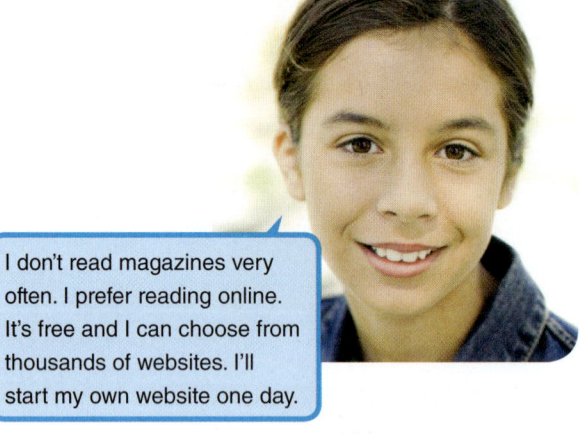

> I don't read magazines very often. I prefer reading online. It's free and I can choose from thousands of websites. I'll start my own website one day.

Louisa said she didn't read magazines very often.

> Mohammad can play the guitar. He practises every day, and he's getting really good at it. He'll be a professional one day!

Jon said that Mohammad could …

Corpus challenge

Find and correct the mistake in the student's sentence.
I said that I want him to come with us.

VOCABULARY say, speak, talk and tell

1 Read the examples. Then match the verbs to the uses.

*Can you **speak** Turkish?*
*I **said**, 'Hello.'*
*I've **told** you the answer.*
*I'm **talking** about blogs.*

1 speak	a someone something
2 say	b about something or someone
3 tell	c something
4 talk	d a language

2 Choose the correct verbs.

1 What did you *tell / say*?
2 I can *say / speak* English.
3 I *spoke / told* him my phone number.
4 She was *talking / telling* about you.
5 Nobody *told / said* anything.
6 Did you *talk / tell* to Mr Marsh?
7 Who is *speaking / saying*?
8 Please *tell / say* us the truth.

WRITING   An online review

1 Do you read reviews of books or films online? Do you ever write reviews?

2 Read the review quickly. Tick (✔) the information that Ali includes.

1 The title of the book
2 The author's name
3 Information about the author
4 The name of the main character
5 The story of the whole book
6 A description of part of the story
7 Details about how the story ends
8 His own opinion of the book

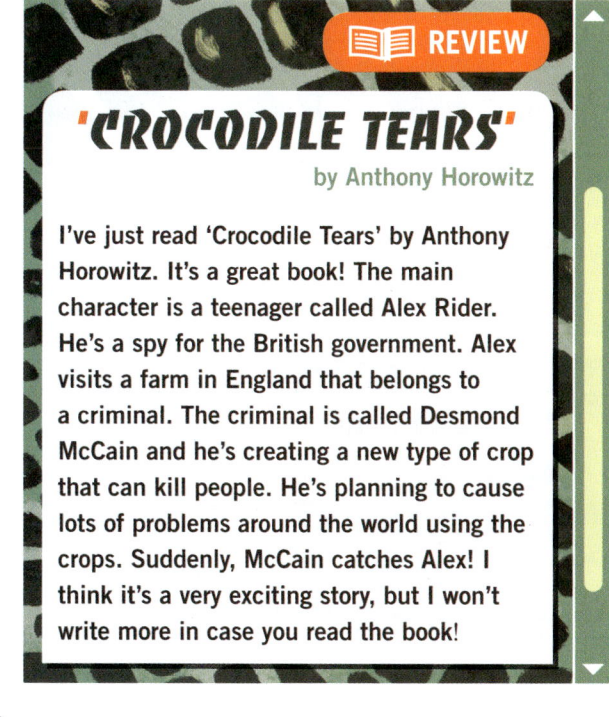

📖 REVIEW

'CROCODILE TEARS'
by Anthony Horowitz

I've just read 'Crocodile Tears' by Anthony Horowitz. It's a great book! The main character is a teenager called Alex Rider. He's a spy for the British government. Alex visits a farm in England that belongs to a criminal. The criminal is called Desmond McCain and he's creating a new type of crop that can kill people. He's planning to cause lots of problems around the world using the crops. Suddenly, McCain catches Alex! I think it's a very exciting story, but I won't write more in case you read the book!

3 Read the *Prepare* box. What is Ali's opinion of *Crocodile Tears*? How do you know?

Prepare to write An online review

In an online review:
- include the title of the book and the author.
- include the name of the main character.
- include some details of the story, but not all.
- give your opinion of the book.

4 Read an online review of *Artemis Fowl*. What is the writer's opinion of the book? Complete the review with the words in the box.

> author   character   incredible   thought   written

I've just read a really good fantasy novel called 'Artemis Fowl'. It was [1] .... by Eoin Colfer, an Irish [2] .... The main [3] .... is a teenage boy called Artemis Fowl II. He comes from a family of criminals and he does all sorts of awful things to make his family richer. He isn't a very nice person, but that doesn't matter because the story is [4] .... It was the first in a series of eight books. I [5] .... it was a really exciting story, and I'll definitely read the rest of the series.

5 You are going to write an online review. Think about a book or film that you like and plan your review. Use the notes to help you.
- What is the title of the book or film?
- Who is the author or director?
- Who is the main character?
- What happens in the story?
- What is your opinion of it?

6 Write your online review.
- Use the tips in the *Prepare* box.
- Write about 100 words.
- Remember to check your spelling and grammar.

20 Puzzles and tricks

VOCABULARY Puzzles

Your profile
Do you like puzzles? Why? / Why not?
What is your favourite kind of puzzle?

1 Look at the pictures. What are the tricks in each one?

2 ▶ 2.31 Listen to two people talking about the pictures. Which picture isn't mentioned?

3 ▶ 2.31 Match the sentence halves. Then listen again and check.

1 No one knows who first
2 **Imagine** that
3 Some animals use colour to
4 However, it's a bit of a **mystery**
5 This picture is similar to
6 You have to use your **imagination**
7 Have you
8 Are you a fan of
9 Street performers like this will never tell you how
10 Their methods are

a **solved** it yet?
b the rabbit's ears are a mouth.
c how they decide which colour to change to.
d **magic** shows?
e **created** this clever picture.
f this **trick** is done.
g **secret**, of course.
h the rabbit–duck **puzzle**.
i **hide** from their enemies.
j to see the second.

4 Complete the sentences with the correct form of **words** from exercise 3.

1 Someone .... my school bag today and I couldn't find it!
2 You need a good .... to be a writer.
3 Can you .... what life was like 100 years ago?
4 It took me ages to .... this puzzle, but I found the answer in the end.
5 My brother knows some really amazing card ....
6 It was hard keeping the surprise party .... from Mum.

5 Ask and answer the questions.

1 What puzzles are you good at solving?
2 Do you enjoy using your imagination?
3 Can you think of more examples of how animals hide from their enemies?
4 Do you enjoy watching magic tricks. Why? / Why not?

EP Word profile *mind*

What's the first animal that comes into your **mind**?

Don't **make up your mind** yet.

page 128

READING

1 Read the article quickly. Choose the main topic of the article.
   a The ways optical illusions are used.
   b How optical illusions work.
   c Optical illusions in nature.

2 Read the article again. Are the sentences correct or incorrect?
   1 Optical illusions are a recent idea.
   2 Akiyoshi Kitaoka designed his optical illusion for a car advertisement.
   3 There are several of Alexander McQueen's 'optical illusion' dresses.
   4 You can find optical illusions in the natural world.
   5 In Professor Wiseman's experiment, people had to draw a brick.
   6 In the experiment, the more creative people found it easier to see the duck and the rabbit.

Tricks of the eye

OPTICAL ILLUSIONS
or 'tricks of the eye' have long been used in art. At first glance, this scene looks 3D. In fact, everything is a flat painting – apart from the person. The artwork actually lets people become part of it!

IN FASHION,
optical illusions are used to make us look better. This dress wasn't just designed to look good. The narrow black and white lines actually make people look thinner! It was designed by Alexander McQueen and cost £2,500. Several famous people have bought one.

SOME ILLUSIONS
can make us feel a picture is actually moving. Look at this picture by Akiyoshi Kitaoka, a Japanese professor. Kitaoka came up with the design while trying to make a New Year's card for his friends and family. Recently it was used in a car advertisement. Can you guess why?

IN THE NATURAL WORLD
some animals depend on optical illusions to stay alive. Many butterflies, snakes and spiders are a similar colour to the place where they live. They don't want their enemies to see them … and eat them!

Can you see the animal on the right?

A BRITISH PROFESSOR,
Richard Wiseman, says these pictures might help us find out how creative we are. He asked 600 people this question: how easy is it for you to see both animals in the duck and rabbit illusion? Then these people were given some creative exercises. For example, in one exercise they had to think of different uses for a brick. What did Wiseman discover? The people who found it easy to see both the duck and the rabbit could think of the most uses for a brick. They seemed more creative.

Talking points
" Why do you think advertisers like using optical illusions?
What do you think of Richard Wiseman's experiment? "

Puzzles and tricks 113

GRAMMAR Past simple passive

1 Match the examples to the passive forms.

1 *The picture **was used** in a car advertisement.*
2 *This dress **wasn't** just **designed** to look good.*
3 *In fashion, optical illusions **are used** to make us look better.*

a present simple positive
b past simple positive
c past simple negative

2 Look at the examples and complete the rules.

ACTIVE: *Kitaoka   created   the picture*
PASSIVE: *The picture was created by   Kitaoka.*

In the past simple passive:
a we use *was* / .... + (not) + ... participle.
b if we want to say the person/thing that did the action, we use ....

→ Grammar reference page 157

3 Read the first part of the article and choose the correct forms of the verb.

Street painting ¹ *appeared / was appeared* first in the 16th century in Italy. The painters ² *called / were called* 'madonnari' and they ³ *painted / were painted* pictures of well-known characters on the pavement.

In 1984, 3D pavement art ⁴ *invented / was invented* by the American, Kurt Venner. When you look at 3D pavement art from a certain place, it looks like it is 3D! A few years later, a TV documentary ⁵ *made / was made* Kurt and his work famous. He ⁶ *asked / was asked* to make 3D art for adverts, festivals and museums. This 3D pavement art ⁷ *didn't do / wasn't done* by Kurt, but by Julian Beever, a British pavement artist.

4 Complete the second part of the article. Use the past simple active or passive form of the verbs.

Recently in England, 3D street painting ⁰ *was used* (use) to make the city safer. Between 1790 and 1820, over 150 kilometres of canals ¹ .... (build) in London. Nowadays, cyclists and pedestrians share the path next to these canals, but many cyclists ride too fast. So a large 3D hole ² .... (paint) on the path by two local artists. As cyclists approached the painting, it ³ .... (look) like there was a large hole in the path. So they ⁴ .... (ride) more slowly. Then, as the cyclists ⁵ .... (pass) the hole, they ⁶ .... (give) information about safer cycling!

5 Rewrite the sentences in the passive. Include *by* … if you think it's necessary.

0 They used her painting in an advertisement.
  Her painting was used in an advertisement.
1 People encouraged the cyclists to go more slowly.
2 A young artist won the prize.
3 They didn't stop cyclists from using the path.
4 They warned her not to cycle on the pavement.
5 Street artists painted them.

Corpus challenge

Find and correct the mistake in the student's sentence.
He born in Paris.

VOCABULARY make and let

1 Read the examples and match the bold verbs to the meanings.

1 *The artwork **lets** people become part of it.*
2 *Some illusions can **make** us feel a picture is moving.*

a force someone to do something, or cause something to happen
b allow someone to do something

2 Complete the sentences with *make* or *let*.

1 My parents .... me stay up late on Fridays.
2 You can't .... people be friends with you!
3 Our teachers always .... us work hard.
4 My brother won't .... me use his laptop!
5 They wouldn't .... us watch the film because we're not old enough.
6 Her jokes always .... me laugh!

LISTENING

1 ▶ 2.32 Listen to three talks by teenagers. What is each teenager's favourite thing?

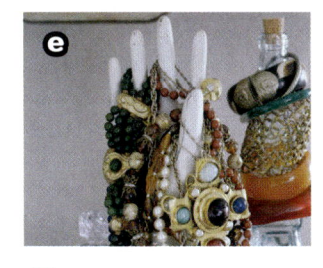

a
b
c
d
e
f

2 ▶ 2.32 Listen to the talks again. Choose the correct answers.

Talk 1

1 Jamie …
   A keeps the cup at home.
   B didn't play well in the final.
   C has borrowed the cup.
2 Jamie …
   A scored a lot of goals in the final.
   B didn't score a goal in the final.
   C only saved one goal.

Talk 2

3 Eleanor …
   A bought her favourite object.
   B was given her favourite object.
   C found her favourite object.
4 Eleanor …
   A has a friend with the same object.
   B uses the object to hold her jewellery.
   C hasn't cleaned the object yet.

Talk 3

5 Harry …
   A has just got the camera.
   B was given the camera.
   C bought the camera himself.
6 Harry's camera is …
   A good but quite large.
   B for experienced photographers.
   C simple to work.

SPEAKING   Talking about a special object

1 Think about a special object that you have. What is it? Why is it special to you?

2 ▶ 2.33 Listen to Alex and Lucy talking about their special objects. Why are the objects special to them?

3 ▶ 2.33 Read the *Prepare box*. Then listen again. Which phrases do Alex and Lucy use?

Prepare to speak — Talking about an object

Describing an object	Saying why it is special
It's/They're made of …	I love it/them because …
It's/They're quite …	The reason I like it/them is …
It's/They're really …	It's/They're special to me because …
Saying where you got it	It's/They're so …
I bought it/them …	
It was/They were given to me by …	

4 Think about an object that is special to you. Make notes.
   • What is it?
   • Where and when did you get it?
   • Why is it important to you?
   • Is there anything else interesting about it?

5 Talk about your special object. Use phrases from the *Prepare* box.

Puzzles and tricks

Biology
The eye

1 Do you know the names of any parts of the eye?

2 In pairs, do the quiz.

Eye didn't know that!

1 How much does an eye weigh?
- A 8 grams
- B 80 grams
- C 800 gram

2 If you look at the sky on a clear night, how far can the human eye see?
- A about 25 kilometres
- B about 25,000 kilometres
- C about 25 billion kilometres

3 What percentage of the world's population is blind?
- A about 0.6%
- B about 1.6%
- C about 6%

4 Is it more common for teenagers to be short-sighted or long-sighted?
- A short-sighted
- B long-sighted

5 When were glasses first used?
- A in the 13th century
- B in the 16th century
- C in the 18th century

6 Which of these foods can improve your sight?
- A beef
- B carrots
- C cheese

7 How many times do people blink in a minute?
- A 5
- B 15
- C 25

8 Which group blinks the most often?
- A children
- B adults
- C cats

3 ▶ 2.34 Listen and check your answers.

4 ▶ 2.34 Can you remember? Answer the questions. Then listen again and check.
1 How is the eye different from other parts of the body?
2 How many planets should humans be able to see from Earth?
3 How many blind people are there in the world?
4 Where were glasses probably invented?
5 What vitamin helps your eyes?
6 How often do cats blink?

5 Read the text on page 117 and answer the questions.

Which part(s) of your body …
1 cleans the eyes?
2 contains something called melanin?
3 is where tears are made?
4 helps to stop dirt getting into your eye?
5 is joined to the eyes?
6 sometimes looks a different colour in photos?

Key words
short-sighted describes people that can only see things that are close to them but not far away
long-sighted describes people that can only see things that are far away but not close
blink open and close both of your eyes quickly

Our eyes are always moving, collecting light and sending messages to the brain. We use them whenever we are awake. When we think of other people and places, we often 'see' a picture in our brain. Even when we are asleep, we 'see' dreams!

EYE CHOO!
All mammals blink when they see a bright light. But do you sneeze when you go from a dark room to a very bright room? About 25% of people do this, but we don't know why!

BLUE-EYED BABIES
The colour of your eyes is decided by your parents' eye colour. However, young babies have often got blue irises. This is because eye colour comes from **MELANIN** and when babies are born, they haven't got much melanin.

The coloured part of the eye is called the **IRIS**. Everyone's irises are different, so in some airports you can use your iris instead of a passport or identification card!

The **PUPIL** is a hole in the eye. This is where light goes into the eye. In the dark, or when there isn't much light, your pupils are larger. This lets more light through the pupil. When there is a lot of light, for example on a sunny day, your pupils are smaller. Have you ever noticed this?

EYEBROWS
stop sweat from our foreheads from getting into the eyes. Under the eyebrows is a tear gland. It produces tears. The corner of each eye is connected to our nose. What happens to your nose when you cry?

EYELIDS
protect the eye from bright light, dirt and dust. When we blink, our eyelids clean our eyes and move the dirt to the corner of our eyes.

EYELASHES
protect the eye from light, dirt and dust. There are about 150 eyelashes at the top of your eye and about 80 eyelashes at the bottom.

RED EYE
Do you notice that people sometimes have red eyes in photographs? When a photo is taken, the eye sees the very bright light of the camera flash, but the pupil hasn't got time to get smaller. So a lot of light from the flash goes into the eye. The red colour we see in photographs is actually blood, inside the eye.

Some people, dogs and cats have got different amounts of melanin in each eye. This means they have different-coloured eyes!

Key words
sweat the salty liquid that comes through your skin when you are hot, nervous or ill
gland a part of the body that makes liquids
sneeze when you sneeze, air suddenly comes out of your nose and mouth in a way you cannot control
tear the liquid that comes from your eye when you cry
melanin a chemical which controls the colour of our eyes and skin

Project
Do a survey about eyes in your class. Use these questions and your own ideas. Then design a webpage with the results of your survey. Use charts and graphs to present the information.
How many students …
1 have got a) brown eyes, b) blue eyes, c) green eyes, or d) eyes of another colour?
2 have had an eye test at an optician's?
3 are a) short-sighted or b) long-sighted?
4 wear a) glasses or b) contact lenses?
5 sneeze when they suddenly see bright light?
6 can blink less than five times in a minute?
7 eat more than ten carrots a week?

The eye

Review 5
Units 17–20

VOCABULARY

1 Choose the odd one out in each group of words.
1. a novel b biography c script d exhibition
2. a poet b audience c painter d writer
3. a painting b drawing c filming d sculpture
4. a artist b series c poet d director

2 Complete the jobs with the missing vowels. Then answer the questions.

b_bys_tt_r	v_t
f_r_f_ght_r	j__rn_l_st
m_ch_n_c	

Who …
1. has the most dangerous job? ....
2. works with children? ....
3. writes about the news? ....
4. repairs cars? ....
5. works with animals? ....

3 Complete the words in the mini conversations.
1. **A:** We have to finish this essay by tomorrow and I've only written a few p ....
   B: I've only written about two l .... !
2. **A:** There's a great a .... in that magazine about Banksy – the graffiti artist.
   B: Thanks. I read a good i .... with him once.
3. **A:** If you see an a .... for a new book, do you usually want to buy it?
   B: No, not really. I usually look for books with an interesting t .... and a good f .... c ....

4 Complete the sentences with the words in the box.

create	hidden	trick	imagined
magic	puzzle	imagination	

1. I used to love doing .... shows when I was younger.
2. The money was .... in a book on his shelf.
3. That's a brilliant card .... Can you teach me how to do it?
4. My sister can .... amazing meals from just a few ingredients.
5. I'd love to be a novelist one day but I don't think I have a good enough ....
6. Have you solved that .... yet? It took me ages!
7. Have you ever .... what life is like for people who are blind?

GRAMMAR

5 Read the first sentence. Then complete the second sentence, including the verbs in the box.

~~advised~~ asked encouraged ordered warned

0. 'You should publish that story.'
   His friends *advised* him *to publish* the story.
1. 'Sit down!'
   The teacher .... the students ....
2. 'Be careful when you do question five.'
   The teacher .... the students .... with question five.
3. 'Can you help me?'
   Harry .... Charlotte .... him.
4. 'You really should enter the art competition.'
   My mum .... me .... the art competition.

6 Complete the sentences. Use the second conditional.
0. My cousins don't live near me, so I don't see them.
   If my cousins lived near me, … *I would see them.*
1. Katie doesn't invite me to her parties, so I don't invite her to mine.
   If Katie invited me to her parties, …
2. They talk all the time, so they are always in trouble.
   They wouldn't always be in trouble if …
3. I never do exercise, so I'm not fit.
   If I did exercise, …
4. He doesn't work hard, so he never gets good marks.
   He would get good marks if …
5. She doesn't like TV, but she plays computer games all the time.
   If she liked TV, …

7 Complete the second sentence so that it means the same as the first. Use no more than three words.
1. Leonardo da Vinci painted 'The Mona Lisa'.
   'The Mona Lisa' was .... Leonardo da Vinci.
2. 'I can't imagine life without my phone,' said Nina.
   Nina said .... life without her phone.
3. In 2006, a collector sold a painting by Jackson Pollock for $151.8 million.
   In 2006, a painting by Jackson Pollock .... for $151.8 million.
4. I don't think you should paint your bedroom black.
   If I were you, I .... your bedroom black.
5. Joe said he was going to the exhibition later.
   'I .... the exhibition later,' said Joe.

118 Review 5

Corpus challenge

8 Tick the two sentences without mistakes. Correct the mistakes in the other sentences.

1. The teacher asked for us to work together.
2. The trainer told us to play together.
3. If you will go, it will be more fun.
4. Fabio called me and said he is going out.
5. If you came here, you will like it.
6. She said she would meet me at school.
7. His old bike was broke.
8. I want to say you that I bought a new game.

9 Read the text and choose the correct word for each space.

DEVELOP YOUR TALENTS!

Many teenagers⁰ ..A.. of becoming celebrities – do you?

If you have a ¹ .... talent for acting, dancing or singing, ² .... not attend our two-week course and develop all three! It ³ .... during the summer holidays and there are ten six-hour classes altogether.

For the first three days, you will concentrate ⁴ .... the three areas – **acting**, **dancing** and **singing** – with a full day for each ⁵ .... Teaching is done in ⁶ .... small groups, to allow you to improve quickly.

The ⁷ .... of the course is about the challenges of doing a live performance. On the final afternoon, you will ⁸ .... part in an amazing show, in front of a real ⁹ .... , which is always great fun.

Book your ¹⁰ .... on the course now!

0	A	dream	B	imagine	C	believe	D	intend
1	A	traditional	B	usual	C	natural	D	final
2	A	how	B	why	C	when	D	who
3	A	stays	B	follows	C	gives	D	happens
4	A	on	B	in	C	of	D	at
5	A	point	B	skill	C	trick	D	range
6	A	very	B	enough	C	so	D	too
7	A	bit	B	part	C	lot	D	rest
8	A	make	B	keep	C	take	D	hold
9	A	public	B	team	C	audience	D	club
10	A	seat	B	place	C	room	D	entry

Pairwork

UNIT 3 PAGE 20 Vocabulary exercise 4
Quiz answers
1 In Britain, the majority of children start school the September before their fifth birthday.
2 In Belgium and Germany, students cannot leave school until they are 18.
3 In some states in the USA, the youngest age you can get a driving licence is 14. However, there are often a lot of rules for drivers of this age. For example, in North Dakota young drivers cannot drive between 10 pm and 6 am.
4 In the UK, 40% of young people go to university but only 30% get a degree. The most common reason for leaving is that students aren't enjoying their course.
5 In almost all European countries, women leave home before men. Over 50% of Italian men leave home in their thirties.
6 In the UK, you can get a job at the age of 13. You can work two hours a day on school days and, until 16, 35 hours a week in the holidays.
7 In Spain, the average age at which women and men marry is 33. In India it is 22. In Japan it is 28.
8 In Sweden, approximately 55% of married couples have children. This is the highest figure in the world.

UNIT 4 PAGE 24 Vocabulary exercise 6
Quiz answers
1 athletics   climbing   cycling   gymnastics   ice skating   jogging   surfing   swimming   windsurfing
2 boxing   squash   table tennis   tennis
3 ice hockey   rugby   volleyball
4 ice hockey   ice skating   surfing   swimming   windsurfing
5 squash   tennis
6 ice hockey   table tennis   tennis   volleyball
7 d   rugby
8 a   Wimbledon = tennis
   b   Tour de France = cycling
   c   World Heavyweight Championships = boxing

UNIT 14 PAGE 82 Grammar exercise 4
Student A

1 Write sentences to describe each person, thing or place. Start each description with *someone*, *something* or *a place* and a relative clause.

Eddie Murphy
He's someone who acts in comedies. He's a black American actor. He's very funny. Who is he?

1 a sports centre   4 a goalkeeper
2 Kristen Stewart   5 a cinema
3 sunglasses   6 graffiti

2 Read Student B's sentences. Can you guess the people, things or places?

UNIT 15 PAGE 88 Grammar exercise 4
1 Most computers are made in China and Taiwan.
2 The most common type of program that people download is anti-virus software. This is software to check for computer viruses.
3 The most common passwords are often quite simple. Many people just use the word 'password' or the numbers '123456'.
4 Lady Gaga was the first person to get one billion hits on YouTube, but the most popular celebrity on search engines changes every year.
5 In the past, actors such as Johnny Depp, Daniel Radcliffe and the Bollywood actor Salman Khan have been the most searched-for actors, but these names will change each year.

UNIT 9 PAGE 54   Vocabulary exercise 4
Key for quiz

Mostly a) answers: You think very carefully about what you spend your money on and you probably find all the best offers. But are you too careful? Money isn't the most important thing in life!

Mostly b) answers: The way you think about money is probably just right. You don't waste it but you don't let it control your life.

Mostly c) answers: You need to start thinking about money or you're going to be short of cash your whole life! You don't *have to* spend everything you have. What about saving a bit?

UNIT 12 PAGE 70   Vocabulary exercise 2
The photos show feathers on a parrot and a frog's eye.

UNIT 12 PAGE 71   Speaking exercise 5
Take turns to describe the photo. Use phrases from the *Prepare* box on page 71.

UNIT 14 PAGE 82   Grammar exercise 4
Student B

1 Write sentences to describe each person, thing or place. Start each description with *someone*, *something* or *a place* and a relative clause.

Eddie Murphy
He's someone who acts in comedies. He's a black American actor. He's very funny. Who is he?

1 a mosquito
2 an expert
3 a novel
4 a boarding pass
5 Brad Pitt
6 Hollywood

2 Read Student A's sentences. Can you guess the people, things or places?

Word profiles

UNIT 1
WORD PROFILE: *right* /raɪt/

CORRECT	In his last test he got almost all the answers *right*.
SUITABLE	Are we going in the *right* direction?
EXACTLY	We live *right* in the centre of town.
DIRECTION	Go *right* at the crossroads.
right away	I'll phone him *right away*.
right now	I'm doing my homework *right now*.

1 Match the questions with the answers.
1. How did you do in the test?
2. Is snowboarding dangerous?
3. Oh, no! Where's my mobile?
4. Is the taxi arriving soon?
5. When are you going to phone your parents?
6. Where's the computer games shop?

a. Calm down! It's right next to you.
b. No, but you need to use the right equipment.
c. It's on the right, next to the library.
d. I only got three answers right!
e. Right away. They go to bed at ten thirty.
f. It's here right now. Come on!

2 In pairs, ask and answer the questions.

UNIT 2
WORD PROFILE: *kind* /kaɪnd/

HELPFUL	She's a very *kind* person.
TYPE	What *kinds* of films do you enjoy?
some kind of	We saw *some kind of* big fish in the sea.
that kind of thing	I collect concert tickets, posters, *that kind of thing*.
all kinds of	There are *all kinds of* jewellery for sale.

1 Match the questions and answers.
1. Can you describe the person you saw?
2. What do you usually do at the beach?
3. Did anyone help you when you fell off your bike?
4. What's the new café like?
5. Does your brother have the same kind of phone as you?

a. No, his is much better than mine!
b. Swim, play volleyball with my friends, that kind of thing.
c. He was in his 30s and he was wearing some kind of uniform.
d. Yes. A really kind woman picked up my things and checked I was OK.
e. Great! They have all kinds of cold drinks and it's not expensive.

UNIT 3
WORD PROFILE: *get* /get/

BECOME	I *get* quite nervous in exams.
OBTAIN	Did you *get* a good mark in the test?
ARRIVE	What time did you *get* here?
get in	I couldn't *get in* your room, it was so messy.
get on	Do you *get on* with your brother?

1 Answer the questions using *get* and the word in brackets. You may need to add some extra words.

0. Are you and your brother good friends?
   Yes, ..*we get on very well*.. (on)
1. Is that your dad's car?
   No, he .... eight o'clock. (home)
2. Ms Parks is going on holiday for two weeks.
   Yes, ... (married)
3. How is your cough?
   It .... (better)
4. Were you late this morning?
   Yes, I .... at 9.15. (school)

2 Answer the questions.
1. How do you get on with your family?
2. Who was the last person to get married in your family?
3. What time do your parents normally get home?
4. Do you want to get a degree?

UNIT 4
WORD PROFILE: *way* /weɪ/

METHOD	There are many *ways* of solving the problem.
ROUTE	Do you know the *way* to the train station?
DIRECTION	Turn your chair the other *way*.
DISTANCE	We walked a long *way* yesterday.
PERIOD OF TIME	The holidays are a long *way* away.
by the way	I know Diane. She's nice. *By the way*, when is the next bus into town?
either way	You can get the train or you can drive, but *either way* it takes about four hours.
no way	*No way*! You can't run 100 metres in 8 seconds!
way of life	Akiko told us about the Japanese *way of life*.

1 Choose the correct answers.

1 I got another letter from Tomasz. .... , can you speak Polish?
   a By the way **b** A long way **c** Either way

2 Email me or text, but .... , contact me later.
   a no way **b** a long way **c** either way

3 Is it .... from Tierra del Fuego to Buenos Aires?
   a way **b** a way of life **c** a long way

4 'I've got my own website.' 'Really? .... !'
   a Way **b** No way **c** By the way

5 Can you tell me the .... to the new stadium?
   a either way **b** way **c** by the way

2 Complete the sentences with *way* and any other words that are necessary.

1 Is it .... from Turkey to Spain?
2 Which .... are the tennis courts?
3 That isn't the best .... to win a game.
4 You can go left or right, ... the path goes past the hockey pitch.
5 .... ! I don't believe that!

UNIT 5
WORD PROFILE: *take* /teɪk/

NEEDS TIME	It *took* us hours to do the homework.
PERFORM ACTION	I *take* a shower every morning.
WRITE	I *took* notes during the talk.
WITHOUT PERMISSION	The thief *took* a laptop.
take a break	Can we *take a break*? I'm really tired.
take a look	*Take a look* at this picture and see if you recognise anyone.
take part	Over 30 different countries will *take part* in the next Olympics.
take place	The concert is *taking place* next Thursday.
take up	I *took up* the guitar when I was about 13.

1 Complete the second sentence so it means the same as the first sentence. Use the correct form of *take* and any other words that are necessary.

0 Come and see our project.
   Take a look at our project.

1 Mary left with my bag, but it was a mistake.
   Mary .... my bag, but it was a mistake.

2 I started doing gymnastics when I was four.
   I .... gymnastics when I was four.

3 We're entering a national sports competition.
   We .... in a national sports competition.

4 I spent an hour tidying my room.
   It .... to tidy my room.

5 Training happens every Thursday at the sports field.
   Training .... at the sports field.

6 Are you going to write anything?
   Are you going to .... ?

UNIT 6
WORD PROFILE: *light* /laɪt/

NOT HEAVY	Here, take this bag – it's quite *light*.
EQUIPMENT	Could you switch the *light* on, please?
BRIGHT	Our living room is the *lightest* room in the house.
BRIGHTNESS	There was hardly any *light* in the street.
NOT MUCH	It's only *light* rain, so you don't need an umbrella.
START FLAMES	We can't *light* the cooker.

1 Match the beginnings and ends of the sentences.
1 Do you know how to
2 I couldn't see because
3 We could hardly see the ball
4 Before our sports lesson
5 As soon as it was
6 Maggie needed help because

a light, we got dressed.
b in the bad light.
c light a barbecue?
d her bags weren't light.
e we did some light exercise to warm up.
f there weren't any lights.

2 Match the meanings of *light* in exercise 1 to the meanings in the *Word profile* box.

UNIT 7
WORD PROFILE: *like* /laɪk/

ENJOY	I *like* cooking.
SIMILAR	My parents aren't at all *like* my grandparents.
SUCH AS	I love team sports, *like* football!
What is sb/sth like?	I don't know *what she's like* but people say she's a good teacher.
it looks like	*It looks like* they had an argument.
likes and dislikes	We've got different *likes and dislikes*.

1 Rewrite the sentences using *like*.
0 They probably don't know the way home.
   It looks like they don't know the way home.
1 Do you enjoy studying?
2 I think it's going to rain later.
3 Tell me some of the things you enjoy and don't enjoy doing.
4 We watched a few cartoons, for example *The Simpsons*.
5 What kind of person is your maths teacher?
6 Is Italian similar to Spanish?

2 Answer the questions.
1 Who in your family are you most like?
2 What is your best friend like?
3 With food, what are your likes and dislikes?

UNIT 8
WORD PROFILE: *around* /əˈraʊnd/

APPROXIMATELY	It happened *around* two months ago.
IN PARTS OF A PLACE	I spent a year travelling *around* Australia.
IN A CIRCLE	We sat *around* a large table.
OPPOSITE DIRECTION	Sally turned *around* and smiled at me.

1 Finish the sentences so they mean the same, using a suitable verb and *around*.
1 Lisbon is a great city to explore on foot.
   Lisbon is a great city to ....
2 Ivan invited about 100 people to his party.
   There .... 100 people at Ivan's party.
3 Looking back, I noticed someone following me.
   I .... and saw that someone was following me.
4 Desmond's flat is near here, but I'm not sure exactly where.
   Desmond .... here, but I'm not sure exactly where his flat is.

2 Answer the questions using *around*.
1 How long is it until your birthday?
2 How much of your country have you visited?
3 How many students are at your school?

UNIT 9
WORD PROFILE: *change* /tʃeɪndʒ/

BECOME DIFFERENT	Our town has *changed* a lot in the last five years.
CLOTHES	Are you going to *change* into something smart for the concert?
JOURNEY	I had to *change* buses twice to get here.
MONEY	Remember to *change* some money into dollars at the airport.
IN SHOP	I decided to *change* those jeans for a different pair.
MONEY	The shop assistant gave me the wrong *change*.
DIFFERENCE	Let me know if there's any *change* to your flight time.
NEW EXPERIENCE	We saw a film in the history lesson, which made a nice *change*!

1 Complete the sentences with the correct form of the verb *change*.
1. I already had that album so I .... it for another one by the same band.
2. We're .... classrooms at school this week because ours needs painting!
3. My uncle has .... so much – he's cut his hair and he's slimmer, too.
4. Could you help me by .... this £20 note?
5. I think Mr Brown .... his tie every day – he seems to have lots of different ones!

2 Write the singular or plural of the noun *change* in the spaces.
1. You haven't given me enough .... – I need another 30 cents.
2. Mum and Dad have made a lot of .... to our living room.
3. It's great to see you smiling for a .... !

UNIT 10
WORD PROFILE: *really* /ˈriːəli/

VERY GREAT	This is *really* tasty. I *really* like it.
EMPHASISING	You *really* shouldn't eat that. It's not fresh.
FACT	I didn't *really* cook this. My dad made it.
Really?	'We're eating in ten minutes.' '*Really*? But it's early.'
not really	'Was the food good?' '*Not really*.'

1 Match the pairs of sentences.
1. Why are you leaving now?
2. Was Simon's curry good?
3. I like Jenny.
4. Did you finish the homework?
5. Are you really going to become a vegetarian?

a. Really? I thought you two didn't get on.
b. Yes, I am. It's much healthier.
c. No, it was really difficult.
d. Not really. But I ate it!
e. I really must get home before 11pm.

2 Match the meanings of *really* in exercise 1 to the meanings in the *Word profile* box.

UNIT 11
WORD PROFILE: *for* /fɔː/

TIME	My Dad's working in Canada *for* two months.
MEANING	What's the Spanish word *for* 'sleep'?
for ever	I'd like this summer to last *for ever*!
for fun	We dressed up as animals, just *for fun*!
for instance	Try to get fit – *for instance*, join a gym or go jogging.
for sale	How many of these paintings are *for sale*?
for sure	I don't know *for sure*, but I think he's from Ecuador.

1 Complete the sentences with a phrase from the *Word profile* box.
1. You can use chillies in so many dishes – .... , in curries or on pizzas.
2. One thing's .... – we need to spend longer on our homework!
3. Everything on this table is .... at £1 or less.
4. Have you ever done something really silly, just .... ?
5. I thought our cat Ossie would live .... , but I was wrong.

2 Answer the questions.
1. How many years have you been at this school?
2. What's the word for 'dragon' in your language?
3. What do you do for fun at the weekends?

UNIT 12
WORD PROFILE: *still* /stɪl/

CONTINUING	I've had dinner, but I'm *still* hungry.
DESPITE	It might be a small insect, but it's *still* an animal.
NOT MOVING	The giraffe stayed very *still*.
DRINK	I prefer *still* water to sparkling.

1 Read the sentences. Match them to the meanings of *still* in the *Word profile* box.
1 They still don't know about every animal on Earth.
2 Elephants haven't got good eyes, but they can still communicate over long distances.
3 Butterflies are never completely still.
4 We'd like still water, please.
5 I think that's right but I still want to check.

2 Look at the *Word profile* box again and notice the position of *still*. Add *still* to each sentence.
1 There are 1,500 wild tigers in India.
2 They haven't found any new species.
3 Bears often sit for a long time.
4 The scientists need more money.
5 This is water. I asked for sparkling water!
6 I only got 60%, but I passed.

UNIT 13
WORD PROFILE: *time* /taɪm/

AVAILABLE OR NEEDED	Have you got *time* to help me?
WHEN SOMETHING HAPPENS	It's *time* for bed.
OCCASION	Every *time* I ask you to help me, you're too busy.
PERIOD	What do you do in your free *time*?
at the same time	We left the party *at the same time*.
in time	We didn't arrive *in time* and missed the train.
on time	Sorry but I won't be here *on time* tomorrow.

1 Finish the sentence for these times in your day.

7.00 am   12.30 pm   3.30 pm   7.30 pm

It's time ...
7.00 am. It's time to get up.

2 Answer the questions.
1 What things don't you have enough time to do?
2 When was the last time you were ill?
3 Do you always arrive on time for school?
4 The last time you ran for a bus, did you get there in time?

UNIT 14
WORD PROFILE: *hope* /həʊp/

WANT TO HAPPEN	I *hope* this film is good.
hope to do sth	We *hope* to go to the cinema this weekend.
POSITIVE FEELING	The main character said, 'You must have *hope*.'
hopeful	We're *hopeful* this novel will be interesting.
hopeless	She felt *hopeless* about the future.
hopefully	*Hopefully*, the cinema won't be full.

1 Complete the sentences with the correct word from the word family of *hope*.
1 .... , we can borrow some more DVDs.
2 I .... my sister remembers to collect my library books.
3 It's .... My grandma will never understand how to use a mobile phone!
4 She .... to meet Ed Sheeran one day.
5 I might not find your comics, but I feel quite .... they're still under my bed.
6 You'll become an actor one day! You mustn't lose ....

2 Answer the questions.
1 What do you hope to do next summer?
2 Are you hopeful about passing your exams?
3 Where do you hope to travel to one day?
4 What are your hopes for the future?

UNIT 15
WORD PROFILE: *turn* /tɜːn/

TIME	It's your turn to do the washing up tonight.
PAGE	Turn to page 45.
CHANGE DIRECTION	Turn left after the cinema.
turn off/on	Can you turn on the light, please?
turn up/down	Turn the sound up. I like this song!

1 Match the beginnings and ends of the sentences.
1 If you need to check the irregular verb list,
2 To get to the sports centre
3 Please don't turn
4 I think it's Mike's turn
5 Unless you turn that computer off right now,

a I'll take it away.
b turn to page 130.
c to have a go.
d turn left at the small shop and go straight on.
e up the TV while I'm on my phone.

2 Match the meanings of *turn* in exercise 1 to the meanings in the *Word profile* box.

UNIT 16
WORD PROFILE: *luck* /lʌk/

luck	Do you believe in luck?
lucky	For Russians, a grey cat is lucky.
unlucky	It's unlucky to walk under a ladder.
luckily	Luckily, I found my mobile again.

1 Look at the *Word profile* box and read the example sentences. Then match the definitions to the uses in the *Word profile* box.
1 good and bad things that result from chance
2 having or causing good luck
3 having or causing bad luck
4 in a lucky way

2 Complete the sentences with the correct word from the word family of *luck*.
1 We went cycling but it didn't rain, ...
2 'I'm going on holiday.' 'You're so .... !'
3 They played well and they were .... to lose.
4 Some people think it's .... to walk under ladders.
5 I've got an exam tomorrow. Wish me .... !

UNIT 17
WORD PROFILE: *own* /əʊn/

BELONGING	Each student has their own dictionary.
HAVE AS A POSSESSION	The film script is owned by the production company.
of your own	I'll have a home of my own someday.
(all) on your own	I like living on my own.
(all) on your own	He performed 21 songs all on his own.

1 Match the definition with the examples in the *Word profile* box.
1 to have something that legally belongs to you
2 without any help
3 alone
4 belonging to someone or something
5 belonging to or done by a particular person or thing

2 Answer the questions.
1 When do you like to be on your own?
2 What can you do on your own now that you needed help with five years ago?
3 When do you think you'll have a home of your own?
4 What's the most valuable thing you own?
5 When will you have your own car?

UNIT 18
WORD PROFILE: *go* /gəʊ/

MOVE / TRAVEL	Are you going by train?
DISAPPEAR	When I got back, my bag had gone.
go blind/grey, etc.	Our dog's 14 and he's going blind.
have a go	I'd love to have a go at snowboarding.
go away	Just go away and leave me alone.
go away	We're going away in the summer.
go on	The party went on until midnight.

127

1 Complete the second sentence so it means the same as the first sentence. Use the correct form of *go* and any other words that are necessary.

0 Matt's dad is losing his hair.
   Matt's dad *is going bald.*
1 I've already had a holiday this year.
   I've already .... this year.
2 Please can I try your new bike?
   Please can I .... on your bike?
3 There's something strange happening here.
   Something strange .... on here.
4 I turned round but he wasn't there.
   I turned round but he ....
5 The party finished at midnight.
   The party .... until midnight.
6 Leave me alone! .... !

UNIT 19
WORD PROFILE: *mean* /miːn/

MEANING	The red light means stop.
EXPRESS	Now I know what you mean when you say this island is beautiful.
HAVE IMPORTANCE	Money means nothing to him.
INTEND	Sorry, I didn't mean to interrupt.
HAVE RESULT	Sunny weather means we can go to the beach.
I mean	We went there in May – I mean in June.

1 Complete the sentences with the correct form of *mean*.

0 I cycle to school so I get there quickly.
   Cycling to school *means I get there quickly.*
1 I don't understand this.
   What .... ?
2 I lost my wallet by accident.
   .... to lose my wallet.
3 Did you intend to give me these books?
   .... these books?
4 I bought a car magazine. Oh, no, it was a cycling magazine.
   I bought a car magazine – I ....
5 I'm sorry if I annoyed you.
   .... to annoy you.
6 I speak English, so I can understand my favourite pop songs.
   Speaking English ....

UNIT 20
WORD PROFILE: *mind* /maɪnd/

POLITE REQUEST	Would you mind if I had some more cake? Would you mind turning your music down?
ABILITY TO THINK	Dan is really clever. He's got a quick mind.
BE CAREFUL	Mind out! That plate is hot.
BE ANNOYED	You don't need to hurry. I don't mind waiting.
change your mind	If you change your mind, call me soon.
make up your mind	'Do you want pizza or salad?' 'I haven't made up my mind yet.'

1 Match the beginnings and ends of the sentences.

1 Carly won't mind taking
2 Would you mind
3 Mind
4 I couldn't make
5 Simon made me change
6 He's got an amazing

a up my mind so I didn't buy anything.
b mind for someone his age, hasn't he?
c if I phoned you later?
d my mind about going out.
e out! There's a car coming.
f out the rubbish.

2 Answer the questions.

1 Do you mind if friends borrow things from you?
2 How good are you at making up your mind?
3 What's the first thing that comes into your mind on Saturday mornings?
4 Do you change your mind a lot?

EP Vocabulary list

adj = adjective   adv = adverb   n = noun   v = verb
pv = phrasal verb   prep = preposition   phr = phrase

UNIT 1

attractive /əˈtræktɪv/ *adj* BEAUTIFUL beautiful or pleasant to look at

bald /bɔːld/ *adj* with little or no hair on the head

careful /ˈkeəfəl/ *adj* giving a lot of attention to what you are doing so that you do not have an accident, make a mistake, or damage something

careless /ˈkeələs/ *adj* not giving enough attention to what you are doing

cheerful /ˈtʃɪəfəl/ *adj* HAPPY happy and positive

confident /ˈkɒnfɪdənt/ *adj* ABILITY certain about your ability to do things well

curly /ˈkɜːli/ *adj* shaped like a curl, or with many curls

dark /dɑːk/ *adj* NOT PALE nearer to black than white in colour

fair /feə/ *adj* HAIR/SKIN having pale skin or a light colour of hair

friendly /ˈfrendli/ *adj* behaving in a pleasant, kind way towards someone

funny /ˈfʌni/ *adj* MAKING YOU LAUGH making you smile or laugh

good-looking /ɡʊdˈlʊkɪŋ/ *adj* If someone is good-looking, they have an attractive face.

(be) in your twenties /ɪn jɔː ˈtwentiz/ *phr* to be aged between 20 and 29

miserable /ˈmɪzərəbl/ *adj* UNHAPPY sad

polite /pəˈlaɪt/ *adj* behaving in a way that is not rude and shows that you do not only think about yourself

rude /ruːd/ *adj* NOT POLITE behaving in a way which is not polite and upsets other people

serious /ˈsɪəriəs/ *adj* PERSON A serious person does not laugh often.

shy /ʃaɪ/ *adj* not confident, especially about meeting or talking to new people

straight /streɪt/ *adj* HAIR not curly

teenage /ˈtiːneɪdʒ/ *adj* aged between 13 and 19 years old

unfriendly /ʌnˈfrendli/ *adj* not friendly

UNIT 2

badly-dressed /bædliˈdrest/ *adj* wearing clothes that are not attractive or are of poor quality

boot /buːt/ *n* SHOE a strong shoe that covers your foot and part of your leg

brand new /brænd njuː/ *adj* completely new

cap /kæp/ *n* a hat with a curved part at the front

casual /ˈkæʒjuəl/ *adj* CLOTHES Casual clothes are comfortable but not smart and not suitable for formal occasions.

comfortable /ˈkʌmftəbl/ *adj* CLOTHES describes clothes, shoes, etc. that provide a pleasant feeling and that do not give you any pain

fashionable /ˈfæʃənəbl/ *adj* popular at a particular time

hard /hɑːd/ *adv* USING EFFORT with a lot of physical or mental effort

jacket /ˈdʒækɪt/ *n* a short coat

jumper /ˈdʒʌmpə/ *n* a piece of clothing usually made of wool which covers the top of your body and is pulled on over your head

loose /luːs/ *adj* NOT TIGHT not fitting closely to the body

narrow /ˈnærəʊ/ *adj* SMALL WIDTH having a small distance from one side to the other, especially in comparison with the length

necklace /ˈnekləs/ *n* a piece of jewellery that you wear around your neck

pocket /ˈpɒkɪt/ *n* IN CLOTHING a small bag for carrying things in, which forms part of a piece of clothing

raincoat /ˈreɪŋkəʊt/ *n* a coat that you wear when it is raining

sandal /ˈsændəl/ *n* a light shoe with straps that you wear in warm weather

second-hand /sekəndˈhænd/ *adj* If something is second-hand, someone else owned or used it before you.

smart /smɑːt/ *adj* STYLISH having a clean, tidy and stylish appearance

suit /suːt/ *n* a jacket and trousers or a jacket and skirt that are made from the same material

sunglasses /ˈsʌŋɡlɑːsɪz/ *n* dark glasses that you wear to protect your eyes from the sun

sweatshirt /ˈswetʃɜːt/ *n* a piece of clothing made of soft cotton which covers the top of your body and is pulled on over your head

tie /taɪ/ *n* CLOTHES a long, thin piece of cloth that a man wears around his neck with a shirt

tight /taɪt/ *adj* CLOTHES fitting your body very closely

tights /taɪts/ *n pl* a piece of women's clothing made of very thin material that covers the legs and bottom

top /tɒp/ *n* CLOTHES a piece of light clothing worn on the upper part of the body

tracksuit /ˈtræksuːt/ *n* loose, comfortable trousers and a top, especially worn for exercising

trainer /ˈtreɪnə/ *n* SHOE a type of light comfortable shoe that is suitable for playing sport

uncomfortable /ʌnˈkʌmftəbl/ *adj* NOT COMFORTABLE not feeling comfortable and pleasant, or not making you feel comfortable and pleasant

unfashionable /ʌnˈfæʃənəbl/ *adj* not fashionable or popular at a particular time

well-dressed /welˈdrest/ *adj* wearing clothes that are attractive, good-quality clothes

wide /waɪd/ *adj* DISTANCE having a large distance from one side to the other

UNIT 3

be born /bi: bɔːn/ *v* When a person or animal is born, they come out of their mother's body and start to exist.

have children /hæv ˈtʃɪldrən/ *n* to give birth to children

get a degree /get ə dɪˈgriː/ *phr* QUALIFICATION get a qualification given for completing a university course

get a driving licence /get ə ˈdraɪvɪŋ laɪsənts/ *phr* get a document which gives official permission to drive a car, received after passing a driving test

get a job /get ə dʒɒb/ *phr* to find regular work in order to earn money

get married /get ˈmærɪd/ *v* to begin a legal relationship with someone as their husband or wife

go to university /gəʊ tə juːnɪˈvɜːsɪti/ *phr* to go regularly to a place where students study at a high level to get a degree

leave home /liːv həʊm/ *phr* to stop living with your parents

leave school /liːv skuːl/ *phr* to stop going to school for ever

start school /stɑːt skuːl/ *phr* to begin going to school

UNIT 4

athletics /æθˈletɪks/ *n* the sports which include running, jumping and throwing

boxing /ˈbɒksɪŋ/ *n* a sport in which two competitors fight by hitting each other with their hands

climbing /ˈklaɪmɪŋ/ *n* the sport of climbing mountains, hills or rocks

coach /kəʊtʃ/ *n* VEHICLE a comfortable bus used to take groups of people on journeys

coach /kəʊtʃ/ *n* PERSON someone whose job is to teach people to improve at a sport, skill, or school subject

cycling /ˈsaɪklɪŋ/ *n* the sport or activity of riding a bicycle

fit /fɪt/ *adj* healthy and strong, especially as a result of exercise

fit /fɪt/ *v* CORRECT SIZE to be the right size or shape for someone or something

gymnastics /dʒɪmˈnæstɪks/ *n* a sport in which you do physical exercises on the floor and on different pieces of equipment, often in competitions

ice hockey /ˈaɪs hɒki/ *n* a sport played on ice in which two teams try to hit a small hard object into a goal using long curved sticks

ice skating /ˈaɪs skeɪtɪŋ/ *n* the activity or sport of moving across ice using ice skates

jogging /ˈdʒɒgɪŋ/ *n* running slowly for exercise

match /mætʃ/ *v* BE THE SAME If two things match, they are the same colour or type.

match /mætʃ/ *n* COMPETITION a sports competition in which two people or teams compete against each other

point /pɔɪnt/ *v* SHOW to show where someone or something is by holding your finger or a thin object towards it

point /pɔɪnt/ *n* SPORT a unit used for showing who is winning in a game or competition

rugby /ˈrʌgbi/ *n* a sport played by two teams with an oval ball and H-shaped goals

squash /skwɒʃ/ *n* a sport in which two people hit a small rubber ball against the four walls of a room

surfing /ˈsɜːfɪŋ/ *n* the sport of riding on a wave on a special board

swimming /ˈswɪmɪŋ/ *n* the activity of moving through water by moving your body

table tennis /ˈteɪbl tenɪs/ *n* a sport in which two or four people hit a small ball over a low net on a large table

tennis /ˈtenɪs/ *n* a sport in which two or four people hit a small ball to each other over a net

trainer /ˈtreɪnə/ *n* SHOE a type of light comfortable shoe that is suitable for playing sport

trainer /ˈtreɪnə/ *n* PERSON a person who teaches skills to people or animals and prepares them for a job, activity or sport

volleyball /ˈvɒlibɔːl/ *n* a sport in which two teams use their hands to hit a ball over a net without allowing it to touch the ground

windsurfing /ˈwɪndsɜːfɪŋ/ *n* a sport in which you sail across water by standing on a board and holding onto a large sail

UNIT 5

catch /kætʃ/ *v* TAKE HOLD to take hold of something, especially something which is moving through the air

clap /klæp/ *v* to hit your hands together, often repeatedly, especially in order to show you enjoyed a performance

drop /drɒp/ *v* FALL to fall or to allow something to fall

fight /faɪt/ *v* USE FORCE to use physical force to try to defeat another person or group of people

hit /hɪt/ *v* WITH HAND/OBJECT to touch someone or something quickly and with force using your hand or an object in your hand

hold /həʊld/ *v* IN HAND to have something in your hand or arms

make a face /meɪk ə feɪs/ *phr* to make a strange or silly expression with your face or to show with your face that you do not like someone or something

point /pɔɪnt/ *v* SHOW to show where someone or something is by holding your finger or a thin object towards it

shake hands /ʃeɪk hændz/ *phr* to hold someone's hand and move it up and down when you meet them for the first time, or when you make an agreement with them

throw /θrəʊ/ *v* IN AIR to make something move through the air by pushing it out of your hand

wave /weɪv/ *v* HAND to raise your hand and move it from side to side in order to attract someone's attention or to say hello or goodbye

UNIT 6

apartment block /əˈpɑːtmənt blɒk/ *n* a large building containing many apartments

bin /bɪn/ *n* a container for waste

bridge /brɪdʒ/ *n* a structure that is built over a river, road, railway, etc. to allow people and vehicles to cross from one side to the other

bus stop /ˈbʌs stɒp/ *n* a place where a bus stops to allow passengers to get on and off

car park /ˈkɑː pɑːk/ *n* an area of ground for parking cars

crowd /kraʊd/ *n* a large group of people who have come together

department store /dɪˈpɑːtmənt stɔː/ *n* a large shop divided into several different parts, each of which sells different things

fountain /faʊntɪn/ *n* a structure that forces water up into the air as a decoration

graffiti /grəˈfiːti/ *n* words or drawings, especially humorous, rude, or political, on walls, doors, etc. in public places

(the) ground floor /graʊnd flɔː/ *n* the floor of a building that is at the same level as the ground outside

park /pɑːk/ *n* a large area of grass and trees in a city or town, where people can walk and enjoy themselves

pedestrian crossing /pəˈdestriːən ˈkrɒsɪŋ/ *n* a place where people can go across a road

pollution /pəˈluːʃən/ *n* damage caused to water, air, etc. by harmful substances or waste

post box /ˈpəʊst bɒks/ *n* a large, metal container in a public place where you can post letters

public transport /pʌblɪk ˈtrænspɔːt/ *n* a system of vehicles such as buses and trains which operate at regular times on fixed routes and are used by the public

recycling bin /riːˈsaɪklɪŋ bɪn/ *n* a container for paper, glass, plastic, etc. that is going to be put through a process so that it can be used again

road sign /ˈrəʊd saɪn/ *n* a notice at the side of a road which gives information, directions, a warning, etc.

rubbish /ˈrʌbɪʃ/ *n* WASTE things that you throw away because you do not want them

speed limit /ˈspiːd lɪmɪt/ *n* the fastest speed that a car is allowed to travel on a particular road

street light /ˈstriːt laɪt/ *n* a light in or at the side of a road or public area that is usually supported on a tall post

street market /ˈstriːt mɑːkɪt/ *n* SELLING PLACE a place outside in the streets of a town or city where people go to buy or sell things

tourist information /ˈtʊərɪst ɪnfəˈmeɪʃən/ *n* information for people who are visiting an area for pleasure or interest

traffic jam /ˈtræfɪk dʒæm/ *n* TRAFFIC a line of cars, trucks, etc. that are moving slowly or not moving

traffic lights /ˈtræfɪk laɪts/ *n* a set of red, green and yellow lights that is used to stop and start traffic

UNIT 7

be on your own /biː ɒn jər əʊn/ *phr* to be alone

be wrong /biː rɒŋ/ *phr* If something is wrong, there is a problem.

do sb a favour /duː ə ˈfeɪvə/ *phr* to do something to help someone

fall out /fɔːl ˈaʊt/ *pv* to argue with someone and stop being friendly with them

get on /get ˈɒn/ *pv* RELATIONSHIP to have a good relationship

get together /get təˈgeðə/ *pv* to meet in order to do something or spend time together

hang out /hæŋ ˈaʊt/ *pv* to spend a lot of time in a place or with someone

have an argument /hæv ən ˈɑːgjuːmənt/ *phr* to have an angry discussion with someone in which you both disagree

have some fun /hæv səm fʌn/ *phr* to do something that gives you enjoyment or pleasure

have sth in common /hæv ɪn ˈkɒmən/ *phr* to share interests, experiences or other characteristics with someone

It isn't my fault /ɪt ɪznt maɪ fɒlt/ *phr* I am not responsible for what has happened.

make friends /meɪk frendz/ *phr* to meet new people and begin to know and like them

UNIT 8

backpack /ˈbækpæk/ *n* a bag that you carry on your back

baggage hall /ˈbægɪdʒ hɔːl/ *n* the place at an airport where passengers collect their luggage after their flight

boarding pass /ˈbɔːdɪŋ pɑːs/ *n* a card or document that a passenger must have in order to be allowed to get on an aircraft or ship

check-in (desk) /ˈtʃekɪn/ *n* the place at an airport where you show your ticket so that you can be told where you will be sitting

check in /tʃek ˈɪn/ *pv* AIRPORT to go to the desk at an airport, so that you can be told where you will be sitting and so that your bags can be put on the aircraft

check in /tʃek ˈɪn/ *pv* HOTEL to say who you are when you arrive at a hotel so that you can be given a key for your room

customs /ˈkʌstəmz/ *n* the place where your bags are examined when you are going into a country, to make sure you are not carrying anything illegal

departure gate /dɪˈpɑːtʃə geɪt/ *n* the part of an airport where passengers wait and then get on a particular aircraft

get back /get ˈbæk/ *pv* to return to a place after you have been somewhere else

go away /gəʊ əˈweɪ/ *pv* HOLIDAY to leave your home in order to spend time in a different place

passport /ˈpɑːspɔːt/ *n* TRAVEL an official document, often a small book, that you need to enter or leave a country

passport control /ˈpɑːspɔːt kənˈtrəʊl/ *n* the place at an airport, port, or border of a country where an official checks your passport

queue /kjuː/ *n* PEOPLE WAITING a group of people standing one behind the other who are waiting for something

security check /sɪˈkjʊərɪti tʃek/ *n* an examination before passengers get on a plane to make sure they are not carrying anything that is dangerous

set off /set ˈɒf/ *pv* to start a journey

sign /saɪn/ *n* NOTICE a symbol or message in a public place which gives information or instructions

take off /teɪk ˈɒf/ *pv* FLY If an aircraft takes off, it leaves the ground and begins to fly.

ticket /ˈtɪkɪt/ *n* a small piece of paper that shows you have paid to do something, for example travel on a bus, watch a film, etc.

UNIT 9

bank account /ˈbæŋk əkaʊnt/ *n* an arrangement with a bank to keep your money there and to allow you to take it out when you need to

change /tʃeɪndʒ/ *n* MONEY the money which is returned to someone who has paid for something which costs less than the amount that they gave

checkout /ˈtʃekaʊt/ *n* SHOP the place in a shop, especially a large food shop, where you pay for your goods

give sth away /gɪv əˈweɪ/ *pv* FREE to give something to someone without asking for payment

price /praɪs/ *n* COST the amount of money that you have to pay to buy something

receipt /rɪˈsiːt/ *n* PIECE OF PAPER a piece of paper that proves that you have received goods or money

save up /seɪv ˈʌp/ *pv* MONEY to keep money so that you can buy something with it in the future

special offer /ˈspeʃəl ˈɒfə/ *phr* If goods in a shop are a special offer, they are being sold at a lower price than usual.

take sth back /teɪk ˈbæk/ *pv* SOMETHING BOUGHT to return something you have bought to a shop

UNIT 10

bitter /ˈbɪtə/ *adj* TASTE with an unpleasantly sharp taste

delicious /dɪˈlɪʃəs/ *adj* having a very pleasant taste or smell

disgusting /dɪsˈgʌstɪŋ/ *adj* extremely unpleasant or unacceptable

fresh /freʃ/ *adj* NOT OLD Fresh food has been produced or collected recently and has not been frozen, dried, etc.

frozen /ˈfrəʊzən/ *adj* FOOD Frozen food has been made so that it will last a long time by freezing.

horrible /ˈhɒrɪbl/ *adj* very unpleasant or bad

juicy /ˈdʒuːsi/ *adj* WITH JUICE full of juice

look (nice/strange, etc.) /lʊk/ *v* used to describe the appearance of a person or thing

raw /rɔː/ *adj* NOT COOKED not cooked

smell (lovely/horrible, etc.) /smel/ *v* to have a particular quality that people notice by using their nose

sour /saʊə/ *adj* having a sharp, sometimes unpleasant, taste or smell, like a lemon, and not sweet

spicy /ˈspaɪsi/ *adj* containing strong flavours from spices

sweet /swiːt/ *adj* TASTE with a taste like sugar

taste (good/sweet, etc.) /teɪst/ *v* to have a particular flavour

tasty /ˈteɪsti/ *adj* Food which is tasty has a good flavour and is nice to eat.

UNIT 11

ache /eɪk/ *n* a feeling of pain over an area of your body which continues for a long time

ankle /ˈæŋkl/ *n* the joint between the foot and the leg, or the thin part of the leg just above the foot

break your arm/leg, etc. /breɪk/ *v* DAMAGE to damage a bone in your arm/leg, etc.

broken arm/leg, etc. /ˈbrəʊkən/ *adj* DAMAGED an arm/leg, etc. with a damaged bone

catch /kætʃ/ *v* ILLNESS to get an illness, especially one caused by bacteria or a virus

chin /tʃɪn/ *n* the bottom part of a person's face, below their mouth

cold /kəʊld/ *n* ILLNESS a common illness which makes you sneeze and makes your nose produce liquid

cough /kɒf/ *n* when you cough or an illness that makes you cough (force air out of your lungs through your throat with a short, loud sound)

cut /kʌt/ *n* INJURY an injury made when the skin is cut with something sharp

cut /kʌt/ *v* INJURE to injure yourself on a sharp object which makes you bleed

earache /ˈɪəreɪk/ *n* pain in your ear

elbow /ˈelbəʊ/ *n* the part in the middle of your arm where it bends

feel better /fiːl ˈbetə/ *phr* to feel less ill than before

feel sick /fiːl sɪk/ *phr* If you feel sick, you think the food or liquid in your stomach is going to come up and out of your mouth.

fever /ˈfiːvə/ *n* ILLNESS when someone's body temperature rises because they are ill

finger /ˈfɪŋɡə/ *n* ON HAND one of the long thin separate parts of the hand, including your thumb

flu /fluː/ *n* an infectious illness which is like a very bad cold, but which causes a fever

forehead /ˈfɒrɪd/ /ˈfɔːhed/ *n* the flat part of the face, above the eyes and below the hair

get (flu, etc.) /ɡet/ *v* to become ill or develop an illness

get better /ɡet ˈbetə/ *phr* to feel well again

have /hæv/ *v* BE ILL If you have a particular illness, you suffer from it.

headache /ˈhedeɪk/ *n* a pain you feel inside your head

hurt /hɜːt/ *v* BE PAINFUL If a part of your body hurts, it feels painful.

hurt /hɜːt/ *v* CAUSE PAIN to cause pain to someone or something

injure /ˈɪndʒə/ *v* to hurt a person, animal or part of your body

knee /niː/ *n* the middle part of your leg where it bends

shoulder /ˈʃəʊldə/ *n* BODY one of the two parts of your body where your arms join your neck

sore /sɔː/ *adj* PAINFUL painful, especially when touched

stomach ache /ˈstʌmək eɪk/ *n* pain in your stomach

throat /θrəʊt/ *n* the front of the neck, or the space inside the neck down which food and air can go

thumb /θʌm/ *n* the short thick finger on the side of your hand which makes it possible to hold and pick things up easily

toe /təʊ/ *n* ON FOOT one of the five separate parts at the end of your foot

toothache /ˈtuːθeɪk/ *n* pain in one or more of your teeth

UNIT 12

ant /ænt/ *n* a small, black or red insect that lives in groups on the ground

bat /bæt/ *n* ANIMAL a small animal like a mouse with wings that flies at night

bear /beə/ *n* a large, strong, wild animal with thick fur

bee /biː/ *n* a yellow and black flying insect which makes honey and can sting you

butterfly /ˈbʌtəflaɪ/ *n* an insect with large, patterned wings

camel /ˈkæməl/ *n* a large animal that lives in the desert and has one or two raised parts on its back

definitely /ˈdefɪnətli/ *adv* without any doubt

definitely not /ˈdefɪnətli nɒt/ *adv* used to emphasise that there is no doubt that something is not true or will not happen

dolphin /ˈdɒlfɪn/ *n* an intelligent animal that lives in the sea, breathes air and looks like a large, smooth, grey fish

donkey /ˈdɒŋki/ *n* an animal like a small horse with long ears

fly /flaɪ/ *n* a small insect with two wings

frog /frɒɡ/ *n* a small, green animal with long back legs for jumping that lives in or near water

giraffe /dʒɪˈrɑːf/ *n* a large African animal with a very long neck and long legs

kangaroo /kæŋɡəˈruː/ *n* a large Australian animal that moves by jumping on its back legs

mosquito /məˈskiːtəʊ/ *n* a small flying insect that sucks your blood, sometimes causing malaria

parrot /ˈpærət/ *n* a tropical bird with a curved beak and colourful feathers that can be taught to copy what people say

penguin /ˈpeŋɡwɪn/ *n* a large, black and white sea bird that swims and cannot fly

perhaps /pəˈhæps/ *adv* used to show that something is possible or that you are not certain about something

probably /ˈprɒbəbli/ *adv* used to mean that something is very likely

rat /ræt/ *n* an animal that looks like a large mouse and has a long tail

shark /ʃɑːk/ *n* a large fish with very sharp teeth

snake /sneɪk/ *n* a long, thin creature with no legs that slides along the ground

tiger /ˈtaɪɡə/ *n* a large wild cat that has yellow fur with black lines on it

whale /weɪl/ *n* a very large sea mammal that breathes air through a hole at the top of its head

UNIT 13

annoying /əˈnɔɪɪŋ/ adj making you feel a little angry

confused /kənˈfjuːzd/ adj NOT UNDERSTAND unable to think clearly or to understand something

confusing /kənˈfjuːzɪŋ/ adj difficult to understand

creative /kriˈeɪtɪv/ adj producing or using original and unusual ideas

disappointed /dɪsəˈpɔɪntɪd/ adj unhappy because something was not as good as you hoped or expected, or because something did not happen

disappointing /dɪsəˈpɔɪntɪŋ/ adj making you feel disappointed

embarrassed /ɪmˈbærəst/ adj feeling ashamed or shy

exhausted /ɪɡˈzɔːstɪd/ adj extremely tired

helpful /ˈhelpfəl/ adj willing to help, or useful

hopeful /ˈhəʊpfəl/ adj FEELING POSITIVE feeling positive about a future event or situation

lazy /ˈleɪzi/ adj PERSON Someone who is being lazy does not want to do any work or use any effort.

lonely /ˈləʊnli/ adj PERSON unhappy because you are not with other people

proud /praʊd/ adj PLEASED feeling very pleased about something you have done, something you own, or someone you know

relaxed /rɪˈlækst/ adj PERSON feeling happy and calm because nothing is worrying you

shocking /ˈʃɒkɪŋ/ adj making you feel surprised and upset

stressed /strest/ adj worried and not able to relax

surprised /səˈpraɪzd/ adj feeling surprise because something has happened that you did not expect

surprising /səˈpraɪzɪŋ/ adj not expected and making someone feel surprised

tiring /ˈtaɪrɪŋ/ adj making you feel tired

UNIT 14

accept /əkˈsept/ v AGREE TO TAKE to agree to take something that is offered to you

action film /ˈækʃən fɪlm/ n a film with an exciting story and which often has good special effects

advice /ədˈvaɪs/ n suggestions about what you think someone should do or how they should do something

advise /ədˈvaɪz/ v to make a suggestion about what you think someone should do or how they should do something

animated film /ˈænɪmeɪtɪd fɪlm/ n An animated film is one in which drawings and models seem to move.

bookshop /ˈbʊkʃɒp/ n a shop where books are sold

borrow /ˈbɒrəʊ/ v GET to get or receive something from someone with the intention of giving it back after a period of time

chat show /ˈtʃæt ʃəʊ/ n a television or radio programme where people are asked questions about themselves

comedy /ˈkɒmədi/ n a film, play, etc. which is funny

documentary /ˌdɒkjʊˈmentəri/ n a film, television or radio programme that gives facts and information about a subject

except /ɪkˈsept/ prep NOT INCLUDING not including a particular fact, thing or person

historical drama /hɪˈstɒrɪkəl ˈdrɑːmə/ n a film or play about events in the past

history /ˈhɪstəri/ n SUBJECT the study of events in the past

horror film/story /ˈhɒrə fɪlm/ /ˈhɒrə ˈstɔːri/ n a film or story that entertains people by shocking or frightening them

lend /lend/ v GIVE to give something to someone for a short period of time, expecting it to be given back

library /ˈlaɪbrəri/ n a room or building that contains a collection of books and other written material that you can read or borrow

loose /luːs/ adj CLOTHES not fitting closely to the body

lose /luːz/ v NOT FIND to not be able to find someone or something

love film/story /lʌv fɪlm/ n a film or story about two people who fall in love

murder mystery /ˈmɜːdə ˈmɪstəri/ n a film or story about detectives trying to find out who killed someone

notice /ˈnəʊtɪs/ v to see something and be aware of it

passed /pɑːst/ v GIVE past tense of pass, meaning gave something to someone by hand

past /pɑːst/ adj UNTIL NOW used to refer to a period of time before and until the present

realise /ˈrɪəlaɪz/ v BECOME AWARE to understand a situation, sometimes suddenly

remember (to do sth) /rɪˈmembə/ v to not forget to do something

remind /rɪˈmaɪnd/ v to make someone remember something, or remember to do something

science fiction film/story /ˌsaɪəns ˈfɪkʃən fɪlm/ n a film or story about life in the future or in other parts of the universe

sensible /ˈsensɪbl/ adj showing good judgment

sensitive /ˈsensɪtɪv/ adj UPSET easily upset by the things people say or do

soap opera /ˈsəʊp ɒpərə/ n TELEVISION PROGRAMME a series of television or radio programmes that continues over a long period and is about the lives of a group of characters

story /ˈstɔːri/ n a description, either true or imagined, of a series of events

thriller /ˈθrɪlə/ n a book or film with an exciting story, often about crime

weather /ˈweðə/ n WIND, RAIN, ETC. the conditions in the air above the Earth such as wind, rain or temperature, especially at a particular time over a particular area

whether /ˈweðə/ conj IF used especially in reporting questions and when expressing doubt to mean if

UNIT 15

app /æp/ *n* abbreviation for application: a computer program that is designed for a particular purpose

delete /dɪˈliːt/ *v* to remove something, especially from a computer's memory

do a search (for) /duː ə sɜːtʃ/ *phr* USE COMPUTER to use a computer to find information, especially on the Internet

download /daʊnˈləʊd/ *v* to copy computer programs, music or other information electronically, especially from the Internet or a larger computer

file /faɪl/ *n* COMPUTER information stored on a computer as one unit with one name

install /ɪnˈstɔːl/ *v* COMPUTER to put a computer program onto a computer or an app onto a phone so that the computer or phone can use it

look (sth) up /lʊk ˈʌp/ *pv* to try to find a piece of information by looking in a book or on a computer

password /ˈpɑːswɜːd/ *n* a secret word that allows you to do something, such as use your computer

podcast /ˈpɒdkɑːst/ *n* a digital recording that you can download from the internet and listen to on your computer or MP3 player. You can also sign up to say that you want to receive a podcast which is then updated and new information is added to it through the Internet when you plug your MP3 player into a computer.

put in /pʊt ɪn/ *pv* to put something into something else

share a link (with sb) /ʃeər ə lɪŋk/ *phr* to give someone a website address

switch (sth) off /swɪtʃ ˈɒf/ *pv* to make a light, television, phone, etc. stop working by using a switch

switch (sth) on /swɪtʃ ˈɒn/ *pv* to make a light, television, phone, etc. start working by using a switch

switch over /swɪtʃ ˈəʊvə/ *pv* to change to a different television station

take (sth) out /teɪk ˈaʊt/ *pv* to remove something from somewhere

turn (sth) down /tɜːn ˈdaʊn/ *pv* to make quieter

turn (sth) off /tɜːn ˈɒf/ *pv* to make a light, television, phone, etc. stop working by using a switch

turn (sth) on /tɜːn ˈɒn/ *pv* to make a light, television, phone, etc. start working by using a switch

turn over /tɜːn ˈəʊvə/ *pv* to change to a different television station

turn (sth) up /tɜːn ˈʌp/ *pv* to make louder

upload /ʌpˈləʊd/ *v* to send a computer program or a document electronically from your computer, using the Internet

virus /ˈvaɪərəs/ *n* COMPUTER PROBLEM a program that is secretly put onto a computer in order to destroy the information that is stored on it

UNIT 16

blow (sth) out /bləʊ ˈaʊt/ *pv* If a flame blows out, or if you blow it out, it stops burning because you or the wind have blown it.

break /breɪk/ *v* to damage something so that it is in two or more pieces

bunch of flowers /bʌntʃ əv ˈflaʊəz/ *phr* a group of flowers which are tied together, often as a present

candle /ˈkændl/ *n* a stick of wax with string going through it which produces light as it burns

cross your fingers /krɒs jɔː ˈfɪŋɡəz/ *phr* to put your third fingers on top of the second ones to show you hope very much that something will happen

gap /ɡæp/ *n* SPACE an empty space between two things

mirror /ˈmɪrə/ *n* a piece of glass with a shiny metallic material on one side which produces an image of anything that is in front of it

pavement /ˈpeɪvmənt/ *n* a path by the side of a road that people walk on

pour /pɔː/ *v* LIQUID to make a liquid flow from or into a container

pull (sth) out /pʊl ˈaʊt/ *pv* to take hold of something and remove it

salt /sɒlt/ *n* a white substance used to add flavour to food

spill /spɪl/ *v* to pour liquid or another substance somewhere without intending to, or to fall or flow out of a container in a way that is not intended

step on sth /step/ *v* to put your foot on something

touch wood /tʌtʃ/ *phr* to put your hand on something wooden to bring you good luck for something you hope will happen

UNIT 17

artist /ˈɑːtɪst/ *n* someone who paints, draws or makes sculptures

audience /ˈɔːdiəns/ *n* GROUP the people who sit and watch a performance at a theatre, cinema, etc.

author /ˈɔːθə/ *n* the writer of a book, article, play, etc.

biography /baɪˈɒɡrəfi/ *n* the life story of a person written by someone else

cheerful /ˈtʃɪəfəl/ *adj* HAPPY happy and positive

colourful /ˈkʌləfəl/ *adj* BRIGHT having bright colours

cultural /ˈkʌltʃərəl/ *adj* ARTS relating to music, art, theatre, literature, etc.

director /daɪˈrektə/ *n* FILM/PLAY someone who tells the actors in a film or play what to do

drawing /ˈdrɔːɪŋ/ *n* a picture made with a pencil or pen

environmental /ɪnvaɪrənˈmentəl/ *adj* relating to the environment, i.e. the air, land and water where people, animals and plants live

exhibition /eksɪˈbɪʃən/ *n* when objects such as paintings are shown to the public

film /'fɪlm/ *v* to make a film

gallery /'gæləri/ *n* a room or building which is used for showing works of art

helpful /'helpfəl/ *adj* useful, or willing to help

musical /'mjuːzɪkəl/ *adj* If you are musical, you are good at playing music or you enjoy music very much.

natural /'nætʃərəl/ *adj* FROM BIRTH If you have a natural ability, it is something you have been born with

novel /'nɒvəl/ *n* a book that tells a story about imaginary people and events

original /əˈrɪdʒənəl/ *adj* INTERESTING special and interesting because of not being the same as others

painful /'peɪnfəl/ *adj* PHYSICAL If a part of your body feels painful, it hurts.

painter /'peɪntə/ *n* someone who paints pictures

painting /'peɪntɪŋ/ *n* PICTURE a picture that someone has painted

peaceful /'piːsfəl/ *adj* CALM quiet and calm

poet /'pəʊɪt/ *n* someone who writes poems

poetry /'pəʊɪtri/ *n* poems in general as a form of literature

political /pəˈlɪtɪkəl/ *adj* relating to politics, i.e. how a country or area is governed

professional /prəˈfeʃənəl/ *adj* EARNING MONEY Someone is professional if they earn money for a sport or activity which most people do as a hobby.

script /skrɪpt/ *n* WORDS the words written for and spoken in a film, play, broadcast or speech

sculpture /'skʌlptʃə/ *n* a piece of art that is made from stone, wood, clay, etc., or the process of making objects like this

series /'sɪəriːz/ *n* BOOKS a set of books published by the same company that deal with the same subject

stressful /'stresfəl/ *adj* making you feel worried and not able to relax

studio /'stjuːdiəʊ/ *n* FILM a film company or a place where films are made

studio /'stjuːdiəʊ/ *n* ART a room in which an artist works

successful /səkˈsesfəl/ *adj* WORK having achieved a lot or made a lot of money through your work

traditional /trəˈdɪʃənəl/ *adj* following or belonging to the customs or ways of behaving that have continued for a long time in a group of people or a society

writer /'raɪtə/ *n* a person who writes books or articles to be published

UNIT 18

author /'ɔːθə/ *n* the writer of a book, article, play, etc.

babysitter /'beɪbɪsɪtə/ *n* someone who takes care of your child while you are out

builder /'bɪldə/ *n* a person whose job it is to make buildings

cleaner /'kliːnə/ *n* someone whose job is to clean houses, offices, public places, etc.

coach /kəʊtʃ/ *n* PERSON someone whose job is to teach people to improve at a sport, skill, or school subject

designer /dɪˈzaɪnə/ *n* someone who draws and plans how something will be made

detective /dɪˈtektɪv/ *n* someone, especially a police officer, whose job is to discover information about a crime

DJ /'diːdʒeɪ/ *n* someone who plays music on the radio or at live events

film director /'fɪlm daɪˈrektə/ *n* a person who is in charge of a film and tells the actors how to play their parts

firefighter /'faɪəfaɪtə/ *n* a person whose job is to stop fires from burning

journalist /'dʒɜːnəlɪst/ *n* a person who writes news stories or articles for a newspaper or magazine or broadcasts them on radio or television

lawyer /'lɔɪə/ *n* someone whose job is to give advice to people about the law and speak for them in court

mechanic /məˈkænɪk/ *n* someone whose job is repairing the engines of vehicles and other machines

model /'mɒdəl/ *n* PERSON someone whose job is to wear fashionable clothes, be in photographs, etc. in order to advertise things

musician /mjuːˈzɪʃən/ *n* someone who plays a musical instrument, often as a job

politician /pɒlɪˈtɪʃən/ *n* someone who works in politics, especially a member of the government

receptionist /rɪˈsepʃənɪst/ *n* someone who works in a hotel or office building, answering the telephone and dealing with guests

runner /'rʌnə/ *n* someone who runs, especially in competitions

scientist /'saɪəntɪst/ *n* someone who studies science or works in science

vet /vet/ *n* someone whose job is to give medical care to animals that are ill or hurt

UNIT 19

article /ˈɑːtɪkl/ *n* NEWSPAPER a piece of writing on a particular subject in a newspaper or magazine

advert /ˈædvɜːt/ *n* a picture, short film, song, etc. which tries to persuade people to buy a product or service

comments section /ˈkɒments ˈsekʃən/ *n* the part of a magazine or newspaper where people give their opinions

front cover /frʌnt ˈkʌvə/ *n* the outside page on the front of a magazine or book

headline /ˈhedlaɪn/ *n* IN NEWSPAPER the title of a newspaper story that is printed in large letters above it

interview /ˈɪntəvjuː/ *n* FOR ARTICLE/TV, ETC. a meeting in which someone is asked questions about themselves for a newspaper article, television show, etc.

line /laɪn/ *n* WORDS a row of words on a page

paragraph /ˈpærəɡrɑːf/ *n* a part of a text that usually contains several sentences and begins on a new line

title /ˈtaɪtl/ *n* the name of a book, article, film, piece of music, etc.

UNIT 20

create /kriˈeɪt/ *v* to make something happen or exist

hide /haɪd/ *v* THING to put something in a place where it cannot be seen or found

imagination /ɪmædʒɪˈneɪʃən/ *n* PART OF MIND the part of your mind that creates ideas or pictures of things that are not real or that you have not seen

imagine /ɪˈmædʒɪn/ *v* FORM PICTURE to form an idea or picture of something in your mind

let /let/ *v* to allow someone to do something

magic /ˈmædʒɪk/ *n* ENTERTAINMENT tricks that are done to entertain people, such as making things appear and disappear and pretending to cut someone in half

make /meɪk/ *v* to force someone to do something, or cause something to happen

mystery /ˈmɪstəri/ *n* something strange or unknown which has not yet been explained or understood

puzzle /ˈpʌzl/ *n* GAME a game or activity in which you have to put pieces together or answer questions using skill

secret /ˈsiːkrət/ *adj* If something is secret, other people are not allowed to know about it.

solve /sɒlv/ *v* to find the answer to something

trick /trɪk/ *n* MAGIC something that is done to entertain people and that seems to be magic

Grammar reference

UNIT 1

PRESENT SIMPLE AND CONTINUOUS

Present simple

- The present simple has two forms.

I, you, we, they	get, study, watch, go	
he, she, it	+ -s	gets
	or + -es	watches, goes
	or -y + -ies	studies

- We use **do/does not** + verb to make negatives.
  I, you, we, they **don't**   get, study, watch, go
  he, she, it **doesn't**   get, study, watch, go
- We use **do/does** + verb to make questions.
  Do I, you, we, they   get, study, watch, go?
  Does he, she, it   get, study, watch, go?
- We use the present simple:
  - for things we do regularly.
    I **walk** to school with a friend every day.
    My sister **doesn't go** to the sports club very often.
    What **do** you **do** on Sundays?
  - for facts.
    We **live** near my grandparents.
    The weather **doesn't get** very cold here.
  - for verbs called **state verbs** (we don't normally use these verbs in a continuous tense) which describe what we think and feel.
    believe, hate, know, like, love, mean, need, own, prefer, understand, want
    Mike **knows** the answer to your question.
    Alice **doesn't understand** what you want.
    I **don't remember** your address.
    What **does** this word **mean**?
    Do you **like** this club?
    Does your teacher **own** a sports car?

Practice

1 Complete the sentences with the verbs in the present simple.

1 .... (you / prefer) volleyball or basketball?
2 Angelo never .... (choose) sandwiches for lunch because he .... (not like) bread.
3 We .... (not see) our cousins very often because they .... (live) in America.
4 Where .... (he / go) after school?
5 We .... (not want) to hang out with Marc.
6 Sara .... (not play) football but she .... (watch) it on TV.
7 .... (they / understand) the questions?
8 Emma .... (study) French and Spanish.

Present continuous

- We use **am, are, is** + **-ing** to make the present continuous.

I	am ('m)	playing
you, we, they	are ('re)	working
he, she, it	is ('s)	helping

- We use **'m not, aren't, isn't** to make negatives.

I	'm not	working
they	aren't	helping
she	isn't	playing

- We use **am, are, is** to make questions.

Am	I	helping?
Are	you	working?
Is	he	playing?

- We use the present continuous:
  - for something that's happening now.
    We're doing our homework. (= we're in the middle of it now)
  - for something temporary around now.
    I'm helping my dad in his office this week.
    (= I don't help him every week)
  - for future plans.
    They're playing table tennis after school. (= they plan to play table tennis)

Practice

2 Complete the sentences with the verbs in the present continuous.

1 I .... (cycle) to the beach with some friends next weekend.
2 My brother .... (not watch) sport on TV this week because of his exams.
3 A: What .... (you do) at the moment?
   B: We .... (watch) a nature film because we .... (study) insects at school this term.

3 Choose the correct form of the verbs.

(1) I sit / I'm sitting on the bus with my friends.
(2) We go / We're going to the match in London. Our team **(3) plays / is playing** in the final this afternoon, so we're very excited. Our team **(4) doesn't play / isn't playing** in the final very often, but this season **(5) they play / they're playing** really well.
(6) We all believe / We're all believing they can win. After the match **(7) we have / we're having** dinner in London. **(8) I want / I'm wanting** to go to a restaurant near the stadium but **(9) they get / they're getting** very busy on match days, so **(10) we eat / we're eating** at a place in another part of the city.

138 Grammar reference

UNIT 2
PAST SIMPLE

Regular verbs
- The past simple of regular verbs is verb + **-ed**.
- Verbs ending consonant + **-y** change **-y** to **-ied**.
- It is the same for *I, you, he, she, it, we* and *they*.
  I **looked**   He **watched**   We **studied**   They **played**

Irregular verbs
- The past simple of irregular verbs has different forms.
- They are the same for *I, you, he, she, it, we* and *they*.

buy	→	bought	make	→	made
do	→	did	meet	→	met
feel	→	felt	put	→	put
get	→	got	run	→	ran
give	→	gave	say	→	said
go	→	went	take	→	took
have	→	had	think	→	thought
know	→	knew	wear	→	wore

→ *See page 158 for a list of irregular verbs.*

Regular and irregular verbs: negatives and questions
- We use **didn't** (**did not**) + verb to make negatives with all verbs in the past simple.
  I, you, he, she, it, we, they **didn't buy, didn't get, didn't look**.
- We use **did** + verb to make questions with all verbs in the past simple.
  Did you **buy**?   **Did** she **get**?   **Did** they **look**?

be
- The verb **be** has two forms in the past simple.

| I, he, she, it | was/wasn't | Was she? |
| you, we, they | were/weren't | Were you? |

- We use the past simple to talk about actions and feelings in the past.
  I **had** coffee with some friends.
  I **didn't eat** anything.
  Did your sister **enjoy** the concert?
- We often mention the time when things happened.
  I **met** my mum **after school**.
  The teacher **didn't give** us any homework **yesterday**.
  Did you **go** out **last night**?

Practice

1 Complete the conversation with the verbs in the past simple.

Lara: I (1) .... One Direction at a concert last Saturday. (see)
Kay: No! Really? Where (2) .... it? (be)
Lara: In Glasgow.
Kay: (3) .... by train or on the bus? (you / go)
Lara: Neither, I (4) .... by car. (go) The chauffeur (5) .... us right to the door. (drive)
Kay: A chauffeur? That's amazing. So, what (6) .... ? (you / wear)
Lara: Jeans and a top and my new necklace.
Kay: Cool! How many people (7) .... at the concert? (be)
Lara: About ten thousand.
Kay: Where (8) .... ? (you / sit)
Lara: In the front row.
Kay: What? How much (9) .... ? (your ticket / cost)
Lara: I (10) .... for it. (not pay)
I (11) .... it in a competition. (win)

2 Make sentences in the past simple.

1 she / be / late again?
....
2 I / not like / Andrea's new dress
....
3 we / sleep / really well last night
....
4 you / remember / my bag?
....
5 he / wear / his new trainers
....
6 they / not know / about Bill Haley and the Comets
....

3 Complete the text with the verbs in the box in the past simple.

| be | not be | catch | come | decide | not eat |
| have | know | start | want | walk | |

My friend Callum and I (1) .... into town yesterday evening. We (2) .... to buy some trainers but there (3) .... any good ones. Callum (4) .... a good café so we (5) .... to try that. We (6) .... some drinks there but it (7) .... very expensive so we (8) .... anything. We (9) .... a bus home because it (10) .... to rain when we (11) .... out of the café.

UNIT 3

COMPARATIVES AND SUPERLATIVES

To make comparative and superlative adjectives:

- one syllable adjectives add **-er** and **-est**, adjectives ending in **-e** add **-r** and **-st**.
  new → newer → (the) newest
  nice → nicer → (the) nicest
- one syllable adjectives ending in vowel + consonant usually double the consonant.
  big → bigger → (the) biggest
- two syllable adjectives ending in **-y** change **-y** to **-i** and add **-er** and **-est**.
  funny → funnier → (the) funniest
- other adjectives with two or more syllables usually use **more** and **the most**.
  friendly → more friendly → (the) most friendly
  beautiful → more beautiful → (the) most beautiful
- some adjectives are irregular.
  good → better → (the) best
  bad → worse → (the) worst

Comparative structures

- To compare two things in a positive way we use comparative adjective + **than**.
  Your laptop is **faster than** mine.
  The girls were **more friendly than** the boys.
- To say two things are not the same we use **not as** (adjective) **as**.
  My laptop **isn't as fast as** yours.
  The boys **weren't as friendly as** the girls.

Superlative structures

- We always use **the** before superlative adjectives.
  This laptop is **the fastest** in the shop.
  The Brazilians were **the most friendly**.

Practice

1 Complete the sentences with the comparative form of the adjectives, adding **than** where necessary.

1 I usually do my homework in the school library because my home internet is .... (slow) my school's and my house is .... (noisy).
2 Exams these days are .... (hard) they were in the past, but the preparation classes are .... (good).
3 Most teenagers prefer to wear casual clothes, partly because they're .... (fashionable) these days and also because they're .... (cheap) formal clothes.
4 I usually take the bus to school. It's .... (fast) walking and it's also .... (warm).
5 Stop worrying! Katy isn't .... (attractive) you and she isn't .... (funny) you either.
6 The weather forecast is for today to be .... (wet) and .... (windy) yesterday.
7 Now I'm even .... (confused). Your brother's explanation was .... (complicated) the original question.
8 We're looking for something a bit .... (bright) and .... (colourful), sorry.

2 Rewrite the sentences using **not as … as**.

1 Football is more tiring than yoga.
  Yoga ....
2 Electric cars are cleaner than petrol cars.
  Petrol cars ....
3 Most ballet dancers are fitter than many athletes.
  Many athletes ....
4 Salads are healthier than burgers.
  Burgers ....

3 Complete the sentences with **the** + the superlative form of the adjectives.

1 This website has .... (cool) music and it's also .... (cheap).
2 My brother's .... (good) student in his class but he is .... (bad) at sport.
3 The beach road is .... (safe) for cycling and it has .... (interesting) views.
4 When we go on holiday, my bag is always .... (light) and my sister's is always .... (big) and .... (heavy).
5 This is a competition to find .... (brilliant) and .... (creative) people in the music industry.
6 It's freezing! Let's go to your house. It's .... (close) and it's always .... (cosy) in winter.
7 Simon really is .... (untidy) person I've ever met. But he's also .... (charming).
8 'You're .... (sociable) person I know. What good cafés can we go to?'
  'Let's go to CoCo's. It's .... (lively) place I know.'

Grammar reference

UNIT 4
PAST CONTINUOUS

- The past continuous is similar to the present continuous, but with the past of the verb **be**.
- We use **was** or **were** + the **-ing** form of a verb.

| I, he, she, it | was | running |
| you, we, they | were | talking |

- We use **wasn't** (**was not**) and **weren't** (**were not**) to make negatives.

| I, he, she, it | wasn't | running |
| you, we, they | weren't | talking |

- We make questions with **was** or **were**.

| Was | he | running? |
| Were | you | talking? |

- We use the past continuous for actions and events in progress at a particular time in the past.
  I **was chatting** to my friends online.
  We **were texting** my mum.
  It **wasn't raining** at that time.
  They **weren't listening** to me.
  Was it **snowing**?
  Were the boys **watching** us?

Practice

1 Complete the sentences with the verbs in the past continuous.

1. I .... (dream) about my holiday last night.
2. How many hours .... (you / play) tennis?
3. You .... (not watch) television in the kitchen.
4. .... (you / talk) to your brother at lunchtime?
5. Belinda .... (not do) her homework in front of the television.
6. The cat .... (sit) on the car.
7. .... (we / use) the wrong kind of paint on that wall?
8. The students .... (chat) quietly in the computer room.
9. Charlie .... (not look) at the cars, he .... (shout) at his friends on the beach.
10. I .... (not ask) your opinion, I .... (explain) my plan.

2 Complete the text with the verbs in the box in the past continuous.

| argue | lie | listen | not listen | look |
| make | not sell | tell | wait | |

It was a peaceful summer afternoon in the park. The students (1) .... on the grass. Derek and Armando (2) .... about football, as usual. Henri (3) .... a story about his holiday in Florida. Penelope and Doris (4) .... to him and Doris (5) .... a necklace of wooden beads. Margherita (6) .... to anyone. She (7) .... at the ice cream van which was near the gate. Twenty people (8) .... to buy an ice cream. There was a burger van as well, but the owner (9) .... many burgers.

3 Look at Exercise 2 and write questions for the answers, using the past continuous.

0. Where *were the students lying*?
   On the grass.
1. What .... ?
   Football, as usual.
2. What .... ?
   His holiday in Florida.
3. What .... ?
   Listening to Henri's story.
4. What .... ?
   A necklace.
5. Who .... ?
   No one.
6. How many people .... ?
   Twenty.

4 Read this paragraph about some students and compare it with your answers to Exercise 2. Some of the facts are wrong. Correct them by completing the sentences using negative verbs.

> The students were sitting on the grass. Derek and Armando were arguing about music. Henri was describing the scenery in Florida. Penelope and Doris were waving at Henri and Doris was making a necklace. Margherita was taking a photo of the other students.

0. The students *weren't sitting on the grass, they were lying on it*.
1. Derek and Armando ....
2. ....
3. ....
4. ....

141

UNIT 5

PAST SIMPLE AND CONTINUOUS

→ See Unit 4, page 141 for past continuous form.

- We use the past continuous for actions and events in progress at a particular time in the past.
  At lunchtime …
  I **was texting** a friend.
  it **was raining**.
  the students **weren't playing** computer games.
  was the teacher **riding** her motorbike?

→ See Unit 2, page 139 for past simple form.

- We use the past simple to talk about:
  - completed actions in the past, often with the time when they happened.
    I **met** my friends at the shopping centre yesterday.
    We **didn't buy** anything but we **looked** at some new phones.
  - two or more actions which happened after one another.
    Amy **showed** me her new bag and then I **went** home.
    When Jules **lost** his key, we all **helped** to look for it.
    I **finished** my drink and **washed** the glass.

- We use the past simple and past continuous together when an action in the past interrupted an action or event that was in progress. We use the past simple for the action that interrupts and the past continuous for the action that was in progress.
  I **was chatting** with some friends when I **saw** you on the bus.
  The singer **threw** his guitar at some fans because they **were annoying** him.
  She **didn't eat** anything for lunch because she **was feeling** nervous.

Practice

1 Choose the correct form of the verbs.

1 I **didn't hear / wasn't hearing** Elinor come into my room because I **wore / was wearing** headphones.
2 We **all celebrated / were all celebrating** when we **got / were getting** our exam results.
3 My grandad **found / was finding** some gold coins when he **worked / was working** in his garden.
4 I **broke / was breaking** my arm when I **learned / was learning** to ski.
5 My mum **drove / was driving** home from work when she **got / was getting** my text, so she couldn't answer it.
6 When Sonja **opened / was opening** the garage door she **discovered / was discovering** her new bike.
7 I **chatted / was chatting** to a friend on the phone when the train **went / was going** into a tunnel and I never **heard / was hearing** the end of her story.
8 Tomas **emailed / was emailing** me twice while I **mended / was mending** my bike but I **didn't check / wasn't checking** my laptop until later.

2 Complete the story with the verbs in the past simple or past continuous.

Marcus Jones was very lucky last weekend. He **(0)** ..was cycling.. (cycle) home from the city centre. It **(1)** .... (snow) and the road was icy. Suddenly his bike **(2)** .... (slip) and he **(3)** .... (fall off) onto the pavement. He **(4)** .... (pick up) his bike off the road when he **(5)** .... (see) something in the sky. It **(6)** .... (move) towards him very fast. He **(7)** .... (jump) back onto the pavement and the object **(8)** .... (hit) the road. It was a piece of a meteorite. 'I was glad I **(9)** .... (not stand) there!' he **(10)** .... (tell) told journalists later.

3 Make sentences. Use the past continuous or past simple form of the verbs.

1 I / visit / my friends. Afterwards, I / take / the bus home.
  ....
2 Luke / walk / into the door because he / not look / ahead.
  ....
3 It / snow / at lunchtime, so I / not go / for walk.
  ....
4 I / not be / hungry, so I / not have / anything to eat.
  ....
5 My sister / crash / into a traffic light when she / ride / her scooter.
  ....
6 I / think / about the holidays. Then suddenly, I / realise / the time.
  ....

UNIT 6

SOME / ANY, MUCH / MANY, A LOT OF, A FEW / A LITTLE

some / any

- We use **some** and **any** with plural countable nouns and uncountable nouns.
- We use **some** in positive sentences.
  We bought **some petrol** and **some sweets** at the garage.
- We use **any** in questions and negatives.
  I haven't got **any homework** tonight.
  Are there **any good clubs** near here?
  Is there **any fruit** in the fridge?
  They don't want **any salad**.

much / many and a lot of

- We use **a lot of** with plural countable nouns and with uncountable nouns, in positive and negative sentences and questions.
  I took **a lot of photos** last night.
  There's **a lot of milk** in the fridge.
  We haven't got **a lot of** money for clothes.
- We use **many** with plural countable nouns in questions and negatives.
  We haven't got **many photos** of our holiday.
  Are **many people** coming to your party?
- We use **much** with uncountable nouns in negative sentences and questions.
  I haven't got **much time** to help you.
  Is there **much traffic** on this road at night?

a few / a little

- We use **a few** and **a little** in positive sentences and questions.
- We use **a few** with plural countable nouns.
  I invited **a few friends** to a barbecue on my birthday.
  Do you want **a few grapes** with the cheese?
- We use **a little** with uncountable nouns.
  I'd like **a little sugar** in my coffee, please.
  Have you got **a little time** to spare?

Practice

1 Complete the sentences with *some* or *any*.

1. Don't make .... noise near the exam room.
2. My brother had .... problems with his phone, so he couldn't text me.
3. Did you have .... help when you made that cake?
4. There isn't .... rubbish in the bin.
5. There's .... fruit in the cupboard if you want it.
6. Were there .... children at the party?

2 Choose the correct words.

1. I didn't play **many / much** matches last season.
2. I haven't got **a little / much** paper, so I need to buy some soon.
3. My earphones aren't working, so I can't listen to **some / any** music on the bus.
4. We had **a little / a few** problems with the password but in the end we remembered it.
5. I've got **a lot of / many** cousins in Germany.
6. How **much / many** students are there at your school?
7. I found **some / much** information for my project online.
8. We haven't got **any / some** time for shopping today.
9. Did you spend **many / a lot of** time at the park?
10. There's **a little / a few** space left for your name at the bottom of the page.

3 Complete the sentences with *much*, *many*, *a few* or *a little*.

1. There isn't .... traffic at this time in the morning, so it only takes .... minutes to get to the centre.
2. I only have .... money with me, so I can't buy .... food.
3. Did you have .... trouble finding the address you needed?
4. We've got .... exercises to do for homework but they won't take .... time.
5. I made .... phone calls about the screen problems with your tablet but I didn't get .... helpful answers.
6. Were there .... traffic jams this morning?
7. We only had .... time at the party but we still made .... new friends.
8. 'Have you got .... sandwiches left?'
   'Yes, there are ....'

UNIT 7

HAVE TO AND MUST; SHOULD

have to and must

- **Have to** changes form.
  I **have to go** to school.
  We **don't have to go** in the car.
  You **had to go** to school.
  She **has to be** home by 10 pm.
  He **doesn't have to do** any homework today.
  They **didn't have to clean** the car.
  We don't use contractions in the positive:
  ~~You've to go. He's to stay.~~

- **Must** has only one form. There is no past tense of **must**; we use the past form **had to**.
  I, you, he, she, we, they   **must catch** the early bus.
  I, you, he, she, we, they   **mustn't be** late.

- We use **must** and **have to** for a rule or something it is necessary to do.
  You **must be** 18 to see that film.
  He **has to practise** the guitar every day.

- In the past tense we use **had to**. There is no past form of **must**.
  You **had to be** 18 to see that film.
  He **had to practise** the guitar every day.

- We use **mustn't** for a negative rule or something it is necessary not to do.
  I **mustn't sleep** in class.
  You **mustn't read** that letter.

- **Don't/didn't have to** means that it is/was not necessary to do something.
  She **doesn't have to answer** that email.
  I **didn't have to do** a test.

should and shouldn't

- **Should** has only one form.
  I, you, he, she, we, they   **should tidy** the living room.
  I, you, he, she, we, they   **shouldn't** make a mess.

- We use **should** when we think it is a good idea to do something.
  I **should buy** a present for my mum.
  They **should build** a new sports centre.

- We use **shouldn't** when we think it is a bad idea to do something.
  You **shouldn't do** your homework in front of the TV.
  We **shouldn't eat** too many chips.

- We use **should** in questions when we ask for advice.
  What **should** I **say** in my interview?
  Which shoes **should** I **wear** with this dress?

Practice

1 Choose the correct verbs.

OUTDOOR ADVENTURE CAMP
Welcome!

PLEASE READ THIS NOTICE CAREFULLY.

There are eight different activities to choose from. You **(1) should / don't have to** look at the list of activities for the week and decide which ones you want to do. You can choose to do something different every day. You **(2) must / should** talk to your friends before you sign up if you want to do the same things.

You **(3) shouldn't / must** try at least three different activities in the week but you **(4) don't have to / must** try everything. You **(5) must / should** sign up for activities before breakfast every day.

You **(6) don't have to / mustn't** miss the safety lesson before each new activity. You **(7) should / have to** ask a teacher if you aren't sure what to do.

2 Rewrite the sentences, using the correct form of *must*, *have to* and *should*. For one sentence three of these verbs are correct. Which sentence is it?

1 We're not allowed to text our friends in lessons.
  We ....
2 It's a good idea to read through your work before you show it to anyone.
  You ....
3 My brother can wear any clothes he likes to school.
  He .... school uniform.
4 Can you advise me which phone to buy?
  Which phone .... ?
5 It wasn't necessary to book seats for the concert.
  We ....
6 It isn't very sensible to wear your best shirt when you mend your bike.
  You ....
7 Seat belts are compulsory for both drivers and passengers.
  Both drivers and passengers ....
  ....

UNIT 8

FUTURE: *BE GOING TO* AND PRESENT CONTINUOUS

Present continuous for plans and arrangements
→ See Unit 1, page 138 for present continuous form.

- We use the present continuous, usually with the time mentioned, for definite plans we already know about.
  I'm flying to Spain at the weekend.
  He's not working next week.
  What time are you leaving?

be going to for intentions

- We use **am/is/are (not)** + **going to** + verb to make the **be going to** future.
  I'm going to run.
  We're going to finish.
  You're not going to win.
  They're not going to arrive.
  Is she going to leave?
  Are you going to play?

- We use **be going to**:
  - for things we intend to do in the future.
    I'm going to visit Italy one day.
    We're going to work really hard.
    I'm not going to eat any more chocolate.
  - for things we know are likely to happen.
    You drive well now, I'm sure you're going to pass your driving test.
    Look at that blue sky! It's not going to rain today.

Practice

1 Choose the correct form of the verbs.

1 The traffic is awful this evening. I'm sure **it's going to take / it's taking** hours to get home.
2 I can't come to the cinema with you on Saturday; it's my parents' wedding anniversary and **we're going to organise / we're organising** a big family party.
3 Look at the mess in this kitchen! **I'm going to get / I'm getting** really angry if you don't clean it up right now.
4 Mum really enjoyed that cake we had at my cousin's party. **I'm going to ask / I'm asking** my aunt how to make it.
5 **I'm going to take / I'm taking** my driving test on Monday morning, so **I'm going to do / I'm doing** lots of practice this weekend.
6 I can't wait to go on holiday! **We're catching / We're going to catch** the train from St Pancras at 9 am tomorrow. **We're going to play / We're playing** card games all the way to Paris.
7 Can you hear thunder? **It's going to rain / It's raining** soon.
8 **We're meeting / We're going to meet** in the library, after lunch.

2 Complete the conversation with the correct form of *be going to*.

A: (1) .... (you, go) to my cousin Felix's party?
B: Yes, I think so.
A: What (2) .... (wear)?
B: I'm not sure. My blue dress, probably.
A: And which shoes?
B: Well, the weather forecast says it (3) .... (be) hot so I (4) .... (buy) some sandals.
A: (5) .... (you, take) him a present?
B: I guess I should give him something.
A: I (6) .... (give) him this belt.
B: Oh, that's cool. I know he (7) .... (be) so pleased with it. But the problem is, I (8) .... (not find) anything as good as that.
A: We can give it as a shared present, if you like.
B: Oh, that's great, thanks very much. But I (9) .... (tell) him you found it for him.

3 Read the descriptions of the situations and write a sentence about what is going to happen, using *be going to* and the verb given.

1 A man is climbing out of a window with a bag in his hand. A police officer is watching him. She's waiting for him.
   She .... (arrest)
2 A boy is walking along the pavement. He's looking at a beautiful motorbike on the road. He doesn't know there's a rubbish bin two metres in front of him.
   He .... (fall over)
3 There are some sausages cooking in a frying pan but there's no one in the kitchen.
   They .... (burn)
4 A man is in bed. The people in the flat downstairs are talking loudly.
   He .... (not sleep well)
5 A girl is singing on a TV talent show. All the judges are smiling and clapping.
   She .... (win)
6 A man and a woman are playing the guitar and drums on a TV talent show. One of the judges has his hands over his ears.
   They .... (not win)

UNIT 9

PRESENT PERFECT

- We form the present perfect of regular and irregular verbs with **has/have** + the past participle.
  I, you, we, they **'ve / have (haven't) bought**
  Have *I, you, we, they* **bought** ...?
  He, She, It **'s / has (hasn't) lived**
  Has *he, she, it* **lived** ...?

- In regular verbs the past participle looks the same as the past simple (verb + -(e)d).

Verb	Past simple	Past participle
turn	turned	turned
like	liked	liked

- In irregular verbs the past participle sometimes looks the same as the past simple and sometimes is different.

Verb	Past simple	Past participle
		The same
make	made	made
find	found	found
		Different
be	was/were	been
do	did	done
break	broke	broken
know	knew	known

→ See page 158 for a list of irregular verbs.

- We use the present perfect for experiences in the past which have some link to the present.
  We've spent all our money. (= we haven't got any now)
  We haven't eaten lunch. (= we're hungry)
  Have you *visited* Paris? (= do you know Paris?)

been and gone

- The verb **go** has two forms in the present perfect: **have gone** and **have been**. They have different meanings.
- **Have / has gone** means that someone is in another place.
  Tessa has gone to the club. (= Tessa isn't here, she's at the club)
  Jack's gone to the city centre. (= he's not here, he's in the city centre)
- **Have / has been** means that someone went to that place in the past but is not there now.
- *Tessa has been to the club.* (= Tessa visited the club some time in the past, but she isn't there now)
  Jack's been to the city centre. (= he's not there now, he was there some time before now)

ever, never and short answers

- We use **ever** and **never** with the present perfect to mean 'in your whole life' or 'not in your whole life'.
- We can use **Yes, I have** and **No, I haven't** to answer these questions.
  Have you ever been to Lapland?
  Yes, I have. (= some time before now)
  No, I haven't. (= he/she has **never** been to Lapland in his/her life)

Practice

1 Complete the sentences with the verbs in the box in the present perfect, adding the words given.

> beat   eat   fall   fly   forget   give   go
> hurt   know   tear   text   write

1 Zoe .... (not) anything all day. I'm going to make her a sandwich.
2 Yolanda .... (never) a thank you letter to anyone.
3 Vincent and I .... Tom all our lives.
4 Urs .... (never) me at chess.
5 I .... to Paris twice, but usually I go by train.
6 Olga .... (not) me her number so I .... (not) her.
7 Nigel .... off his bike. He .... (not) himself but he .... his best jeans.
8 Mark .... to the sports club but he .... his membership card. I hope they let him in without it.

2 Complete the conversations with the verbs in the present perfect.

A: (1) .... (you / finish) your history homework?
B: Not quite. I (2) .... (find) three websites with the right sort of information but I (3) .... (not read) it all.
A: Well, I (4) .... (go) to the library and I (5) .... (borrow) this old book for you. I (6) .... (look) at the pictures and I think it could be useful.
B: Thanks, that's great.

C: (7) .... (you / tidy) your room?
D: No, I (8) .... I'm going to do it now.
C: But I (9) .... (make) a pizza for our lunch. It's going to be cold before you can eat it.
D: That's OK. I (10) .... (have) some chips, so I'm not really hungry.
C: Oh, thanks for telling me!

E: Where (11) .... (you / be)? The match starts in five minutes!
F: I (12) .... (be) in that café. Look, I (13) .... (buy) you some chocolate.
E: But I don't like chocolate. (14) .... (you / ever / see) me eating chocolate?
F: Oh, sorry. No, I (15) ....
E: Well, I hope you (16) .... (remember) our tickets?
F: Of course I (17) .... Here they are!

146 Grammar reference

UNIT 10

PRESENT PERFECT AND PAST SIMPLE; HOW LONG? AND FOR/SINCE

Present perfect
→ See Unit 9, page 146 for the present perfect form.

- We use the present perfect for experiences in our life up to the present.
- We don't use past time phrases with the present perfect.
  She's **seen** that film.
  They've **heard** that song.
  We **haven't visited** this museum.
  Have you **tried** Thai food?

Past simple
→ See Unit 2, page 139 for the past simple form.

- We use the past simple to talk about when things happened.
  She **saw** the film last week.
  They **heard** that song at a concert.
  We **visited** this museum last time we came to London.
  Did you **try** Thai food when you were in Bangkok?

How long? and for/since

- We use **How long** + present perfect to ask a question about a period of time up to now.
  How long have you lived here?
  How long have you known your best friend?
- We use **for** to introduce the length of time something lasted.
  for ten years, **for** a long time, **for** six weeks
- We use **since** to say when something began.
  since six o'clock, **since** my birthday party, **since** last year
- When there is a verb after **since**, it is in the past simple.
  I have known him **since** I **was** eleven, **since** I **started** school, **since** I **arrived** in Madrid.

Practice

1 Choose the correct form of the verbs.
1. I hope you're all hungry. **I've made / I made** a big paella and a salad.
2. Emerald **has gone / went** to the cinema with her friends, I'm not sure when she'll be home.
3. Gary **has cooked / cooked** a fantastic meal last night. I **haven't met / didn't meet** anyone who can cook as well as he can.
4. I don't know why Toby **hasn't come / didn't come** to see me. **I've asked / I asked** him yesterday to come as soon as possible.
5. My friends **haven't enjoyed / didn't enjoy** the trip to the beach at the weekend because the wind **has been / was** so cold.

2 Complete the sentences with *for* or *since*.
1. I've supported Liverpool .... I was at primary school. They've always been a great team although they haven't won the cup .... quite a long time.
2. We haven't eaten meat .... five years. It was a bit difficult at first but we've all been very healthy .... we became vegetarians.
3. They've only owned that car .... about three months but they've had two accidents .... they bought it.
4. I'm so tired! I've cycled ten kilometres .... breakfast and I've had all this shopping in my backpack .... most of the time.
5. My dad hasn't seen his parents .... the beginning of the year. They've been in Australia .... six months, visiting my aunt and her family.

3 Complete the text with the verbs in the present perfect or the past simple.

I (1) .... (be) a member of the swimming team for two months. I (2) .... (enjoy) swimming since I (3) .... (be) small. Last year I (4) .... (start) using the swimming pool at our local sports club and one day I (5) .... (see) a notice about the team. The next week they were practising in the pool when I (6) .... (arrive) and I (7) .... (think) it looked like fun.

We train twice a week. I (8) .... (not miss) any training sessions although sometimes it's hard to find the time. When I (9) .... (have) exams last summer I almost (10) .... (give) up. But I'm so pleased I (11) .... (not leave) because since then we (12) .... (enter) three competitions and we (13) .... (have) a lot of fun together. Unfortunately, we (14) .... (not win) any prizes for quite a long time.

UNIT 11

WILL AND BE GOING TO

will

- We form the future with **will/won't** + verb.
  We'll (will) write
  She won't go
  Will they want … ?
- We use **will**:
  - for general predictions about the future.
    People will be healthier.
    Medicines won't cure everything.
    Will everyone live longer?
  - for decisions which we make at the same time as we are speaking.
    I'll have a cake with my coffee.
    I won't wait any longer.

be going to

→ See Unit 8, page 145 for the form of **be going to**.

- We use **be going to**:
  - for plans we have already made.
    Our teacher is going to give us the test results soon.
    I'm not going to spend a lot of money today.
    What are we going to eat tonight?
  - for predictions based on what we know or can see when we speak.
    Business is good – we're going to be rich!
    Look at the crowd round the table – the food's going to run out.

Practice

1 Choose the correct form of the verbs.

1 Scientists are working on new crops that **will help / are going to help** feed us all.
2 I can't meet you tomorrow, **I'll help / I'm going to help** my brother paint his bedroom.
3 This new bike **will save / is going to save** me lots of money on bus fares.
4 I've got a headache now but I think **I'll feel / I'm going to feel** OK when I get outdoors.
5 Please hurry up, the bus **will leave / is going to leave** any minute.
6 I must get another pen. This one **will run / is going to run** out of ink in a minute.
7 Some people say that air fares **will be / are going to be** much more expensive in the future.

2 Complete the conversation with the correct form of the verbs, *will* or *be going to*.

Jane: Hi, Angie, what are you doing?
Angie: I'm trying to pack, but I'm not getting on very well. I've got so much stuff, my case **(1)** …………………… (be) too heavy.
Jane: Don't worry, I **(2)** …………………… (help) you. I'm good at packing. What **(3)** …………………… (do) on your holiday?
Angie: Oh, I **(4)** …………………… (have) a good rest after my exams. I **(5)** …………………… (lie) on the beach under an umbrella and listen to the waves.
Jane: OK. So you need a swimming costume. What else?
Angie: Well my dad wants to visit some ancient city so probably I **(6)** …………………… (walk) around there with him one day.
Jane: Right, shorts and a T-shirt and a pair of trainers. But what are all these heavy bottles?
Angie: Shampoo, shower gel, face cream …
Jane: I don't think you **(7)** …………………… (use) that much in one week! I've got some small travel bottles. I **(8)** …………………… (lend) them to you. They **(9)** …………………… (not weigh) as much. Now, what about sun cream?
Angie: I've got that in my hand luggage, see?
Jane: But that tube's 120 millilitres. The security people at the airport **(10)** …………………… (take) it away from you. I **(11)** …………………… (put) it in your suitcase.
Angie: Thanks. I hope we can have a holiday in this country next year. Then I **(12)** …………………… (not care) about the weight of my bag!

3 Write sentences using *will* or *be going to*.

1 Lucy and Linda are running a race. Lucy is running very fast, Linda is tired.
   …………………………………………………… (win)
2 Jonah is on a boat. The sea is very rough. Jonah feels ill.
   …………………………………………………… (be sick)
3 Jo has got a difficult science project. His sister is good at science.
   …………………………………………………… (help)
4 Alicia and Paula are in a beauty salon preparing for a birthday party.
   …………………………………………………… (look / great)
5 Inez is cooking some burgers on a barbecue and talking to her friends at the same time.
   …………………………………………………… (burn)
6 Tomasz likes studying.
   …………………………………………………… (go / university)

UNIT 12
MODALS OF PROBABILITY

- Modal verbs do not change form. Modal verbs of probability are always followed by another verb.
  I, you, he, she, it, we, they **must be / might die / could bite / can't exist**

- We use the modal verbs **must, could / might** and **can't** + verb to show that we think something is certainly true, or possibly true, or that it is impossible.

- When we think that something is certainly true, we use **must** + verb.
  *The explorers found two new species. They **must be** very excited.*
  (= I'm certain they're very excited.)
  *They've walked through the jungle for four days. They **must feel** tired.*
  (= I'm certain they feel tired.)

- When we think something is possibly true, we use **might** or **could** + verb.
  *I've never seen an animal like this before, it **could / might be** a new species.*
  (= Perhaps it's a new species.)
  *Other new species **could exist** in these mountains.*
  (= Perhaps other new species exist in these mountains.)
  *Don't touch it, it **might bite** you.*
  (= Perhaps it will bite you if you touch it.)

- When we feel certain that something is impossible, we use **can't** + verb. (**NOT** mustn't + verb).
  *I've seen a picture of this animal in an old book, so it **can't be** a new species.*
  (= I'm sure it isn't a new species.)
  *He's an intelligent person; he **can't believe** those silly stories!*
  (= I'm sure he doesn't believe those stories.)

Practice

1 Rewrite the underlined words in the sentences using *must*.

1 Jon's gone out without a coat. <u>I'm sure he's cold</u>.
....

2 I put the potatoes in the oven an hour ago. <u>I'm certain they're ready to eat by now</u>.
....

3 <u>I know this parcel is my new phone</u> because I ordered it last week.
....

2 Rewrite the underlined words in the sentences using *might*.

1 That cat wants something. <u>Perhaps he's hungry</u>.
....

2 I don't know where my phone is. <u>Perhaps it's in the car</u>.
....

3 <u>It's possible that my teacher speaks three languages</u>, I'm not sure.
....

3 Look at your answers to Exercise 2. Can you replace *might* with a different modal verb?

4 Rewrite the underlined words in the sentences using *can't*.

1 This fish smells terrible. <u>I'm certain it isn't fresh</u>.
....

2 <u>I don't believe that coat belongs to you</u>, it's much too small.
....

3 <u>It's not possible that you feel tired</u>. You've been asleep for twelve hours!
....

5 Choose the correct verbs.

Liz has come to visit Becca on her birthday.

Becca: Hi, Liz, come in. I'm having a great day. I've got lots of cards and some great presents. But what's this parcel? I didn't notice it before. Oh dear, there's no card with it.
Liz: Is it from your sister?
Becca: It **(1) can't be / must be** from her – I've already opened her present.
Liz: Is it from your parents?
Becca: No, it **(2) can't be / could be** from them either because they're giving me a new bike. We're going to get it later.
Liz: Is it from your grandparents?
Becca: It **(3) could be / must be** from them, I guess. They usually send me something, but I don't know how it got here.
Liz: Well, the card **(4) might be / can't be** inside.
Becca: Yes, but it's a strange shape. I wonder what it is. The wrapping paper is really beautiful. It **(5) must be / can't be** something special.
Liz: It's not very big. It **(6) could be / must be** a new phone. Did you ask for one?
Becca: No. Anyway, it's hard at one end and softer at the other, so it **(7) can't be / might be** a phone. OK, I'm going to open it. Oh, wow, it's some of those brushes I saw in the art shop last week! And here's the card. It says 'Love from Liz'! I didn't see you bring the parcel in.
Liz: Well, I knew you wanted some and so I thought perhaps they **(8) could be / must be** a good present.
Becca: They're perfect, thank you so much!

UNIT 13

JUST, ALREADY AND YET

We use *just*, *already* and *yet* with the present perfect.

Just
- means 'a short time before now'.
- emphasises that it is only a short time.
- goes before the main verb in positive sentences.
  I've just passed my driving test.
  The match *has just started*.
  We've just moved house.

Already
- means 'some time before now'.
- emphasises that the action is now complete – we are not so interested in how long ago.
- sometimes means 'earlier than expected'.
- goes before the main verb in positive sentences.
  I've already driven five hundred kilometres, I don't want to drive any more.
  My brother *has already left* school. He's at university now.
  My dad had flu last week but he*'s already gone* back to work.
  Our little sister*'s already learned* how to open cupboards although she's only one!

Yet
- means 'up to now'.
- often emphasises that we expected something to happen before now or around now.
- goes at the end of a negative sentence.
  I haven't finished my sandwich *yet*. (= I'm eating it now, I need more time.)
  We *haven't decided* which film to watch *yet*. (= We're still thinking about it.)
- sometimes suggests that something might happen in the future.
  You *haven't seen* my new bike *yet*. (= You might see it sometime soon.)
- goes at the end of a question.
  Have you *phoned* Jade *yet*?
  (= I think you planned to phone Jade around now.)
  Has Francis *bought* mum a birthday card *yet*?
  (= I think he should do it soon.)

Practice

1 Choose the correct words.
1 That's amazing! I've **just / yet** seen our street on television.
2 I've worked at the café for the last two weekends but I haven't been paid **already / yet**.
3 We've **just / yet** heard our exam results.
4 Oh no! I've **already / just** dropped a litre of olive oil on the kitchen floor! Can you help me clear it up?
5 Have you had an invitation to Janie's party **just / yet**?

2 Put the words in brackets in the correct position in each sentence.
1 The lesson has begun. (already)
2 Have you been to the new shopping centre? (yet)
3 This parcel has arrived for you. (just)
4 I haven't saved much money for my holiday. (yet)
5 It's only eleven o'clock but everyone's gone home. (already)
6 My parents have bought a new car. (just)
7 Have you done this exercise? (yet)
8 We've finished the last sentence. (just)

3 Mark the sentences S if they mean the same thing or D if they mean different things.
1 I saw the doctor a few minutes ago. ....
  I've just seen the doctor.
2 We've already had one holiday this year. ....
  We haven't had a holiday yet.
3 My brother has a job although he only left school last week. ....
  My brother left school last week and he's already found a job.
4 I've already been to Australia twice but I haven't visited New Zealand yet. ....
  I've just left Australia and I'm going to New Zealand.
5 I've just finished cleaning the kitchen and I'm going to have a shower. ....
  I've already cleaned the kitchen but I haven't had a shower yet.

4 Nick has an exam tomorrow. He's made a list of things to do. Write sentences about what he's already done and what he hasn't done yet.

> Read through my revision notes.
> Buy some new pens. ✓
> Set my alarm for 7 a.m.
> Decide what to wear.
> Text my mates about meeting after the exam. ✓
> Ask Mum to give me a lift to school. ✓

0 He hasn't read through his revision notes yet.
1 ....
2 ....
3 ....
4 ....
5 ....

UNIT 14
RELATIVE CLAUSES

Relative clauses:
- give the information a listener needs to understand which things or people a speaker is talking about.
  *The film **that we saw last night** was really funny.*
  (We need the words **that we saw last night** to know which film the speaker is talking about.)
  *The actor **that played Mrs Wood** was brilliant.*
  (We need the words **that played Mrs Wood** to know which actor the speaker is talking about.)
- begin with the relative pronouns **who** or **that** for people.
  *There's the woman **who** I met at the singing competition.*
  *I preferred the singer **that** got the second prize.*
- begin with the relative pronouns **which** or **that** for things.
  *I enjoy singing songs **which** make people laugh.*
  *My friend sang a song **that** she wrote about her home town.*
- can have **who, which** or **that** as their subject or as their object.
  *I preferred the singer **that** got the second prize.*
  (**that** is the subject of the relative clause)
  *I enjoy singing songs **which** make people laugh.*
  (**which** is the subject of the relative clause)
  *There's the woman **who** I met at the singing competition.*
  (**who** is the object of the relative clause, **I** is the subject)
  *My friend sang a song **that** she wrote about her home town.*
  (**that** is the object of the relative clause, **she** is the subject)
- begin with the relative pronoun **where** for places.
  *We went to the house **where** the film director lives.*
  (= which the film director lives in)
  *I know a website **where** you can find all kinds of films.*
  (= you can find all kinds of films there)

Practice

1 Complete the sentences with *who* or *which*.

1 I've just met someone .... has a part in a soap opera.
2 The chat show .... I usually watch has lots of interesting people on it.
3 I like programmes .... make me laugh.
4 This is the animated film .... my teacher recommended to me.
5 The hero has a cat .... is called Hannibal.
6 I really admire the actor .... plays the main character in this thriller.
7 I'm not a big fan of murder mysteries .... have complicated stories.
8 I know a girl .... is a TV actor.
9 This documentary is by a woman .... my mum was at school with.

2 Malcolm is telling Kirsty about a film. Read what they say, then complete what Malcolm says using the clauses from the box.

> who was always unkind to him
> who hasn't seen it
> who was called Millie Moop
> who lived in an old bus
> which you need to see to understand
> which was really funny
> where Millie put shampoo into a toothpaste tube
> where Mr Scratch lived

Malcolm: I saw this film last weekend (1) .... There was a family called the Moops (2) .... They had a teenage daughter (3) .... and she was very intelligent. Her dad had a job which he hated, and he worked for a man called Mr Scratch (4) .... So one day, Millie went to the house (5) .... and got a job as a cleaner. Then she played all kinds of tricks on Mr Scratch and his family. The best scene was one (6) .... I laughed all the time.
Kirsty: Really?
Malcolm: Oh, well, perhaps it's one of those films (7) .... It doesn't sound so funny to someone (8) ....

3 Make each pair of sentences into one sentence, using a relative clause. Make other changes if necessary.

1 This is a photo of my friend. She wants to be a TV presenter.
   ....
2 We have a goldfish. He is called Bubbles.
   ....
3 That man wrote a song. Everyone knows it.
   ....
4 I visited a house. John Lennon lived there as a boy.
   ....
5 Do you remember the woman? She had 20 cats.
   ....
6 Our teacher gave us some exercises for homework. No one could understand them.
   ....
7 I have a neighbour. He is a famous designer.
   ....

UNIT 15

PRESENT SIMPLE PASSIVE

- We form the present simple passive with the present tense of **be** + the **past participle** of a verb.

I	**am given**
you, we, they	**are helped**
he, she, it	**is recommended**

  I'm given a maths test every week.
  I'm not given a maths test every week.
  Are you **given** a maths test every week?
  Robbie **is helped** with his homework.
  Robbie **isn't helped** with his homework.
  Is Robbie **helped** with his homework?
  These apps **are recommended** on lots of websites.
  These apps **aren't recommended** on many websites.
  Are these apps **recommended** on many websites?

- When we include who or what does the action, we use **by**.
  My teacher gives me a maths test every week. (active)
  I'm given a maths test **by my teacher** every week. (passive)
  The teacher doesn't help Robbie with his homework. (active)
  Robbie **isn't helped** with his homework **by the teacher**. (passive)
  Do a lot of people admire the girls for their courage? (active)
  Are the girls **admired by a lot of people** for their courage? (passive)

- We use the passive:
  - when it isn't important to say who or what does the action.
    This app **is used** for sharing photos.
    Our exam results **are published** online.
    Teenagers **are allowed** to drive in my country.
  - when we do not know who or what does the action.
    These new phones **are made** in China.
    The streets **are cleaned** at night.
    My dad **is sent** lots of brochures.

- We include **by** when we want to emphasise who or what does the action.
  This app **is used by millions of people** for sharing photos.
  My dad **is sent** lots of brochures **by car companies**.

Practice

1 Rewrite the passive sentences in the active form.

1 I'm always given money for my birthday by my granny.
   My granny .... for my birthday.
2 All our vegetables are grown by my parents.
   My parents .... vegetables.
3 Cambridge is visited by lots of tourists.
   Lots of tourists .... Cambridge.
4 Computers are used by most schoolchildren nowadays.
   Most schoolchildren .... nowadays.

2 Rewrite the sentences using the passive form of the verb. Only include *by* if it is important.

1 You need a password to enter this website.
   A password .... this website.
2 My brother cleans Dad's car once a month.
   Dad's car .... once a month.
3 We don't send children to prison in this country.
   Children .... in this country.
4 Thieves steal ten bicycles every day in this town.
   Ten bicycles .... in this town.
5 People play football all the year round.
   Football .... all the year round.
6 My parents don't allow me to have a TV in my bedroom.
   I .... a TV in my bedroom.
7 Someone designs a clever new app every day.
   A clever new app .... day.
8 A local company pays for our school trips.
   Our school trips ....
9 Criminals hide viruses in software.
   Viruses .... in software.
10 A film star owns that house on the corner.
   That house ....

UNIT 16

ZERO AND FIRST CONDITIONAL

- Conditional sentences tell us about a possible situation, called the conditional clause, and another clause, which is the result.
- The conditional clause begins with *if* or *unless*.
- The conditional clause or the result clause can come first without changing the meaning.

Zero conditional

- The zero conditional uses the present simple in the conditional clause and in the result clause.
- *If* + present tense, + present tense
  If plants **have** enough light, they **grow** well.
  If plants **don't have** enough light, they **don't grow** well.
  NOTE we use a comma when the *if* clause comes first.
- OR present tense + *if* + present tense
  Plants **grow** well *if* they **have** enough light.
- We use the zero conditional to describe a condition with a result which is always true.
  If you **water** plants regularly, they **grow** well.
  If you **don't water** plants regularly, they **don't grow** well.
- *If* usually means the same as *when* in zero conditional sentences.
  Plants **grow** well *when* you **water** them regularly.

Practice

1 Complete the sentences with the correct form of the verbs.

1. Everyone .... sleepy if the weather .... too hot. (feel, be)
2. If my brother .... any money, he always .... it on clothes. (earn, spend)
3. Students .... stressed if their teacher .... too many tests. (get, give)
4. If I .... a film, I .... it to the end. (not like, not watch)
5. If I .... well in my school exams, my parents usually .... me extra pocket money. (do, give)
6. It .... difficult to remember facts if you .... studying that subject. (be, not enjoy)

First conditional

- The first conditional uses the present simple in the conditional clause and the *will* future in the result clause.
- *If* + present tense, + *will/won't*
  If we **share** a taxi, we'**ll save** money.
  If we **take** a taxi, we **won't get** wet.
  If we **don't take** a taxi, we'**ll get** wet.
  NOTE we use a comma when the *if* clause comes first.
- OR *will/won't* + *if* + present tense
  We'**ll save** money *if* we **share** a taxi.

- We use the first conditional to describe a possible or probable future situation and its likely result.
  If this café **closes**, we'**ll lose** our jobs.
  We'**ll lose** our jobs *if* this café **closes**.
  We **won't lose** our jobs *if* this café **doesn't close**.
- *If* does not mean the same as *when* in first conditional sentences.
  If this café **closes**, we'**ll lose** our jobs. (The speaker believes it is possible that the café will close, but is not sure.)
  When this café **closes**, we'**ll lose** our jobs.
  (The speaker knows that the café is going to close.)

Practice

2 Choose the correct form of the verbs.

1. If **I don't go / I won't go** to bed right now, **I'm not able / I won't be able** to get up in the morning.
2. **I'll buy / I buy** some ice cream later if the café **is / will be** still open.
3. **You pass / You'll pass** your driving test if **you won't forget / you don't forget** to wear your lucky ring.
4. **We'll phone / We phone** my dad after the party if **we'll need / we need** a lift home.
5. If anyone **finds out / will find out** where my brother is today, **he'll be / he's** in big trouble when he comes home.
6. **You won't feel / You don't feel** cold if **you put / you'll put** this sweater on.

unless

- *Unless* means *if ... not*.
  Plants don't grow *unless* they **have** light. (= if they **don't have** light)
  I'll walk home *unless* it **rains**. (= if it **doesn't rain**)

Practice

3 Rewrite the sentences using *unless*.

1. I can't get up in the morning if I don't have enough sleep.
   ....
   ....

2. We'll all have dinner together if my mum doesn't get home too late.
   ....
   ....

3. My parents will go mad if we don't clear up this mess.
   ....
   ....

4. If we don't find a taxi soon, we'll miss the train.
   ....
   ....

UNIT 17

REPORTED COMMANDS

- When we want someone to do something or not to do something, we say things like:
  Open the door! / Don't open the door! **(Command)**
  Please open the door. / Please don't open the door. **(Request)**
  You must open the door! / You mustn't open the door! **(Command)**
  You should open the door. / You shouldn't open the door. **(Advice/suggestion)**
- When we report commands, requests, suggestions, etc., we use:
  - a reporting verb + object pronoun + **to** + infinitive for positive commands and requests.
    Dad said to me, 'Open the door!' → Dad **told me to open** the door.
    Dad said to me, 'Please open the door!' → Dad **asked me to open** the door.
    I said to the boys, 'You must close the door!' → I **told them to close** the door.
    I said to the boys, 'You should close the door.' → I **advised them to close** the door.
  - a reporting verb + object pronoun + **not to** + infinitive for negative commands and requests.
    Dad said to me, 'Don't open the door!' → Dad **told me not to open** the door.
    Dad said to me, 'Please don't open the door!' → Dad **asked me not to open** the door.
    I said to the boys, 'You mustn't close the door!' → I **told them not to close** the door.
    I said to the boys, 'You should close the door.' → I **advised them not to close** the door.

Reporting verbs

- In sentences like the ones above, we can use different verbs to tell people what we want them to do,
  e.g. She **convinced** me to stay, but my friend **warned** me not to listen to her.
  advise, ask, convince, encourage, order, persuade, remind, tell, warn
  NOTE We cannot use *say* in this way. (**NOT** He said me to open the door.)

Practice

1 Write what the speakers said. Include the words in brackets.

0 Our teacher reminded us not to leave our bags on the bus.
He said, '*Don't leave your bags on the bus...*' (don't)

1 My brother persuaded me to try a new hairstyle.
He said, '..' (should)

2 The inspector asked us to show him our tickets.
He said, '..' (please)

3 My cousin convinced me not to put my address on the website.
She said, '..' (shouldn't)

4 I told my friends not to text me in the morning.
I said, '..' (mustn't)

5 The police officer ordered the driver to get out of his car.
She said, '..' (please)

6 I asked my sister to help me with the washing-up.
I said, '..' (please)

7 My friend encouraged me to join the sports club.
He said, '..' (should)

8 My mum advised me to phone the school.
She said, '..' (should)

9 The fire officer warned us not to go into the house.
He said, '..' (mustn't)

2 Report what each speaker said, using the reporting verb and a suitable pronoun.

1 The detective shouted to the thief, 'Put the gun on the floor!' (order)
The detective ....

2 The electrician said to us, 'You mustn't open that box.' (warn)
The electrician ....

3 The hairdresser said to me, 'You shouldn't use this shampoo.' (advise)
The hairdresser ....

4 I texted my friends, 'Remember to come to my party.' (remind)
I ....

5 The teacher said to the students, 'Please tell me your names.' (ask)
The teacher ....

6 I whispered to my brother, 'Please don't tell anyone!' (ask)
I ....

7 My friend said to me, 'You should tell your mum about your problem.' (encourage)
My friend ....

8 My dad said to my brother, 'You really should apply for another job.' (persuade)
My dad ....

9 My mum said to my dad, 'Don't invite the neighbours on Saturday.' (tell)
My mum ....

10 My sister said to the shop assistant, 'Come on! Please give me a discount.' (persuade)
My sister ....

UNIT 18
SECOND CONDITIONAL

- Conditional sentences tell us about a possible situation, called the conditional clause, and another clause, which is the result.
- The conditional clause begins with *if* or *unless*.
- The conditional clause or the result clause can come first without changing the meaning.
- The second conditional uses the past simple in the conditional clause and *would* (*'d*) / *wouldn't* + verb in the result clause.
  If + past tense, + *would* + verb:
  If I was a journalist, I'd (would) meet lots of famous people.
  NOTE We use a comma when the *if* clause comes first.
  OR *would* + verb + *if* + past tense:
  I'd (would) meet lots of famous people if I was a journalist.
- We sometimes use *were* instead of *was* in the conditional clause.
  If I were a journalist, I'd (would) meet lots of famous people.
- We can never use *when* instead of *if* in second conditional sentences.
- We use the second conditional to describe something in the present or future which is unlikely, impossible or imaginary.
  If I were a millionaire, I'd buy a desert island.
   (= I'm not a millionaire, so I won't buy a desert island.)
  We wouldn't send many texts if they cost a lot of money.
  (= It's cheap to send texts, so we send lots.)
  If my brother got up earlier, he wouldn't have to run for the train every morning.
  (= My brother doesn't get up early enough, so he has to run for the train every morning.)
  If I could get a job, I'd (would) have enough money to go out.
  (= I can't get a job, so I don't have enough money to go out.)
  The students wouldn't play football unless they enjoyed it.
  (= They enjoy playing football, that's why they do it.)
- We often use the second conditional to ask questions.
  If you had the chance, would you visit California?
  Wouldn't you be angry if you were me?
  What would you do if someone told you a secret?
  If you could do any job at all, what would you choose?
- We answer the questions with the conditional tense.
  I wouldn't visit California, I'd go to Florida.
  Yes, I would. / No, I wouldn't.
  I wouldn't tell anyone else.
  I'd be a racing driver.

Practice

1 Match the questions and answers.
1 If you could leave school tomorrow, what would you do? ☐
2 If you saw someone stealing, who would you tell? ☐
3 What would you say if I told you I'd bought a motorbike? ☐
4 How would you get to school if you missed the bus? ☐
5 What colour would you choose if you repainted your room? ☐

a I'd go for light blue, I think.
b I'd probably talk to my dad about it.
c I'd travel round Europe with a friend.
d I'd say you were mad!
e I'd have to walk, I suppose.

2 What would be your answers to the questions in Exercise 1?

3 Make questions for the answers using a second conditional.
1 What / you / do / if / you / win / lots of money?
  ....
  I'd buy presents for all my friends.
2 Who / you / ask / if / you / not / understand / some grammar?
  ....
  I'd ask my teacher.
3 What / you / do / if / you / see / a burger for $50?
  ....
  I'd find somewhere cheaper to eat.
4 What / you / do / if / someone / ask / you / about advanced physics?
  ....
  I'd try to find some information online.
5 Who / help / you / if / you / miss / the school bus?
  ....
  My dad would give me a lift.

4 Complete the sentences using *would* and the past simple.
1 You .... (have) more friends if you .... (not tell) stories about people.
2 If I .... (be) you, I .... (take) a warm coat today, but I guess it's up to you.
3 If Kirsty .... (stay) in France, she .... (learn) French quickly.
4 My parents .... (not get) angry with us unless we .... (do) something very bad.
5 If we all .... (eat) as much as you, there .... (not be) any food in the fridge!
6 If you .... (save) a little money every week, you .... (have) enough to buy new boots quite soon.

UNIT 19

REPORTED SPEECH

When we report what people said in the past:
- the tense of the verbs changes.
- the pronouns change if necessary.
- we sometimes, but not always, use *that* after *said*.

Direct speech	Reported speech
Present simple →	**Past simple**
'I often **go** sailing,' said Ed. →	Ed said (that) **he** often **went** sailing.
Present continuous →	**Past continuous**
'Doug **is cycling** fast,' said Megan. →	Megan said (that) Doug **was cycling** fast.
will →	**would**
'Olga **will win** the race,' said the coach. →	The coach said (that) Olga **would win** the race.
can →	**could**
They said to us, '**You can** sit with **us**.' →	They said (that) **we could** sit with **them**.

Practice

1 Change the sentences from reported to direct speech.

1 Andy said he was texting his parents.
  Andy said, 'I .... my parents.'
2 My brothers said they couldn't find any pictures of their favourite singers.
  My brothers said, 'We .... pictures of our favourite singers.'
3 Andrea said she always laughed at the letters page in her magazine.
  Andrea said, 'I always .... the letters page in my magazine.'
4 My sister said I could borrow her new shoes.
  My sister said, 'You .... new shoes.'
5 Phil said he often bought a newspaper for his dad.
  Phil said, 'I often .... for my dad.'
6 Alexi said he was looking for an article about his local team.
  Alexi said, 'I .... an article about my local team.'
7 We said we'd design the front cover.
  We said, 'We .... the front cover.'

2 Complete the reported sentences.

1 'I'm starting a blog about my sailing club,' said Saskia.
  Saskia said .... a blog about her sailing club.
2 'Readers can get free gifts with fashion magazines,' said Lewis.
  Lewis said that readers .... gifts with fashion magazines.
3 'The writers don't know much about teenagers, in my opinion,' said my mum.
  My mum said that in her opinion the writers .... about teenagers.
4 'I'll take some photos for you,' said Derek.
  Derek said .... take some photos for me.
5 'We are making a lot of progress with our stories,' said the twins.
  The twins said .... a lot of progress with their stories.
6 'The celebrities are sitting in my garden,' said the photographer.
  The photographer said that the celebrities .... his garden.
7 'I'll change the headline,' said the editor.
  The editor said she .... headline.

3 Read what Alessandro said. Underline all the verbs and pronouns that you need to change, then rewrite what he said as reported speech.

> "I'm writing a blog about fashion. I make some of my clothes and my mum helps me sometimes. We buy second-hand clothes from markets and update them. I can't sew as well as my mum, but I'm learning a lot. I'm taking photos of everything I make to put on my blog. I won't sell the clothes, but I'm hoping people will tell me their opinions. I'm planning to study fashion at a college in London next year."

UNIT 20
PAST SIMPLE PASSIVE

- We form the past simple passive with the past tense of *be* + the **past participle** of a verb.
  I **was told** to phone home.
  She **wasn't told** the correct time.
  Were you **told** what to do?
  The story **was told** to a journalist.
  The journalist **wasn't told** the truth.
  Was the story **told** to make trouble for someone?
  The pictures **were found** in a second-hand shop.
  They **weren't found** in good condition.
  Were the pictures **found** by chance?

- When we include who or what did the action, we use *by*.
  Two school students found the pictures in a second-hand shop. (active)
  The pictures **were found** in a second-hand shop **by two school students**. (passive)
  The shop owner didn't tell the journalist the truth. (active)
  The journalist **wasn't told** the truth **by the shop owner**. (passive)
  Did the students find the pictures? (active)
  Were the pictures **found by the students**? (passive)

- We use the passive:
  - when it isn't important to say who or what did the action.
    That picture **was sold** for a thousand pounds.
    My brother's drawings **were shown** in a gallery.
    I **wasn't allowed** to watch horror movies when I was younger.
  - when we do not know who or what did the action.
    My friend **was interviewed** about his invention.
    The story **wasn't published** until yesterday.
    The students **were offered** a reward.

- We include *by* when we want to emphasise who or what did the action.
  That picture was sold **by the artist's mother** for a thousand pounds.
  My friend was interviewed **by several journalists** about his invention.
  The story wasn't published **by the national newspapers** until yesterday.
  The students were offered a reward **by the owner of the painting**.

Practice

1 Rewrite the sentences in the active form.
  1 The celebrity artist was interviewed by lots of journalists.
    Lots of journalists .... the celebrity artist.
  2 The best drawing wasn't done by Picasso.
    Picasso .... the best drawing.
  3 Were the pictures copied by the students?
    Did .... the pictures?
  4 These sculptures weren't made by Henry Moore.
    Henry Moore .... these sculptures.
  5 These pictures aren't described in the course book.
    The course book .... these pictures.

2 Rewrite the sentences using the passive form of the verbs.
  1 Our teacher **reminded** us about the school trip.
    We .... teacher.
  2 Someone **copied** my card details and **stole** all my money.
    My card details .... and all my money ....
  3 My classmates **gave** me a good luck card before my interview.
    I .... my classmates before my interview.
  4 Did you **prepare** these salads this morning?
    Were .... this morning?
  5 No one **told** me where to sit.
    I .... to sit.

3 Choose the correct form of the verbs.
  Last month a class of secondary school students **(1) was given / gave** a half-day holiday by their school after their exams. Two of the students went for a walk but it **(2) was started / started** to rain, so they went into a second-hand shop to keep dry. All kinds of old furniture **(3) piled up / were piled up** around the shop. There were bowls and plates everywhere and old photographs and paintings **(4) were pushed / pushed** under tables. The students **(5) were decided / decided** to look at the pictures to pass the time. Most of them **(6) were covered / covered** in dust. Then one of the students **(7) was noticed / noticed** a small picture which **(8) was almost hidden / almost hid** behind a cupboard.
  It **(9) was shown / showed** a vase of flowers which **(10) were painted / painted** in great detail. The picture **(11) wasn't signed / didn't sign** but the shop owner thought it **(12) was probably painted / probably painted** about fifty years ago. The students **(13) were paid / paid** £5 for it and **(14) were taken / took** it away. Later they **(15) were discovered / discovered** it was five hundred years old. It **(16) was sold / sold** by a gallery in London last week for one million pounds!

157

List of irregular verbs

Infinitive	Past simple	Past participle
be	was were	been
become	became	become
begin	began	begun
break	broke	broken
bring	brought	brought
build	built	built
burn	burnt/burned	burnt/burned
buy	bought	bought
catch	caught	caught
choose	chose	chosen
come	came	come
cost	cost	cost
cut	cut	cut
do	did	done
draw	drew	drawn
dream	dreamed/dreamt	dreamed/dreamt
drink	drank	drunk
drive	drove	driven
eat	ate	eaten
fall	fell	fallen
feel	felt	felt
find	found	found
fly	flew	flown
forget	forgot	forgotten
get	got	got
give	gave	given
go	went	gone/been
grow	grew	grown
have	had	had
hear	heard	heard
hit	hit	hit
hold	held	held
hurt	hurt	hurt
keep	kept	kept
know	knew	known
learn	learned/learnt	learned/learnt
leave	left	left

Infinitive	Past simple	Past participle
lend	lent	lent
lie	lay	lain
lose	lost	lost
make	made	made
mean	meant	meant
meet	met	met
pay	paid	paid
put	put	put
read	read	read
ride	rode	ridden
ring	rang	rung
run	ran	run
say	said	said
see	saw	seen
sell	sold	sold
send	sent	sent
show	showed	shown
shut	shut	shut
sing	sang	sung
sit	sat	sat
sleep	slept	slept
speak	spoke	spoken
spell	spelled/spelt	spelled/spelt
spend	spent	spent
stand	stood	stood
steal	stole	stolen
swim	swam	swum
take	took	taken
teach	taught	taught
tell	told	told
think	thought	thought
throw	threw	thrown
understand	understood	understood
wake	woke	woken
wear	wore	worn
win	won	won
write	wrote	written

Acknowledgements

The authors would like to thank Annette Capel, Diane Hall and Sheila Dignen for their hard work and dedication to *Prepare!* James Styring dedicates this book to Livia Florence Luz Styring. Nicholas Tims thanks Clare, Ismay and Elodie for their endless support and patience.

The authors and publishers are grateful to the following for reviewing the material during the writing process:

Argentina: Silvia Bautista, Celeste Hayet; Mexico: Paty Cervantes; Mexico and Spain: Louise Manicolo; Russia: Catherine Lee; Turkey: Ali Kemal Yumurcak

Development of this publication has made use of the Cambridge English Corpus, a multi-billion word collection of spoken and written English. It includes the Cambridge Learner Corpus, a unique collection of candidate exam answers. Cambridge University Press has built up the Cambridge English Corpus to provide evidence about language use that helps to produce better language teaching materials.

This product is informed by English Profile, a Council of Europe-endorsed research programme that is providing detailed information about the language that learners of English know and use at each level of the Common European Framework of Reference (CEFR). For more information, please visit www.englishprofile.org

The authors and publishers acknowledge the following sources of copyright material and are grateful for the permissions granted. While every effort has been made, it has not always been possible to identify the sources of all the material used, or to trace all copyright holders. If any omissions are brought to our notice, we will be happy to include the appropriate acknowledgements on reprinting.

Peter Menzel/menzelphoto.com for the text on p.19 adapted from *Material World*, by Peter Menzel, Charles Mann and Paul Kennedy. Copyright © Peter Menzel/menzelphoto.com. Reproduced with permission;

Kids Can Press Ltd for the text and illustration on p.51 from *If the World Were a Village: A Book about the World's People* (second edition). Text © 2011 David J Smith. Illustration © 2011 Shelagh Armstrong. Used by permission of Kids Can Press Ltd, Toronto;

Peter Menzel/menzelphoto.com for the text on p.62 adapted from *What I Eat: Around the World in 80 Diets*, by Peter Menzel and Faith d'Aluisio, published by Material World 2010. Copyright © Peter Menzel/menzelphoto.com. Reproduced with permission.

For the sound recordings on p.40, track 1.23: *Yoga Tantrum*, artist – RFM. Copyright ©Sound Express/Getty Images; p.71, track 2.05: *Yo Curtis*, artist – Sony/ATV Music Publishing. Copyright © Spin City, from Sony/ATV/Getty Images.

Photo acknowledgements

p.12: Stanislaw Pytel/Alamy; p.13 (TL), p.75, p.91 (TR), p.116 (B): Radius Images/Alamy; p.13 (BL): Nick Tim's; p.14 (a): Rotello/MCP/REX; p.14 (b): Aflo Co. Ltd/Alamy; p.14 (c): Broadimage/REX; p.14 (d): CAU/ROCHON/VOLLET/SIPA/REX; p.14 (e), p.14 (f): REX; p.15 (TL): Steve Vidler/Alamy; p.15 (TR): Photograph by Camera Press London; p.15 (BL): Rick Diamond/Getty Images; p.15 (BR): Mirrorpix; p.17 (TR): Agencja Fotograficzna Caro/Alamy; p.17 (BL): Shawshots/Alamy; p.17 (BR): RosalreneBetancourt 2/Alamy; p.18–19 (B), p.19 (B), p.63: © Peter Menzel www.menzelphoto.com; p.19 (C): Louie Psihoyos/Getty Images; p.20 (a): 2/Cohen/Ostrow/Ocean/Corbis; p.20 (b): craftvision/Getty Images; p.20 (c): Rawpixel/Shutterstock; p.20 (d): Mint Images Limited/Alamy; p.20 (e): JanVicek/Shutterstock; p.20 (f): Julia Wheeler and Veronika Laws/Getty Images; p.21 (TL): Blend Images/SuperStock; p.23: PYMCA/Getty Images; p.24 (a): thinkomatic/Getty Images; p.24 (b): Dennis O'Clair/getty Images; p.24 (c), p.24 (d), p.64 (R): PCN Photography/Alamy; p.24 (e): Stephen Bisgrove/Alamy; p.24 (f): EpicStockMedia/Shutterstock; p.24 (g): Inge Schepers Sports and Events Photography/Alamy; p.24 (h): dotshock/Shutterstock; p.24 (BR): Ron Chapple Stock/Alamy; p.25 (B): Neil Tingle/Loop images/Corbis; p.27 (TL): Rajah Bose/AP/Press Association Images; p.27 (TC), p.76 (Alfie): OJO Images Ltd/Alamy; p.27 (TR): Jason Smalley Photography/Alamy; p.27 (CL): Jonathan Larsen/Diadem Images/Alamy; p.27 (BL): Mike Hewitt/Getty Images; p.29 (a): Denkou Images/Alamy; p.29 (b): Photopat/Alamy; p.29 (c): Sandro Di Carlo Darsa/PhotoAlto/Corbis; p.29 (d): slobo/Getty Images; p.29 (e): Jan-Otto/Getty Images; p.29 (B): tom carter/Alamy; p.31: ALAN EDWARDS/Alamy; p.32 (a): Bruce Bennett/Getty Images; p.32 (b): Keystone/Getty Images; p.32 (c): Jason LaVeris/Getty Images; p.32 (d), p.85 (Seven Samurai): Everett Collection/REX; p.32 (e): Jamie Squire/Getty Images; p.32 (f): ROBYN BECK/Getty Images; p.33 (TR), p.41 (B), p.76 (Jack), p.103 (BL): Image Source/Alamy; p.33 (BL): ARTHUR SASSE/Getty Images; p.33 (BC): B.A.E. Inc/Alamy; p.33 (BR): Bettmann/Corbis; p.34 (B): Steven Day/AP/Press Association Images; p.35: Paula Solloway/Alamy; p.36 (a): Dmitriy Bryndin/Shutterstock; p.36 (b): David Freund/Getty Images; p.36 (c): Nicola Longobardi/Getty Images; p.36 (d): William Perugini/Shutterstock; p.36 (e): DanielW/Shutterstock; p.37 (TR): Boston Globe/Getty Images; p.37 (CL): Ross Parry Agency; p.38 (1), p.38 (6): incamerastock/Alamy; p.38 (2): Hemera Technologies/Getty Images; p.38 (3): Stu/Alamy; p.38 (4): Peter Gudella/Shutterstock; p.38 (5): Gabriele Maltinti/Shutterstock; p.38 (7): mike lane/Alamy; p.38 (8): Keith Lewis Archive/Alamy; p.39 (TR): Malcolm Brice/Alamy; p.39 (CL): Peter Eastland/Alamy; p.39 (BL): colinspics/Alamy; p.40 (TR): Hannah Peters/Getty Images; p.40 (BL): PhotoAlto/Alamy; p.40 (BR): bikeriderlondon/Shutterstock; p.41 (TR): stock_shot/Shutterstock; p.41 (CL): Xinhua/Alamy; p.42 (TL): Ysbrand Cosijn/Shutterstock; p.43: Bruce Ayres/Getty Images; p.46 (a): Agencja Fotograficzna Caro/Alamy; p.46 (b): Jupiterimages/Getty Images; p.46 (c): Henry George Beeker/Alamy; p.46 (d): Barry Lewis/Alamy; p.46 (e), p.89: SAUL LOEB/Getty Images; p.46 (f): david pearson/Alamy; p.47 (BL): Vladyslav Danilin/Shutterstock; p.47 (BR): Ioannis Tsouratzis/Alamy; p.48 (T): nagelestock.com/Alamy; p.48 (B): mikecphoto/Shutterstock; p.49 (T): Roberto Caucino/Shutterstock; p.49 (B): Michael Ventura/Alamy; p.50: Tupungato/Shutterstock; p.51: Material sourced from *If the World Were a Village: A book about the World's People* (Second Edition) is used by permission of Kids Can Press Ltd., Toronto. Illustration © 2011 Shelagh Armstrong; p.53: moodboard/Alamy; p.54 (a): F1online digitale Bildagentur GmbH/Alamy; p.54 (b): Brent Lewis/Getty Images; p.54 (c): Izel Photography/Alamy; p.54 (d): Denys Prykhodov/Shutterstock; p.54 (e): RosalreneBetancourt 5/Alamy; p.54 (f): age fotostock/Alamy; p.54 (g): allesalltag/Alamy; p.54 (h): Judith Dzierzawa/Alamy; p.55: panco971/Getty Images; p.57: LWA/Dann Tardiff/Blend Images/Corbis; p.58 (a): Joy Skipper/Getty Images; p.58 (b): marco mayer/Shutterstock; p.58 (c): hfng/Shutterstock; p.58 (d): photogal/Shutterstock; p.58 (e): Poprotskiy Alexey/Shutterstock; p.58 (f): funkyfood London-Paul Williams/Alamy; p.58 (g): Zadorozhnyi Viktor; p.58 (h): SteveWoods/Shutterstock; p.59 (TR): Miguel Romero Gorria/Alamy; p.59 (BL): Africa Studio/Shutterstock; p.59 (BR): Life on white/Alamy; p.59 (ants): Mario Cruz/fotoLIBRA; p.59 (durian): 33333/Shutterstock; p.59 (berries): ZUMA Press, Inc/Alamy; p.60 (TL): Bogdan Shahanski/Shutterstock; p.60 (TR): Joshua Resnick/Shutterstock; p.60 (BL): Kzenon/Shutterstock; p.60 (BR): cobraqphotography/Shutterstock; p.61 (burger), p.102 (c): Brand X Pictures/Getty Images; p.61 (salad): Robyn Mackenzie/Getty Images; p.61 (chips): RedHelga/Getty Images; p.61 (cola): Evgeny Karandaev/Getty Images; p.64 (L): ABEL F. ROS/Alamy; p.65: Ariel Skelley/Getty Images; p.66 (TL): Pressmaster/Shutterstock; p.66 (TR): Olga Rosi/Shutterstock; p.66 (BL): Hill Street Studios/Blend Images/Corbis; p.66 (BC): altrendo images/Getty Images; p.67 (TL): lewis jackson/Alamy; p.67 (TR), p.83 (B): Image Source/Getty Images; p.68 (a): paytai/Shutterstock; p.68 (b): Betty Shelton/Shutterstock; p.68 (c): Andrew JK Tan/Getty Images; p.68 (d): Steven Kazlowski/Getty Images; p.68 (e): Raisa Kanareva/Shutterstock; p.68 (f): Pete Oxford/Minden Pictures/Corbis; p.68 (g): Steven Cooper/Getty Images; p.68 (h): Stephen Frink/Getty Images; p.68 (i): Tim Graham/Getty Images; p.68 (j): anshu18/

Shutterstock; p.68 (k): Radu Bercan/Shutterstock; p.68 (l): Andrey Pavlov/Shutterstock; p.68 (m): Dr. Martin Oeggerli/Visuals Unlimited/Corbis; p.68 (n): Brandon Alms/Shutterstock; p.68 (o): E.O./Shutterstock; p.68 (p): Leo Shoot/Shutterstock; p.68 (q): Andy Rouse/Nature Picture Library/Corbis; p.68 (r): Christopher Meder/Shutterstock; p.68 (s): saluha/Getty Images; p.68 (t): Xavier MARCHANT/Shutterstock; p.69 (TL): Photography by David Thyberg/Getty Images; p.69 (TR): Gerard Lacz/FLPA; p.69 (BL): Mark Newman/FLPA; p.69 (BR): Mary Evans Picture Library/Alamy; p.70 (TL): Buddy Mays/Alamy; p.70 (a): ritfuse/Shutterstock; p.70 (b): imageBROKER/Alamy; p.70 (c): John Kimbler/Tom Stack & Associates/Alamy; p.70 (d): Eric Isselee/Getty Images; p.70 (CR): Photoshot Holdings Ltd/Alamy; p.70 (BR): Nature Picture Library/Alamy; p.71 (TL): Jeff Rotman/Alamy; p.71 (TC): Arterra Picture Library/Alamy; p.71 (TR): dpa picture alliance/Alamy; p.71 (BL): ALEXANDER JOE/Getty Images; p.71 (BR): Valeriy Kirsanov/Getty Images; p.72 (lion): Deborah Kolb/Shutterstock; p.72 (giraffe): Volodymyr Burdiak/Shutterstock; p.72 (grass): orangecrush/Shutterstock; p.72 (bird): johnbraid/Shutterstock; p.72 (snake): Patrick K. Campbell/Shutterstock; p.72 (mouse): Piotr Krzeslak/Shutterstock; p.72 (eagle): Mark Caunt/Shutterstock; p.72 (fish): Vlada Z/Shutterstock; p.72 (frog): Eduard Kyslynskyy/Shutterstock; p.72 (insect): encikAn/Shutterstock; p.72 (plants): mexrix/Shutterstock; p.76 (Ellen): Goodshoot RF/Getty Images; p.76 (Evie): AdiniMalibuBarbie/Getty Images; p.76 (Lily), p.76 (Grace): Design Pics Inc/Alamy; p.76 (Ollie): MISHELLA/Shutterstock; p.77: Alfred Mitz/Alamy; p.79: MJTH/Shutterstock; p.80 (a), p.80 (f), p.84, p.85 (Jean De Florette), p.85 (Avatar), p.85 (Manon Des Sources): Photos 12/Alamy; p.80 (b), p.80 (h), p.80 (j), p.85 (Sherlock Holmes)p.102 (e): AF archive/Alamy; p.80 (c), p.111 (TR): CBW/Alamy; p.80 (d): Murder On The Orient Express, FILM Copyright © 1974 Studiocanal Films Ltd. All Rights reserved/The Kobal Collection; p.80 (e): Marguerite Smits Van Oyen/Nature Picture Library; p.80 (g): Dreamworks/20th Century Fox/The Kobal Collection; p.80 (i): NBC/Douglas Gorenstein/NBCU Photo Bank/Getty Images; p.80 (k): Atmosphere Entertainment MM/The Kobal Collection; p.81 (Liz): Huntstock, Inc/Alamy; p.81 (Steve): Tetra Images/Alamy; p.81 (Jenny), p.119: Blend Images/Alamy; p.81 (Phil): Johner Images/Alamy; p.82 (B): Universal/The Kobal Collection; p.83 (T): Directphoto Collection/Alamy; p.85 (Godzilla): Warner Bros/The Kobal Collection; p.86 (TL): NetPhotos3/Alamy; p.86 (TR): Hero Images Inc./Alamy; p.86 (CR): JMiks/Shutterstock; p.86 (BL): kay/Shutterstock; p.86 (BC): PSL Images/Alamy; p.86 (BR): Peter Dazeley/Getty Images; p.87: ra2studio/Shutterstock; p.88 (TL): LIONEL BONAVENTURE/Getty Images; p.88 (BL): nevarpp/Getty Images; p.90 (a): Flashon Studio/Shutterstock; p.90 (b): Thinkstock Images/Getty Images; p.90 (c): Exra Bailey/Getty Images; p.90 (d): cagan/Getty Images; p.90 (e): Yganko/Shutterstock; p.90 (f): PathDoc/Shutterstock; p.90 (g): Alan Bailey/Shutterstock; p.90 (h): focal point/Shutterstock; p.90 (i): M.Sobreira/Alamy; p.91 (BL): CORDIER Sylvain/Getty Images; p.91 (BR): Photoman29/Shutterstock; p.92 (TL): Gannet77/Getty Images; p.92 (TR): Bildagentur Zoonar GmbH/Shutterstock; p.92 (BL): Alain Daussin/Getty Images; p.92 (BR): Johannes Mann/Corbis; p.93 (a): Pavel Klimenko/Getty Images; p.93 (b): Clive Brunskill/Getty Images; p.93 (c): PHILIPPE HUGUEN/Getty Images; p.93 (d): Szasz-Fabian Jozsef/Shutterstock; p.93 (TR): david sanger photography/Alamy; p.93 (BR): Tim Gainey/Alamy; p.94 (a): Image Source Plus/Alamy; p.94 (b): Nik Taylor/Alamy; p.94 (c): snapgalleria/Shutterstock; p.94 (d): Oleksiy Mark/Shutterstock; p.95 (cake): Dasha Petrenko/Shutterstock; p.95 (gold): cigdem/Shutterstock; p.97: Ruth Amos StairSteady Products Ltd; p.98 (TR): Tom Merton/GettyImages; p.98 (CL): Allyson Scott/Alamy; p.98 (BL): New Line Cinema/The Kobal Collection; p.99 (TL): WENN Ltd/Alamy, p.99 (TR): WENN UK/Alamy, p.99 (BL): PAUL ELLIS/Getty Images, p.99 (BR): Antoine Antoniol/Getty Images; p.101: Startraks Photo/REX; p.102 (a): Digital Vision/Getty Images; p.102 (b): Robert Warren/Getty Images; p.102 (d): Dmitry Kalinovsky/Shutterstock; p.102 (f): Catherine Yeulet/Getty Images; p.102 (g): Jaimie Duplass/Shuttterstock; p.102 (h): Digital Storm/Shutterstock; p.103 (TR): Ian Walton/Getty Images; p.103 (BR): Ed Freeman/Getty Images;

p.104: 26kot/Shutterstock; p.106 (TL): Erik Pendzich/REX; p.106 (TR), p.114 (B): epa european pressphoto agency b.v./Alamy; p.106 (BL): Aflo Co. Ltd./Alamy; p.106 (BR): PRAKASH MATHEMA/AFP/Getty Images; p.107 (TR): RIA Novosti/Alamy; p.107 (CL): Nancy Brown/Getty Images; p.107 (CR): Brent Winebrenner/Getty Images; p.107 (BL): ableimages/Alamy; p.108 (TC): iStock.com/pictafolio; p.108 (TR): pictafolio/Getty Images; p.108 (CR): BONNINSTUDIO/Shutterstock; p.108 (BL): Pixellover RM4/Alamy; p.108 (BR): David L. Moore/Alamy; p.109 (B/G): Julian Cartwright/Alamy; p.110 (T): PT Images/Shutterstock; p.110 (B): Cultura RM/Nancy Honey; p.112 (a): Trevor Smith/Alamy; p.112 (d): Lakeview images/Shutterstock; p.112 (e): Gaschwald/Shutterstock; p.113 (TL): CHRISTOPHER JUE/epa/Corbis; p.113 (TR): viphotos/Shutterstock; p.113 (BL): Luca Ghidoni/Getty Images; p.113 (BR): Gavriel Jecan/Corbis; p.114 (T): Dan Kitwood/Getty Images; p.115 (a): Alex Kalmbach/Shutterstock; p.115 (b): taelove7/Shutterstock; p.115 (c): mark wragg/Getty Images; p.115 (d): Viorel Sima/Shutterstock; p.115 (e): Andreas von Einsiedel/Alamy; p.115 (f): maigi/Shutterstock; p.115 (TR): bbostjan/Getty Images; p.115 (BR): Heike Richter, New Zealand/Getty Images; p.116 (T): Arnau Ramos Oviedo/Alamy; p.117 (T): caia image/Alamy; p.117 (C): Chris George/Alamy; p.117 (B): mariait/Shutterstock; p.121: Y-tea/Shutterstock.

Commissioned photography by Neil Matthews: p.10, p.11, p.17 (TL), p.17 (TC), p.25 (TR), p.42 (TR), p.42 (BL), p.42 (BR), p.45, p.47 (TR), p.66 (BR), p.78, p.81 (TR), p.81 (L), p.105 (T), p.109 (T), p.109 (C), p.109 (B), p.111 (TL)

Front cover photo by Leon van den Edisvag/Shutterstock

Illustrations

Mark Duffin p.88; Stuart Harrison pp.16, 34, 56, 78, 95, 100, 112; Alek Sotirovski (Beehive Illustration) pp.26, 61, 105.

The publishers are grateful to the following contributors:
text design and layouts: emc design Ltd; cover design: Andrew Ward; picture research: Alison Prior and Ann Thomson; audio recordings: produced by IH Sound and recorded at DSound, London; Texts and exercises on pp.11, 25, 47, 81, 106-7, 109: Emma Heyderman; Grammar reference section: Louise Hashemi.